# Brunch Basket

T.H.

A Collection of Recipes
for Brunch and Light Meals from
The Junior League of Rockford

Cover and illustrations
by Tom Heflin

The purpose of the Junior League is exclusively educational and charitable and is to promote voluntarism; to develop the potential of its members for voluntary participation in community affairs; and to demonstrate the effectiveness of trained volunteers.

Manufactured by
Favorite Recipes® Press
an imprint of

**FRP**

P.O. Box 305142
Nashville, Tennessee 37230
800-358-0560

| First Printing | February 1985 | 10,000 copies |
| Second Printing | November 1985 | 10,000 copies |
| Third Printing | June 1989 | 5,000 copies |
| Fourth Printing | January 1992 | 5,000 copies |
| Fifth Printing | October 1997 | 5,000 copies |

Proceeds from the sale of *Brunch Basket* will be returned to the community through projects sponsored by the Junior League of Rockford, Inc.

Library of Congress Catalog Card Number: 84-81269

International Standard Book Number: 0-9613563-0-8

Printed in the United States of America

# Table of Contents

## Brunch Basket Committee
## 1982-1984

Jan Rebman George . . . . . . . . . . . . . . . . . . . . . . . . . . . . . . Chairman & Editor
Kay Lievens Galloway . . . . . . . . . . . . . . . . . . . . . . . . . . . . . . . Co-Chairman
Joyce Blum DeWallace . . . . . . . . . . . . . . . . . . . . . . . . . . . . . Assistant Editor
Diane Anderson Hedberg . . . . . . . . . . . . . . . . . . . . . . . Recipe Chairman
Renate Fischer Pendleton . . . . . . . . . . . . . . . . . . . . . Recipe Co-Chairman
Sanchia Bruer Leach . . . . . . . . . . . . . . . . . . . . . . . . . Marketing Chairman
Betsy Nash Homewood . . . . . . . . . . . . . . . . . . . . . . . Promotion Chairman
Debbie Beckstrand Brearley . . . . . . . . . . . . . . . . . . . . . . . . . Art Director
Ellen Baitinger Erkert . . . . . . . . . . . . . . . . . . . . . . . . . . . Index Chairman
Carlyn Bruce Peterson . . . . . . . . . . . . . . . . . . . . . . . . Business Manager
Darlene Koning Furst . . . . . . . . . . . . . . . . . . . Administrative Manager
Kathy Ginestra Guzzardo . . . . . . . . . . . . . . . . Executive Committee Liaison
Karen Reinhold Shifo . . . . . . . . . . . . . . . . . . . Executive Committee Liaison

## Committee

Diana Gifford Cobb
Kirby Johnson Doyle
Marsha Lewis Hess
Judy Vosburg Hirsch
Barbara Severson Johnson
Deb VanAtta Laughlin
Elizabeth Brearley McDonald
Pat Fedro Norten
Debbi Reitsch Pauletto
Dale Hart Peel
Susan Stolar Polivka
Betsie Kramp Trejo
Maureen O'Brien Volkmann

# About The Artist

Tucked away down an Illinois country road, amidst overgrown fields of thistles and cockleburs, stands a faded, ramshackle farm house — Tom Heflin's studio. There are no telephones, no clocks, no passing cars…time is defined only by the morning song of birds, the evening chirp of crickets. In this distilled environment of a world at peace with itself, Heflin finds inspiration for his work.

One of the Midwest's pre-eminent artists, Tom Heflin is listed in "Who's Who in American Art" and "Who's Who in the Midwest." His exhibitions have spanned the country from New York to California, including exhibits at the American Watercolor Society, New York; Chicago Art Institute; Central Wyoming Museum; and Dallas' Southwestern Watercolor Society. He is represented by the Overland Trail Gallery in Scottsdale, Arizona; the Omni Gallery in Dallas, Texas; and the Heflin Gallery in Rockford, Illinois. .

when the junior league asked me to
do some paintings for its upcoming
recipe book i was hesitant because
i thought i would be obliged to approach
it from a commercial point of view and
i had no interest in painting
chicken casseroles and such.
as it turned out, the only requirement
was that i include some form of a
basket in each painting.
this gave me plenty of creative room
to work.
i didn't go out and purchase "neat"
little baskets.
i made use of baskets that were already
in my environment, either in our
home or at my country studio.
the result is that each work functions
as a legitimate painting in its own
right while still relating to, and
hopefully, enhancing the rockford junior
league's brunch basket recipe book.
                                    tom heflin

tori heflin

# Baskets
# & Brunches

Anthropologists mark, as one beginning of human development, the ability to gather food and carry it back to the tribe using crude containers made from long leaves.

These early baskets soon became an expression of the ingenuity and creativity of their makers. In fact, basketry is thought to be the oldest form of handicraft—useful not only to form containers for food, but for every imaginable content.

The famous voyage of author Thor Heyerdahl proved it was possible for people to sail across the oceans in small, basket-like woven boats, centuries before the beginning of recorded history. Baskets uncovered in the Nile River Basin are dated from 8000 B.C. The Bible includes many references to basketry—such as the story of Moses being kept alive because his mother floated her baby among the reeds in a pitch-covered basket of intertwined bulrushes.

In the United States, coiled and twined baskets dating from 9000 to 7000 B.C. have been unearthed in Nevada and Utah.

Most of America's goods were once carried and stored in baskets. Crops were harvested into sturdy baskets of hickory or ash and carried in large panniers. Cheeses were aged in open, hexagonally woven containers, and ladies' hats were protected from dust in finely woven, lidded bonnet baskets.

Field baskets were designed according to the crop they were to hold. Baskets for tomatoes showed slightly raised, cone-shaped bottoms to distribute the weight of the produce and prevent crushing. Baskets used to collect root crops or mushrooms had bottoms loosely woven to allow dirt to pass through. Smaller berry baskets were woven tightly to keep the fruit from being wedged into the openings. Basket sizes gave us the familiar dry measures of pints, quarts, pecks and bushels.

Today, antique baskets are valued for their varied shapes, natural colors, careful craftmanship and simple rustic charm. What we think of as the American country basket is usually one of three types: the splint basket, constructed of thin strips of cane or wood; the straw basket, coiled, plaited or woven from hollow stalks of rye or other grain; and the wicker basket, woven from strips of willow.

Baskets are still used for gathering, storing and displaying goods. They are modeled from wire, plastic, clay, synthetics and every type of growing plant whose fibers remain intact when dry. Baskets are available in every imaginable color and form. Whether made by hand or machine, their size and shape are dictated by the function of the finished product.

Imagination is the only limit to designing beautiful baskets and using them creatively. **Brunch Basket** is brimming with hints on using the baskets you have made or collected to add pizzazz to your family meals and inspire your entertaining.

Make some baskets, edible or not. Use them lavishly, formally, in an off-beat grouping, or an unexpected place—and fill them with the bounty of **Brunch Basket**.

## *Using Baskets As Centerpieces . . .*

Fill an old-fashioned market basket with a bounty of fruits and vegetables in season and surround with shiny, cored apples to hold candles.

Combine the June abundance of fresh strawberries and daisies in a wicker basket with English ivy.

Stack a flat round basket with a pyramid of peaches sprigged with green mint leaves. Another time try lemons and limes with curly parsley.

Use an arrangement of both Bosc and D'Anjou pears in a low basket draped with cascades of grapes for a totally edible centerpiece.

In early spring gather bunches of forget-me-nots and intersperse them with crisp snow peas in a small basket set on its side, trailing a blue ribbon.

After filling a flat basket with florist's foam, cover it with fresh button mushrooms held with toothpicks and add the contrast of small fern fronds . . . charming in any season.

Line an oversize oblong bread basket with checked napkins, excelsior (fine wood shavings), a bottle of wine, and a loaf of bread for an Italian dinner.

For a fall buffet, use a colorful arrangement of gourds and squash with dried leaves overflowing from a cornucopia basket.

For a winter supper, place an assortment of small cabbages (red, green, and Savoy) in a low flat basket lined with a few of the large outer cabbage leaves.

Stain or paint a wooden mushroom basket in a pastel color. At Easter fill it with cellophane grass, colored china eggs and ceramic or stuffed bunnies.

For the winter months, place in a low basket assorted pine cones wired with small bows.

Arrange small pots of flowering annuals in a handled basket. Fill in the niches with wood chips and Voila! You have a summer patio table centerpiece.

Using acrylic paint, spray a large handled basket. Add garlands of greens and flowers. This makes a wonderful container for a silk trailing plant such as ivy or ferns.

## *Using Baskets As Servers . . .*

Fit plain bowls or simple casserole dishes into baskets and use them for serving containers, eliminating the need for hotpads. Great for potlucks!

Small baskets lined with bandanas can hold flatware or serving utensils. Matching bandanas can be used as napkins or sewn together for a tablecloth.

Center a round, flat-bottomed basket with a bowl of dip and surround with chips or pretzels.

Use a divided basket, perhaps an old wire bottle carrier, to hold wine glasses for a casual supper.

Small cylindrical baskets can hold bread sticks or pretzel rods. Raw vegetable sticks can also stand in these containers by lining the basket with slightly smaller glasses.

For children's parties, small plastic pint baskets lined with a paper napkin can hold a sandwich and munchies.

Wrap individual place settings of flatware in napkins and tie with a contrasting ribbon; pile in a large basket with a matching ribbon on the handle.

Keep a wicker hamper filled with a tablecloth, napkins, plastic utensils, and disposable cups to take advantage of perfect evenings for pick-up-and-go picnics.

## *Baskets For the Holidays . . .*

Decorate a small, table-top Christmas tree or an evergreen wreath with a collection of miniature baskets, each holding a tiny arrangement of evergreens and baby's breath. Tie these on the tree with shiny satin ribbons.

Fill a silver basket with fancy decorated chocolates. Tuck in a few holly sprigs.

Polish every silver, brass, crystal or pewter basket you have. Fill with an assortment of shiny ornaments, pine cones, candies, crudites or cocktail napkins. Group with candles for a glittering holiday.

Fill a brass log basket with a generous assortment of bread loaves for a sandwich smorgasbord.

# Baskets You Can Make...

In the fall, gather a bunch of wild grapevines. Weave them into a low, flat basket. Twist two or three vines to form a simple handle.

Another easy-to-make flat basket can be nailed together using five pieces (4 to 5 inches wide) of rough-sawn cedar. Use 4 boards for the sides, and nail together corners. Cut bottom to fit and nail in place. Add a twined grapevine handle. Use the handle only for decorative purposes, not for carrying.

For the holidays, sweeten your tabletop with a red-and-white-striped peppermint stick basket. Plastic food storage containers, such as a one-pound margarine tub, form the base. Run a thick ribbon of white glue around the container and let it dry for ten minutes to become tacky. Then press the upright candy sticks all around the base. Finish with a trim of ribbon and spray with a clear fixative. Larger peppermint sticks may be glued together to form a U-shaped handle.

Form a basket from fragrant cinnamon sticks. Using whole cinnamon sticks and household containers as the bases, use the same method as for peppermint stick baskets. Garden shears are best for cutting the woody sticks to size. For a larger container, glue a row of the sticks inside the container for a thicker effect. Thin satin cording provides an effective contrast to the rough texture of the bark. Handles can be formed by gluing 3-inch cinnamon sticks crosswise to both sides of a 2-inch wide piece of poster board bent to shape and cut to size.

Sew a quilted fabric basket using 20 vertical strips (2-1/4 inches by 5 inches) of fabric for sides, a square of fabric (9-1/2 inches by 9-1/2 inches) for bottom, a strip (35 inches by 2-1/2 inches) for rim, another strip (22 inches by 2-1/2 inches) for handle, and a piece of coordinating fabric for the lining. You will also need heavy wire, a piece of cardboard (8-1/2 inches square), and quilt batting. Sew the vertical strips together using 1/4-inch seam allowances on the 5-inch sides, until all strips are connected in a long rectangle. Cut a piece of batting and one of lining the same size as rectangle. Sandwich batting between strips and lining; sew exactly over each vertical seam. Join ends to form a cylinder. Apply rim at top of cylinder as you would bias tape — but before final stitching, insert a narrow length of batting and a length of wire. With right sides together, stitch square bottom piece to bottom of cylinder, 1/4 inch from edge. Turn basket inside out; pin right side of a 9-1/2-inch square lining piece to right side of fabric bottom. Sew halfway around. Turn right side out. Cover cardboard with batting; insert into bottom. Finish bottom by handstitching to close. For handle, cut batting to fit handle strip and pin to wrong side. Fold lengthwise, right sides together, and stitch. Turn right side out, placing seam in center. Stitch over seam line down center of tube. Insert a length of wire into handle. Stitch ends closed and sew by hand to inside of basket.

## Never-Fail Bread Dough Basket with Alum
Makes a very hard, permanent container                    Makes 1 basket

| | |
|---|---|
| **1-1/2 c. water**<br>**2 c. flour**<br>**2 c. salt**<br>**1 T. alum (available**<br>**at pharmacy)** | In a medium saucepan, bring water to a boil. Mix together the flour, salt, and alum. Gradually add flour mixture to the boiling water, stirring constantly over medium heat, to form a very stiff dough. Use an additional 1/2 cup of water if needed, but add only enough to let mixture form a ball. Remove from heat and cover with a damp towel until cool. |

Knead dough for 7-10 minutes until smooth. Roll out on a well-floured board 1/4 to 1/2-inch thick. Cut into 1-inch strips at least 14 inches long, using a plain knife or fancy scalloped cutter depending on the kind of basket you want. Use an ovenproof bowl as your base. An 8-inch, 1-1/2-quart glass or metal bowl works well, but any shape may be used. Spray the base well with vegetable oil spray.

Lay the strips in a lattice design over the outside of base, weaving them to form the basket. Trim carefully and finish with a 1/2-inch band made from the rerolled scraps. Use another container of the same diameter to form a handle 2 inches wide and about 12 to 16 inches long. Three smaller strips can be braided together for handle.

Place both dough-covered bowls on cookie sheets and bake overnight at 140° or approximately 3 hours at 300° until dough is hard and dry. Let cool and remove carefully, loosening the edges with a blunt knife. If a piece breaks off, it may be glued back on. After the basket is completely cool, glue the handle in place and finish with varnish, acrylic paints, or spray varnish as desired.

## Easy-Do Dough Basket
Less durable but easier                                    Makes 1 basket

| | |
|---|---|
| **4 c. flour**<br>**1 c. salt**<br>**2 t. dry mustard**<br>**1-1/4—1-/12 c. water**<br>**1 egg, beaten** | Mix flour, salt and mustard in mixing bowl, gradually adding water until dough forms a ball. If a dough hook is used, knead for 5-10 minutes. Or, turn out onto a floured board and knead until as smooth as putty. Follow directions for alum basket for forming the basket and the handle over well-greased bowls. Brush both the basket and handle with beaten egg. Bake at 300° for 2-3 hours until dry and hard. Let cool; glue on handle. |

## *Edible Baskets...*

### *Dip in a Bread Bowl*

Serves 6

1-1/2 c. mayonnaise
1-1/2 c. sour cream
3 T. dill seed
1 t. garlic salt .
1 round loaf dark rye
   bread

One day before serving, mix mayonnaise, sour cream, dill seed and garlic salt. Refrigerate, covered. Hollow out bread loaf in the shape of a bowl. To serve, fill the bread bowl with dip. Use bread from the center in chunks for dipping. An extra loaf may be needed for dippers.

### *Puff Pastry Bowl*

Serves 6

2/3 c. water
1/4 c. butter
1 c. biscuit mix
4 eggs

Generously grease a 9-inch pie pan. Heat water and butter to boiling in a sauce pan. Add the biscuit mix all at once. Stir vigorously over low heat until the mixture forms a ball, about 1 minute. Remove from heat. Beat in the eggs one at a time. Continue beating until smooth. Spread in the pie pan, but do not spread up the sides. Bake at 400° until puffed and dry in the center, 35-40 minutes. Cool. This versatile container can be used for mounds of scrambled eggs, main dish or vegetable salads, or 1-1/2 quarts of ice cream topped with sliced fruit or sundae sauce.

### *Phyllo Basket*

Makes 1 Basket

9 sheets phyllo pastry,
   thawed
1/4 c. butter, melted

Remove one sheet phyllo from package. Keep the remaining sheets covered tightly with foil as you work. Brush the sheet lightly with melted butter. Top with a second sheet and repeat until 8 layers are stacked. Trim to a 14 x 9-inch rectangle. Use a round cookie cutter or a glass to scallop the edge of the rectangle. Fit pastry into a buttered 10 x 6-inch baking dish. Bake at 350° for 10-15 minutes. Cool. Remove from pan.

To make handle, butter 1 sheet of phyllo and roll up. Curve the roll and place on a buttered cookie sheet. Bake at 350° for 8-10 minutes. When cool, trim handle and fit into basket. Use toothpicks to hold handle firmly.

Fill the basket with hot herb-buttered vegetables just before serving. Serve a piece of the basket along with the vegetables.

## Salad Baskets

**oil for deep frying**
**egg roll wrappers**

Heat oil to 375° in a deep fat fryer. Plunge one egg roll wrapper into hot oil and immediately press down its center with a soup ladle. Keep the ladle in place until "basket" is nicely browned. Remove and drain upside down on paper towels. Repeat process with remaining wrappers. Use these edible baskets to serve green salads or vegetable salads. Fill just before serving. These are best made and served the same day.

## Taco Shells

Makes 8 Baskets

**8 flour tortillas**
**oil for deep frying**

Drop one tortilla into a deep fat fryer filled with oil preheated to 375°. Press down in center with a long handled ladle, letting the sides rise to form the shell. Cook 1 minute, or until golden brown. Drain on paper towels. Repeat with remaining tortillas. When cool, place each in a glass bowl and fill with taco salad. Prepare 8 shells for Best Ever Taco Salad.

## Best Ever Taco Salad

Serves 8

**1 lb. ground beef**
**1 pkg. taco seasoning**
  **mix**
**1 c. water**
**1 head lettuce, shredded**
**1—8-oz. pkg. shredded**
  **taco or cheddar cheese**
**1—15-oz. can dark**
  **kidney beans, drained**
  **and rinsed**
**1—5-3/4-oz. pkg.**
  **crushed Dorito chips**
**1/2 c. thousand island**
  **dressing**
**1—16-oz. can black**
  **olives, drained and**
  **sliced**

**2 tomatoes, cubed**
**1 avocado, peeled and**
  **cubed**
**1 medium onion,**
  **chopped or 6 green**
  **onions, sliced**
**sour cream for topping**
**Mexican sauces, optional**

Brown ground beef in skillet; drain. Add taco seasoning mix and water; cook and stir 10 minutes; cool to room temperature. Mix and toss all ingredients together just before serving. Fill prepared taco shells, and serve with side dishes of sour cream, red and green Mexican sauces.

## Baskets From Fresh Fruits . . .

Nature has provided fruit containers that need just a few deft strokes of the knife to hold any number of fillings beautifully. Fruits are colorful and sturdy, two traits that lend themselves to many basket uses.

## Citrus Fruit Baskets

The familiar oranges, grapefruits, lemons, and limes and lesser known tangelos, tangerines, calamondins, and kumquats are easy to hollow out for individual baskets. Use a sharp paring knife and a curved, serrated grapefruit knife. Holding the fruit by its stem end, cut away wedges to form a handle in the middle. Very carefully, scoop out the fruit under the handle; and then using the serrated knife, loosen the pulp from the peel in the fruit's base. Start the original wedge cuts about 2/3 up from the base and make the handle flare a bit wider as it meets the basket. After the fruit is removed, you may want to make a sawtooth or scalloped edge for a fancier container.

Larger orange and grapefruit baskets can hold fresh or frozen fruit salads. Try a salad made from the segmented fruit, halved grapes, coconut, and light rum. When citrus baskets are used as buffet servers, they can be lined with custard cups or small glass mixing bowls to hold sauces, whipped butter, cream cheese, or other spreads as well as dips.

The smaller fruits are ideal as containers for meat sauces, jellies, preserves, berries, or individual scoops of sorbets and ices.

## Strawberry Sorbet

1—3-oz. pkg. strawberry
  gelatin
1 c. water, boiling
2—16-oz. pkg.
  unsweetened frozen
  whole strawberries,
  thawed

Dissolve gelatin in water in saucepan. Measure 2 cups of the berries and add to the gelatin mixture. Cook and stir until mixture comes to a boil. Crush fruit and simmer for 2 minutes. Place remaining berries in mixing bowl or food processor, and pour hot strawberry mixture over them. Then beat until thick and smooth and light in color. Freeze until solid, but not hard; then beat again. Freeze and beat once more before serving or storing in a tightly covered container. Serve small scoops in a fruit basket as a sorbet between courses of a formal dinner, or larger scoops for dessert topped with a teaspoon of an orange-flavored liqueur.

## Frosted Fruit Shells

Makes 6

1 egg white
1/2 c. sugar
6 fruit shells

Beat egg white until frothy. Lightly coat fruit shells with egg white. Roll the shells in the sugar and allow to dry on a rack for 15 minutes. Fill as desired.

## Melon Baskets

For melon baskets, the technique is much the same as for smaller fruits. Use a medium-to-large knife, and scoop the fruit out with a melon baller. Then, with a lemon zester or small knife, carve floral or geometric designs on the melon rind; or, carve the guests' names.

When serving several melons, it is easy to use some very thin slices of the melon to make flowers. Spiral the melon slice around itself and secure with a toothpick. Insert a small melon ball of a constrasting color into the center. Place on a leaf of salad greens or atop your melon basket.

## Shrimp and Melon Basket

Serves 8

1 large honeydew melon, cut into a basket
honeydew melon balls
1/2 c. bottled French dressing
1-1/2 lb. shrimp, cooked, cleaned, deveined
1/3 c. diced celery
1/3 c. mayonnaise
1 c. sour cream
2 T. curry powder
1/4 c. shredded coconut

Marinate melon balls in French dressing for 15 minutes. Set aside a few shrimp for garnish. Combine the remaining shrimp, celery, mayonnaise, sour cream, and curry powder. Fold in the marinated melon balls. Spoon this mixture into the melon basket. Chill until serving. Sprinkle with shredded coconut and garnish with remaining shrimp.

## Pineapple Baskets

With their quilted golden brown shells, pineapples look like woven baskets. Their size makes them ideal for festive luncheon or supper containers. Split a green-tufted ripe pineapple in half, cutting carefully through the leaves. Scoop out the fruit; turn the empty shells upside-down to drain. Fill as desired with chicken, seafood, fruit salad, or dip.

## Pineapple Appetizers

Serves 8

1 pineapple
2 T. green creme de
  menthe
maraschino cherries

Slice a ripe pineapple into fourths, cutting carefully to include part of the green tuft. Then slice parallel to the base to loosen the fruit. Cut this wedge of fruit lengthwise once, then horizontally to form chunks; do not remove fruit from the shell. Push alternate slices slightly in opposite directions. Arrange the four wedges on a round or oval platter with the leaves toward the edge. Pour cream de menthe over each wedge and garnish with maraschino cherries. Or, place 1 cup of sour cream in a small lined basket in the center of the four wedges; sprinkle generously with dark brown sugar. Serve with cocktail picks.

## Polynesian Dip

Serves 6

1—3-oz. pkg. cream
  cheese
1 c. mayonnaise
1/4 c. finely minced
  green onions,
  including tops
1/4 c. chopped candied
  ginger
1 c. sour cream
1/4 c. chopped water
  chestnuts
1/4 c. minced fresh
  parsley
1 T. soy sauce
1/8 t. garlic powder

Blend cream cheese and mayonnaise. Add green onion and ginger and fold in sour cream. When well-blended, add water chestnuts, parsley, soy sauce and garlic powder. Stir and refrigerate to let flavors blend. Remove from refrigerator 30 minutes before serving in a pineapple basket with chunks of pineapple, green pepper strips, and crackers.

## Pineapple Hibachi

Serves 6

1 pineapple
assorted fruits, in chunks
dark rum
sugar
1 small can Sterno fuel

Cut crown from pineapple. Carefully hollow pineapple from the top, leaving a 1/2-inch shell. On a large tray surround pineapple shell with fruits and small dishes of rum and sugar. Place Sterno can in pineapple (set on a wooden block if necessary) and light. Guests may spear fruit on fondue forks, dip in rum, then sugar, and glaze over flame.

# Vegetable Baskets . . .

Just as fruits lend themselves to use as serving baskets, vegetable cases offer versatility and variety both cooked and uncooked. From artichokes to zucchini, the garden provides a cornucopia of serving ideas.

## Artichoke Baskets

Clean and trim a fresh artichoke, removing the choke. Use a scissors to cut off the thorny leaf tips. Use an aritchoke basket for Hollandaise Sauce, Bernaise Sauce, or Bechamel Sauce.

## Cabbage Baskets

Use cabbages which still have the outer leaves intact. Gently wash and curl back these outer leaves. Carefully cut away wedges of the solid inside head until the remaining outer wall is 3/4-inch thick. If the cabbage is too firm, use the looser outside leaves to surround a glass bowl, curling the leaves over the rim to conceal the bowl. Savoy is the showiest, but red cabbage can be equally attractive. Even a pale green cabbage makes a striking container for coleslaw, and adds drama to cold soups, like Vichyssoise or Borscht.

## Eggplant Baskets

With its natural basket shape and striking color, an eggplant can be studded with appetizers on toothpicks, or hollowed and used as a container for this refreshing vegetable medley:

## Summer Garden Ratatouille

Serves 6-8

1—2-3 lb. eggplant
1/4 c. olive oil
1 medium zucchini,
    cubed
1 medium yellow
    summer squash, cubed
1 onion, sliced
1 green pepper, diced
4 tomatoes, peeled and
    cubed
1 clove garlic, crushed
1 bay leaf
1/2 t. oregano
salt and pepper

Cut eggplant just under the green cap. Scoop out the pulp, leaving a 1/2-inch shell. Make a sawtooth edge. Set aside.

Heat oil and add zucchini, squash, onion, green pepper, tomato, garlic and bay leaf. Stir to coat with oil. Stir in oregano, salt and pepper. Simmer until tender, about 20 minutes. Remove bay leaf. Fill eggplant basket with mixture, draining slightly with a slotted spoon. Heat at 400° for 10 minutes. Extra ratatouille tastes delicious chilled.

## Mushroom Baskets

The basket shape of mushrooms, plus the elegance they add to whatever food they accompany, makes them suitable to any number of fillings. This hors d'oeuvre wins raves:

## Baked Stuffed Mushrooms

2 lb. mushrooms
1 T. olive oil
1 T. butter
3 cloves garlic, minced
1 T. flour
1/2 c. dry white wine
1 egg yolk
1/4 t. pepper
3 T. olive oil
1/2 c. dry bread crumbs
3 T. butter

Remove stems from mushrooms; chop. In skillet, heat 1 T. oil and 1 T. butter. Saute stems and garlic; then add flour and stir to combine. Slowly add the wine, stirring constantly. Cook until liquid is absorbed. Cool 10 minutes; then mix in egg yolk and pepper. Stuff the caps with mixture. Place 3 T. oil in a baking pan. Put stuffed caps in pan. Top with bread crumbs and dot with 3 T. butter. Bake at 375° for 15 minutes. Serve hot or cold.

## Potato Baskets

Baked stuffed potatoes and filled potato skins are not the only way to turn this ever-popular vegetable into an edible serving container. These Oriental Potato Nests are unique, delicious with any filling, and well worth the time and effort for a special company meal.

# Oriental Potato Nests

*Serves 8*

**Potato Baskets:**
**8 medium baking**
 **potatoes, peeled and**
 **shredded**
**salt**
**1-1/2 t. cornstarch**
**vegetable oil**

**Chicken and Vegetable**
**Filling:**
**2 eggs**
**2 T. cornstarch**
**1-1/2 lb. boneless,**
 **skinless chicken**
 **breasts, cut in 1-inch**
 **pieces**
**1—4-oz. can sliced**
 **bamboo shoots**
**1—4-oz. can sliced**
 **mushrooms**
**4 large stalks celery, in**
 **1-inch diagonal pieces**
**1 medium green pepper,**
 **in 1-inch chunks**
**1 medium sweet red**
 **pepper, in 1-inch**
 **chunks**

**Sauce:**
**1 T. cornstarch**
**1 T. water**
**1 c. water**
**2/3 c. soy sauce**
**3 T. sugar**
**2 T. rice wine**
**1 T. vinegar**
**1 slice fresh ginger,**
 **peeled and minced**
**1 clove garlic, crushed**

To make baskets:
Place potatoes in colander and sprinkle with salt. Rinse under cold water until water runs clear. Pat dry with paper towels and mix with cornstarch. Heat oil in deep fryer to 350°. Spray a 4 to 5-inch metal strainer with non-stick spray.* Fill with a layer of the potato mixture and press with a ladle. Plunge into the hot oil and deep fry until crisp and brown, about 8-10 minutes. Continue until all baskets are cooked. Drain on paper plates, after carefully removing from the strainer.

*Note: Alternatives to using a metal strainer and ladle are either two strainers which fit inside each other or a special utensil for basket-making which can be purchased in a cooking specialty shop.

To make filling:
Beat eggs and mix with cornstarch. Coat chicken completely with mixture. Deep fry in 350° oil for 2 minutes, removing with slotted spoon. Sear vegetables in oil for 30 seconds and remove. Prepare sauce.

To make sauce:
Blend cornstarch and water. In a wok, mix rest of ingredients and heat to boil. Add cornstarch mixture and stir to thicken. Add chicken and vegetable filling and return to boil. Cook 1 minute and spoon mixture into prepared potato nests. Serve immediately.

# Pumpkin & Squash Baskets

Most cookbooks as well as most cooks seem to ignore the pumpkin as a vegetable, yet the pulp is rich and tasty. Best of all, the container itself makes for a conversation-stopping presentation. Both pumpkins and squash are firm enough to withstand long baking, and make excellent containers for soups and stews.

## Chili in a Pumpkin

Serves 8

2 lb. ground beef
1 clove garlic, minced
1 c. onion, minced
1 c. celery, chopped
1/2 c. green pepper, chopped
1 t. salt
1/4 t. pepper
1-1/2 T. chili powder
1 T. paprika
1 t. ginger
1 T. sugar
1—4-oz. can tomato paste
1—8-oz. can tomato sauce
1—1 lb.-12 oz. can tomatoes
1/2 c. water
2—15-oz. cans kidney
   beans, drained
2 T. flour
3 T. water
1—8-lb. pumpkin
vegetable oil

Fry beef, garlic, onion, celery and green pepper together lightly. Drain. Add salt, pepper, chili powder, paprika, ginger, sugar, tomato paste, tomato sauce, tomatoes and water. Simmer gently 1 hour. Stir in kidney beans. Make a paste of the flour and water; stir in. Simmer 15 minutes.

While chili simmers, cut off the top of the pumpkin and scrape out the seeds and stringy pulp. Place cleaned pumpkin on a sturdy shallow baking pan. Replace the top. Brush the surface of the pumpkin with oil and bake until tender, about 70 minutes. Pour chili into baked pumpkin. To serve, spoon some of the chili into a large soup plate. Scoop out some of the pumpkin and mound in the center of each serving.

## Fall Fondue

Serves 8

8 small acorn squash
vegetable oil
4 slices white bread,
   cubed
3 c. milk
1/4 c. butter, melted
1 t. salt
1/2 t. nutmeg
1/4 t. pepper
4 oz. imported aged
   Swiss cheese, grated

Cut tops from squash and remove seeds. Coat outside surface of squash with oil. Toast bread cubes on a cookie sheet at 350° for 5 minutes, until golden. Mix milk, butter, salt, nutmeg and pepper. Layer bread cubes and cheese in the squash, filling cavities 3/4 full. Pour in milk mixture just to cover bread and cheese. Place close together on a baking dish; cover with caps. Bake at 350° for 1 hour 15 minutes, stirring contents occasionally. Serve hot.

## Tomato & Zucchini Baskets

Bright in color, rich in nutrients and flavor, tomatoes and zucchini are old favorites as containers for fillings. They adapt well to hot or cold fillings, and to baking, grilling, or broiling. They are equally versatile as main dishes or accompaniments.

## Horseradish Mayonnaise in Tomato Baskets

*Serves 8*

8 small, firm tomatoes,
  peeled and tops removed
salt
1/2 c. whipping cream,
  whipped
1/2 c. mayonnaise
2 t. lemon juice
2 T. horseradish
2 T. fresh chives, chopped

Scoop out the seeds and juice from the peeled tomato cups. Sprinkle the insides with salt and stand upside-down to drain and chill for 2 hours. For sauce, fold cream into mayonnaise, lemon juice and horseradish. Cover and chill. Just before serving, spoon the horseradish sauce into the tomato baskets and sprinkle with the chopped chives. Serve with cold meats.

## Zucchini Boats

*Serves 4*

4 medium zucchini
1 lb. bulk pork sausage
1/4 c. chopped onion
1/2 c. grated Parmesan
  cheese, divided
1/2 c. fine cracker
  crumbs
1 egg, beaten
1/4 t. salt
1/4 t. thyme
1/8 t. garlic salt
1/8 t. pepper

Cook whole zucchini in boiling salted water for 7-10 minutes, until barely tender. Remove and cool. Cut in half lengthwise; scoop squash from shells to form "boats"; reserve pulp. Cook sausage with onion in large skillet until thoroughly cooked, breaking up with fork. Reserving 2 T. cheese, mix all ingredients into zucchini pulp. Spoon into zucchini boats. Place boats in shallow baking dish; sprinkle with reserved cheese. Bake at 350° for 25-30 minutes. Serve hot, as a main dish. To use as side dish, decrease amount of sausage to 1/4 pound.

## Zucchini Mini-Baskets

*Serves 6-8*

2 medium zucchini
2 stalks broccoli
1/4 head cauliflower
2 carrots
2 T. water
4 T. butter, melted

Cut both ends from zucchini. Cut into 2-inch segments. Hollow out the segments to form a 1/4-inch shell. Fill each shell with some of vegetables. Place in glass baking dish with water. Cover with plastic wrap and microwave 10 minutes on high, or until tender. The baskets can also be steamed for 6-8 minutes. Serve hot with melted butter or cold with a vinaigrette dressing.

## *Dessert Baskets . . .*

## *Easy Berry Basket Cake*

Serves 6-8

1—9-inch round yellow
  cake layer
2 egg whites
1/4 t. cream of tartar
1/2 c. sugar
1 qt. fresh strawberries,
  sliced
4 T. sugar

Place cake layer on a baking sheet. Make meringue by beating egg whites with cream of tartar until soft peaks form. Gradually beat in sugar. Pipe circles of meringue (using star tip) around edge of cake, building up sides to form a basket. Bake at 400° for 8-10 minutes. Cool. Gently mix strawberries with sugar. Pile berries into center of cake. Serve immediately.

## *Raspberry Meringue Baskets*

Serves 8

1—10-oz. pkg. frozen
  raspberries in syrup,
  thawed
2 t. cornstarch
8 meringue shells
  (recipe follows)
1—6-oz. pkg. vanilla
  pudding, prepared and
  chilled

Drain berries, reserving juice. Combine juice and cornstarch in sauce pan, stirring to dissolve completely. Cook over low heat, stirring until clear and thickened. Add berries and cool.

For each serving, place a meringue shell on a dessert plate. Fill with vanilla pudding and top with a spoon of raspberry sauce, drizzling some sauce over the shell and filling.

## *Meringue Shells*

Makes 8

3 egg whites
1/2 t. cream of tartar
3/4 c. sugar

Line baking sheets with brown paper. Beat egg whites with cream of tartar until foamy. Add sugar, one T. at a time, beating until stiff and glossy. Drop meringue by half-cupfuls onto lined sheets. Shape into baskets, building up sides. Bake 1 hour, at 250°, then turn off oven and let dry out completely for at least 1-1/2 hours with oven door closed. Cool completely. These keep well in a covered tin.

# Sundae Bubble Ring

Serves 12-16

1 c. water
1/2 c. butter
1 c. flour
1/2 t. salt
4 eggs
2 qt. chocolate almond
  fudge ice cream (or
  other flavor)
Microwave Chocolate
  Sauce (recipe follows)
1/2 c. sliced almonds
1 t. butter
salt
whipped cream
6 maraschino cherries,
  halved

Heat water and butter in a large saucepan to boiling. Stir in flour and salt quickly, stirring until mixture forms a ball. Remove from heat and let cool for 5 minutes. Stir in eggs one at a time, beating until very smooth. Drop batter by slightly rounded tablespoons onto ungreased baking sheet. Bake at 400° for 30-35 minutes until golden brown. Cool.

Let ice cream soften while preparing nuts. Roast almonds by melting butter in a shallow pan. Add nuts and sprinkle lightly with salt. Toss to coat and toast over medium heat to a light brown, about 10 minutes.

To assemble bubble ring, cut off tops of puffs to open, but leave hinged. Scoop out any soft dough and fill with softened ice cream. Arrange filled puffs upside down in a well-buttered 10-inch tube pan, forming the ring. Sprinkle with toasted almonds between the layers of puffs as you assemble. Place in freezer at least one hour. Prepare sauce.

Remove from freezer about 15 minutes before serving. With spatula, loosen ring from pan and invert on serving plate. Drizzle sauce over ring, reserving some to pass. Top with dollops of whipped cream and cherries.

# Microwave Chocolate Sauce

Makes 1 cup

2—1-oz. squares
  unsweetened chocolate
2 T. butter
3/4 c. sugar
1/4 t. salt
2/3 c. milk
1 t. vanilla

In a deep glass bowl, microwave butter and chocolate until melted, about 2 minutes on high. Add sugar and salt and stir in milk. Return to microwave and cook on high for three minutes. Stir in vanilla and serve.

## Chocolate Dessert Baskets

Makes 16

8—1-oz. squares
    semisweet chocolate
1 T. butter
1/2 t. vegetable oil
pleated foil baking cups

Melt chocolate, butter and oil in the top of a double boiler over hot, not boiling water. Beat thoroughly when completely melted. Pour the warm mixture into the baking cups, swirling to cover the inside. Chill the coated cups in a muffin pan until hard. To serve, peel off the foil carefully and fill with ice cream, sherbet, or mousse. Top each basket with a teaspoon of liqueur.

## Chocolate Nests

Makes 16

1—12-oz. pkg. semi-sweet
    chocolate chips
2—1-oz. squares
    unsweetened chocolate
1—4-oz. pkg. shredded
    coconut
2 c. crushed cereal
    flakes

Melt chocolate chips and chocolate together over hot water in a double boiler. Stir in coconut and cereal. The mixture will be quite stiff. Using two spoons, form the chocolate into nests on waxed paper. Refrigerate to harden. Fill as desired. These appeal to children at Easter to hold small candies.

## Drizzled Chocolate Basket

Makes 1

12 oz. semi-sweet
    chocolate
    (squares or bits)
1—9-inch pie pan or
    similar sized container
aluminum foil

Melt chocolate over hot water in a double boiler. Line container with foil, pressing tight and smooth and leaving a rim to use when removing basket. Using a large serving spoon, pour a stream of chocolate 4-6 inches above container. Drizzle in a random pattern, making sure sides are firm enough to hold shape. Chill until hard. Carefully remove foil. Use to hold homemade candies or cookies or as a very special gift.

# Brunch Ideas . . .

To provide a bit of inspiration for your entertaining, **Brunch Basket** offers thirty suggestions for brunches, breakfasts and light meals. We hope they bring sunshine to your mornings and friends to your table:

1. Brunchercise—A shape-up lunch
   Decorate with assorted sports balls in baskets; towels for tablecloths and napkins. Everyone wears jogging clothes and works out to exercise records. Serve an assortment of salads.

2. Balance-Due Brunch—To commiserate at tax time
   Invitations are printed on old tax forms. Guests come in old clothes and sit on the floor. Brunch is served in paper bags; tablecloth is newspaper and centerpiece is a striking arrangement of dead flowers. Serve Empty-Pocket Sandwiches (pita bread) to which guests add the fillings.

3. Blarney Brunch—Celebrate the wearin' o' the green
   Green linens and ivy baskets set the mood. Our Reuben Casserole and homemade Irish Cream are perfect on St. Patrick's mornin'.

4. Bunny Brunch—Set a festive Easter morning table
   Tie pastel ribbons around napkins and arrange daffodils and Easter eggs in baskets. Eggs Oliver, a festive coffeecake, and Lemon Layer Cake will please all.

5. South of the Border Brunch—For Mexican Festival Day, May 5
   Fill an upside-down sombrero with cactus; surround with colorful pottery dishes and Mexican foods. Line your walk or driveway with luminarias (paper bags punched with holes and filled with lighted candles). Offer Margarita Slush, Chiles Rellenos and Layered Tortilla Pie.

6. Derby Day Breakfast—Join the Run for the Roses
   Long-stemmed roses are a must! Wear your jockey's colors and decorate with racing forms and play money for placing bets. Serve the World's Best Mint Juleps.

7. Blueprint Brunch—A Housewarming
   Blueprint invitations. Garb friends in hard hats and carpenters' aprons. Guests will sit on boxes and eat at a sawhorse table. Set out flowers in paint cans. Serve Screwdrivers and Rusty Nails, of course.

8. Bonnet Brunch—For Mother's Day
   Make this an elegant luncheon. Ask your female guests to wear hats and gloves, and serve from gleaming china and silver. Pots of flowers can be set in children's hats, and later planted in Mom's garden. Your menu: Vegetable Vichyssoise, Citrus Chicken, Butterhorns and Frozen Grand Marnier Souffle.

9. Battle the Bugs Brunch—A summer cookout
   Gather on the patio or at the lake. Enjoy volleyball, croquet, and the aroma of coffee bubbling over the coals. Cook a one-dish brunch, like German Farmer's Breakfast, in a hugh skillet on the grill.

10. Beach Brunch—For a lazy family get-away
    Pack individual picnic baskets for each. Bring beach balls, rafts, squirt guns and frisbees; award a prize for the best sand castle. Pack Italian Pasta Salad, French Loaves, and Chocolate Chip Cake.

11. Bridal Brunch—An elegant shower
    Parisienne Chicken Crepes, Sacramento Fruit Bowl and Champagne Punch highlight a formal brunch. Use lacey white placemats and orange blossoms in crystal baskets.

12. New Baby Brunch—Or a shower for the parents-to-be
    Use pastel gingham and stuffed animals in baskets. Serve New Orleans Milk Punch, French Toast Fondue and Grasshopper Flower Pots "planted" with gingham flowers.

13. Bogey Brunch—Before or after a golf game
    Use golf score cards for invitations, tees to hold placecards. Your entree could be Bunch O'Brunch.

14. Old Buddy Brunch—To honor out-of-town guests
    Small doll suitcases filled with fruit or flowers make clever centerpieces. For easy hostessing, begin with a drink called Morning Smile, and make ahead Any-Kind-Of-Strata.

15. Bidders' Bridge Brunch—A grand slam party
    Decorate with red and black, using king-size playing cards as coasters. Serve a variety of hot or cold soups, Swedish Rye Bread and Veiled Country Lass.

16. Baseball Brunch—For the Little Leaguers
    After a backyard campout, serve up Funnel Cakes with syrup and Disappearing Marshmallow Brownies.

17. Breakfast at Wimbledon—After an early doubles match
    Ask the florist to place a small arrangement in a pair of baby tennis shoes. Cool off with chilled Berry Soup and celebrate with Champion Chicken Crepes. White-Chocolate Ice Cream scores on this menu!

18. Block Party Brunch—Fourth of July celebration
    Organize a Neighborhood Olympics and potluck brunch. Contribute a beautiful Fruit Pizza or "Everyone Wants This Recipe" Casserole.

19. Bastille Day Brunch—Make an occasion of July 14
    Invitations should be hand-delivered, written in French and tucked into small baskets of croissants. Pair some excellent French wines with Champignons Lyonnaise, Beignets and Cafe au Grand Marnier.

20. Back-to-School Brunch—Just for Moms
    Host a salad luncheon on burlap-covered tables with Crayola-colored napkins.
    Pile red apples in a basket with pencils, rulers and school supplies. Begin the
    celebration with Orange Blossoms.

21. Balloon Buffet—A bon voyage party
    Ask guests to bring small travel gifts. Use balloons lavishly, inside and out. Put
    each guest's name on a balloon and tie to chairs. Serve ethnic dishes from the
    area to be visited.

22. Bewitching Breakfast—At midnight on Halloween
    You'll want dim lighting and Jack-O-Lantern centerpieces. Serve buffet-style,
    offering Finger Salad, an assortment of quiches, and steaming apple cider.
    Pumpkin Log, decorated with tiny witches, completes the menu.

23. Touchdown Brunch—A tailgate feast
    Take along a hibachi for heating Maple Barbecued Baby Ribs. Accompany
    with Artichoke Salad, Herbed Pinwheel Rolls and Chocoho-Licks.

24. Boss' Brunch—An elegant feast
    Pull out all the stops! Forget the cost and calories, and prepare Brunch Lobster
    and Triple Chocolate Sin.

25. Bavarian Brunch—Don't forget Octoberfest
    Black, red and gold, the colors of the German flag, blend beautifully with the
    color of fall leaves. Plan the menu around German Pancake Pie.

26. Take the Bench Brunch—For Superbowl Sunday
    Pennants and pom-pons stuck into a football helmet make an easy centerpiece.
    Stuff a child's football uniform to make your own "player", and have all guests
    autograph a football to be given as a prize. Offer Hot Bloody Marys, Bacon
    Crisps and Chili in a Pumpkin.

27. A Bullish Brunch—To beat the winter blahs
    Ask your friends to invest in a bullish brunch, and provide blue-chip foods and
    festivities. Serve over-the-counter. Highlight of the party can be a make-your-
    own-sundae bar, using a vareity of homemade ice cream sauces.

28. Ballot Brunch—A campaign special
    Introduce your candidate, or provide a forum for opponents. Decorate with
    campaign posters, and serve Sugar Cookies cut into elephant and donkey
    shapes. Zucchini Boats garnished with tiny flags will be a winner!

29. Break-A-Heart Brunch—For Valentine's Day
    Go old-fashioned with antiques, hearts and flowers. Try an all-pink dessert
    menu to include Pink Champagne Punch and Strawberry/Raspberry Cream
    Puffs.

30. Committee Brunch—A Junior League Special!
    Our **Brunch Basket** Committee's choice: Baskets of Spinach-Strawberry
    Salad; Wild Rice, Chicken and Ham Casserole; and Peppermint Freeze. Enjoy!

## OCTOBER APPLES

picked a few apples today. the sun is warm but its a
little cool in the shade. pumped a cup of cold water,
came inside and sat the apples on a chair.
while i was sipping the water i decided my blue denim
jacket, leather hat, and the old rusty cup would make
a good painting.

monday october 3, 1983 partly sunny, warm    tom heflin

# Beverages

## Rosé Sparkle Punch
Very festive                                                    Serves 24

2—10-oz. pkg. frozen
   raspberries, thawed
1/2 c. sugar
2—4/5-qt. bottles
   rosé wine
1—12-oz. can frozen
   lemonade
1—4/5-qt. bottle pink
   champagne, chilled
ice ring

In a mixing bowl combine raspberries, sugar and 1 bottle wine. Cover and let stand at room temperature 1 hour. Strain mixture into punch bowl. Add frozen lemonade and stir until completely thawed.

Pour in remaining bottle of wine and sparkling champagne. Add block of ice. Serve at once.

Decorate around punch bowl according to season.

## Welcome Punch
Easy to carry along on a picnic                                 Serves 10-15

2 c. reconstituted
   orange juice
1—6-oz. can frozen
   lemonade, thawed
1 c. orange liqueur
1 bottle (750 ml) dry
   white wine, chilled
1—28-oz. bottle
   club soda
ice

In a large pitcher, combine orange juice, lemonade concentrate, orange liqueur and wine. As guests arrive, add soda and ice. Stir and serve.

## Artillery Punch
Packs a punch, so beware!                                       Serves 30

1 c. sugar
juice of 6 lemons
2 T. bitters
1 qt. dry red wine
1 qt. brandy
1 qt. sherry
1 qt. bourbon
1 qt. club soda

In a punch bowl, mix all ingredients but soda and ice. Pour in soda just before serving.

## Ice Ring
Fill a ring mold half full of cold water and freeze until solid. Arrange one or more of the following fruits in a design over the surface of the ice: maraschino cherries, mandarin orange slices, pineapple chunks, lemon or lime slices.

Cover with water and freeze. To unmold, dip in warm water.

## Pink Champagne Punch

Pretty with a pink color scheme                                    Serves 12-14

1—6-oz. can frozen pink
   lemonade concentrate,
   thawed
1 c. orange juice
1/2 c. Cointreau
1/3 c. sugar
orange slices
1 pt. fresh strawberries
   or raspberries,
   washed and hulled
1 bottle pink champagne
club soda to taste
ice cubes or ice ring

In a punch bowl, mix lemonade concentrate, orange juice, Cointreau and sugar. Add orange slices and berries. At serving time, add champagne and club soda to taste. Float ice on top.

## Champagne Punch

Quick and easy                                                     Serves 32

1-1/2 c. orange juice
6 T. lemon juice
2 c. pineapple juice
1 c. sugar
2 c. rum, chilled
4 bottles champagne,
   chilled
fresh strawberries for
   garnish

In a pitcher, mix juices and sugar. Chill. Just before serving, pour into punch bowl and add chilled rum and champagne. Serve with a fresh strawberry in each glass.

## East Coast Champagne Punch

A punch that men really enjoy                                      Serves 30

1 fifth champagne
1 fifth dry white wine
16 oz. light rum
1 qt. club soda
6 oz. frozen orange juice,
   thawed
6 oz. frozen lemonade,
   thawed
4 oz. grenadine syrup
fruit slices for garnish
decorated ice ring

Chill all ingredients before mixing. In punch bowl, combine and gently stir all ingredients over ice ring.

## Brandy Slush

Keep this on hand for summer guests                    Serves 18

7 c. water
2 c. sugar
2 c. boiling water
4 tea bags
1—12-oz. can frozen
   orange juice
1—12-oz. can frozen
   lemonade
2 c. brandy
club soda or 7-Up

In a pan, bring water and sugar to boil. Cool. Steep tea bags in boiling water for 5 minutes. Cool. Stir sugar and tea mixtures together with remaining ingredients. Freeze at least 8 hours.

May be frozen in ice trays or large freezer-proof container.

To serve, fill 8 oz. glass 3/4 full of slush and add 7-Up or soda to fill.

## Strawberry Daiquiri Slush

Easy and thirst-quenching                    Serves 20

3—12-oz. cans frozen
   lemonade
1—12-oz. can frozen
   limeade
14 c. water
4 c. light rum
1—1/2-oz. envelope
   unsweetened powdered
   strawberry drink mix
7-Up
strawberries for garnish

In a large freezer container, mix all ingredients except 7-Up and strawberries well. Freeze at least 8 hours. Mixture will not freeze solid.

To serve, fill glass halfway with slush. Fill with 7-Up. Garnish each with a strawberry.

## World's Best Mint Juleps

A sure sign of spring                    Serves 12

1 c. cold water
2 c. superfine granulated
   sugar
1/2 c. mint leaves,
   packed tightly
bourbon
crushed ice
mint leaves for garnish

In a quart jar with tight-fitting lid, mix water and sugar. Cover and shake vigorously until sugar dissolves completely. Stir in mint leaves. Cover and let stand overnight, shaking several times. Next day strain syrup and discard mint leaves.

To serve, pour 2 ounces bourbon and one ounce minted syrup over crushed ice in each glass. Stir briefly. Garnish with mint sprigs and serve with straws.

Syrup will keep several weeks, covered. Do not refrigerate.

## Margarita Slush
Great beginning for a Mexican meal                                    Serves 4

1—6-oz. can frozen
   limeade
6 oz. tequila
2 oz. triple sec
3/4 blender container
   of ice
1 lime, sliced
salt

In a blender, mix limeade, tequila and triple sec until just mixed. Add ice and blend until slushy.

To serve, rub a lime slice around rim of glass and turn rim in salt. Pour drink into salted glass and garnish with lime slice.


## Spicy Bloody Mary
Everyone's favorite morning cocktail                                 Serves 6

8 c. tomato juice
2 c. clam-flavored
   tomato juice
3 T. green chilies,
   seeded and chopped
1 T. chopped onion
2 T. Worcestershire
   sauce
2 T. lemon juice
2 t. celery salt
2 t. sugar
1/2 t. hot pepper sauce
1-1/2 c. vodka
celery stalks with leaves,
   or unpeeled zucchini sticks

In blender container, mix all ingredients except celery stalks. Blend 1 minute. Serve over ice cubes in tall glasses, garnished with celery stalks or zucchini sticks.


## Egg Nog
A classic for the holidays                                          Serves 12

6 eggs, separated
3/4 c. sugar,
   divided
2 c. milk
1 c. whiskey
1 t. vanilla
1 c. whipping cream,
   whipped
nutmeg

Beat egg whites and yolks separately. While beating yolks, add 1/2 c. sugar. After beating whites stiff, add 1/4 c. sugar. Fold egg yolks into whites with milk, whiskey and vanilla. Fold in whipped cream. Serve cold with nutmeg grated on top.

# Quick Egg Nog
Fast and fancy                                    Serves 8-10

4 c. dairy egg nog
1/3 c. creme de cacao,
  chilled
2/3 c. brandy, cognac,
  or whiskey, chilled
1/3 c. rum, chilled
1 c. whipping cream,
  whipped
nutmeg

In a mixing bowl, mix egg nog and chilled liquors with whipped cream. Beat with an electric mixer until frothy. Sprinkle with nutmeg and serve.

# New Orleans Milk Punch
Serve in a punch bowl or champagne glasses          Serves 6-8

1-1/2 c. milk
1-1/2 c. half & half
1/2 c. plus 2 T. white
  creme de cacao
1/4 c. plus 2 T. bourbon
2 T. powdered sugar
2 egg whites
cracked ice
cinnamon

In a blender, combine all ingredients except ice and cinnamon. Blend until frothy. Serve over cracked ice and sprinkle with cinnamon.

# Iced Coffee
For the coffee lover                                Serves 8-10

4 c. brewed regular
  blend coffee
4 c. brewed chicory
  coffee
1/4 c. sugar
10 whole allspice
10 whole cloves
4 cinnamon sticks
1/2 c. coffee-flavored
  liqueur
1 tray ice cubes made
  from freezing brewed
  regular blend coffee

In large bowl, combine hot brewed regular coffee with hot brewed chicory coffee. Add sugar and spices. Cover with plastic wrap and set aside at room temperature for 1 hour.

Just before seving, add liqueur. Place ice cubes in glass pitcher and strain coffee into pitcher.

## Creamy Coffee Punch
For dessert, add chocolate liqueur                                                Serves 30

4 qt. cold, strong coffee
1 qt. cold milk
1 T. vanilla
1 c. sugar
2 qt. vanilla ice cream
whipped cream

In a large container, combine coffee, milk and vanilla. Add sugar and stir until dissolved. (This may be done the day before.)

To serve, pour over ice cream in punch bowl. Serve in punch cups. Top with dollop of whipped cream.

## Cappuccino
Elegant any time of day                                                            Serves 6

3 c. brewed coffee
3 c. half and half cream
1/2 c. Kahlua
1/4 c. dark rum
1/4 c. brandy
6 cinnamon sticks

In a medium saucepan, combine coffee, cream and liquors. Cover and heat; do not boil. Serve immediately with cinnamon sticks for stirrers.

## Café au Grand Marnier
Delightful alternative to Irish Coffee                                             Serves 1

1-1/2 oz. Grand Marnier
3/4 c. freshly brewed
   coffee
whipped cream

Fill mug 3/4 full of coffee. Pour Grand Marnier into cup. Top with whipped cream.

## Orange Blossoms
Nice for a ladies-only brunch                                                      Serves 1

1/2 c. orange sherbet
1/2 c. orange juice
1-1/2 oz. vodka or
   champagne

In a blender, mix all ingredients until well blended. Pour into stemmed glass. To serve, garnish with mint sprig.

## Morning Smile
A nutritious twist on the Screwdriver                                              Serves 1

1-1/2 c. orange juice
1/4 c. vodka
1 egg
1 T. honey

In a blender, mix ingredients for 30 seconds. Serve over ice.

## Hot Buttered Wine
Make this just for the aroma!                                    Serves 12

2 c. Chianti
2 c. cranberry juice
2 c. pineapple juice
1/3 c. brown sugar
1/4 t. cinnamon
1/4 t. ground cloves
1/4 t. ground ginger
1/8 t. salt
1/4 c. butter (approx.)

Combine all ingredients except butter in a saucepan. Heat slowly, stirring often, until steaming. Ladle into mugs and dot each with one teaspoon butter.

For a stronger brew, allow to cool after heating. Let stand several hours at room temperature. Reheat to serve.

## Hot Bloody Mary
Fill a big thermos for apres-ski                              Serves 8-10

1 qt. tomato juice
1 cinnamon stick
4 whole cloves
1 T. Worcestershire
  sauce
1/4 t. salt
1/4 t. pepper
1/4 c. lemon juice
1-1/2 c. vodka

In a pan, combine tomato juice, cinnamon, cloves and Worcestershire sauce. Heat over low flame 10-15 minutes. Add salt and pepper. Pour in lemon juice and vodka just before serving.

## Swedish Glögg
One of Rockford's delicious Swedish traditions               Serves 6

1/2 c. sugar
1—3-inch strip
  orange peel
1—3-inch strip
  lemon peel
1 t. whole cloves
1/3 c. blanched whole
  almonds
1/4 c. raisins
1/4 t. Angostura bitters
4 pods cardamom seeds
2 c. light port wine
2 c. sherry
1 c. blackberry brandy
3-inch cinnamon sticks
  for stirring

In a pan, mix all ingredients except cinnamon. Heat until very hot; do not boil. Cover and simmer for 10 minutes. Strain. Pour Glögg into mugs and serve with cinnamon sticks while hot.

## Vintage Tomato Bouillon
Also good served cold                                    Serves 8

6 c. canned tomato juice
2 thick slices onion
2 celery stalks, sliced
2 bay leaves
8 whole cloves
2—10-oz. cans condensed
   beef consomme
1 c. dry red wine
salt and pepper
1 lemon, sliced

In a pan, combine juice, onions, celery, bay leaves and cloves. Bring to a boil and simmer, covered, for 20 minutes. Strain, add consomme, wine, salt and pepper. Serve hot in mugs with a slice of lemon.

This may be done in microwave. It may be frozen.

## Bavarian Mint
A warm winter welcome                                   Serves 1

1 oz. peppermint
   schnapps
1 oz. light creme
   de cacao
1 c. hot chocolate
whipped cream
cinnamon for garnish

Add liqueurs to cup of hot chocolate. Garnish with whipped cream and cinnamon. Serve in tulip glass.

## Irish Cream
Better and less expensive than commercial brands        Makes 1 quart

3 eggs
1—14-oz. can sweetened
   condensed milk
2 T. chocolate syrup
1/2 t. coconut extract
1 pt. frozen non-dairy
   creamer, thawed
1-1/2 c. whiskey, brandy
   or rum

In blender, blend first 5 ingredients until well mixed. Add whiskey and blend well.

Refrigerate. Will keep 2 weeks in refrigerator.

Serve in liqueur glasses or over ice.

## Homemade Kahlua
Bottle as gifts at Christmas                             Makes 2-3 bottles

4 c. sugar
4 c. water
3/4 c. dry instant coffee
5 T. vanilla (or 1 long
   vanilla bean)
1 qt. vodka

In a pan, bring sugar and water to a boil and remove from heat. Add coffee and vanilla. Let cool completely.

Add vodka and stir well. Store in dark location for 1 month. Strain and bottle in attractive bottles or place in your decanter.

## Swedish Wassail
Easily made and served in a coffeepot      Serves 16-20

1 gal. apple cider
1—6-oz. can frozen
   orange juice
   concentrate, thawed
1—6-oz. can frozen
   lemonade, thawed
2/3 c. brown sugar
1 t. nutmeg
1 T. whole cloves
1 T. allspice
cinnamon sticks
rum (optional)

In a pan, mix together first five ingredients. Fill cheesecloth bag or loose tea holder with cloves and allspice. Simmer together for 20 minutes. Serve piping hot in mugs with cinnamon stick as garnish.

Add 1/2 to 1 oz. rum to each mug, if desired.

## Fruit Punch
Inexpensive way to serve a crowd      Serves 50

5 lb. sugar (10 c.)
1/2 gal. strong tea
1—46-oz. can
   unsweetened
   grapefruit juice
1—46-oz. can
   unsweetened
   pineapple juice
1—40-oz. bottle
   unsweetened grape
   juice
6 oranges, sliced
6 lemons, sliced
ice ring

In a large container, dissolve sugar in hot tea. Add other ingredients. Pour over ice ring. Garnish with orange and lemon slices.

## Strawberry-Peach Cooler
Nourishing, quick and easy      Serves 4-6

1 pint strawberries,
   hulled and sliced
1—16-oz. can peaches in
   light syrup, drained
1 c. plain yogurt
2 T. wheat germ,
   optional
honey, to taste
freshly grated nutmeg
   to taste
6 whole strawberries
   for garnish

Place all ingredients except whole strawberries in blender. Process until smooth. Refrigerate one hour, until well chilled. Serve garnished with whole berries.

## Strawberry Lemonade
A treat for any age                                          Serves 6

1—10-oz. pkg. frozen
  strawberry halves
1—6-oz. can frozen
  lemonade
6 c. cold water
1/2 c. sugar
1/3 c. instant powdered
  tea (unsweetened)

In a blender, combine strawberries and lemonade. Pour into pitcher. Add water, sugar and tea. Chill and serve over ice.

## Banana/Buttermilk Drink
A quick and nourishing breakfast                            Serves 2-4

2 bananas
2 T. sugar
1 c. orange juice
2 c. buttermilk
orange slices

In a blender, puree bananas, sugar and orange juice. Add buttermilk and blend briefly.

Serve in glass with a slice of orange as garnish.

## Cantaloupe Carrot Whip
Try it — you'll like it                                      Serves 4

2 carrots, peeled and
  chopped
1 c. milk
2 c. cantaloupe, diced
2 T. honey or sugar
dash cinnamon
carrot, grated (optional)
cinnamon sticks
  (optional)

In a blender, combine chopped carrots and milk and blend until liquified. Add cantaloupe; blend. Stir in honey or sugar and pour into glasses over crushed ice. Sprinkle with cinnamon. Garnish with grated carrot and cinnamon stick, if desired.

## Hot Chocolate Mix
Makes a winter's supply                                      Serves 50

1—14-oz. jar powdered
  cream
25.6 oz. powdered milk
1 lb. powdered sugar
1 lb. unsweetened
  instant cocoa mix

In a large bowl, combine all ingredients. Mix well. Store in air-tight container (coffee can works well).

To serve, place 1/3 cup of cocoa mix in a coffee cup. Fill with hot water. Stir. Add marshmallows, if desired.

## WILD IRIS

around the second week in june the irises start blooming.
emmerts brother, herbert, planted a whole garden of irises.
since herbert went away, fifteen years ago, the irises have
had to make it on their own. they push through knee
high weeds and bloom in all their glory.
herbert would be proud of them. and i thought of him
when i did this painting.

turday june 18, 1983                    tom heflin

# Appetizers

## Avocado-Bacon Dip
For dippers, use fresh vegetables or nacho chips                    Serves 8

**2 ripe avocados, peeled,
  pitted and sliced
1/2 c. mayonnaise
2 T. sliced green onion
1 T. lemon juice
3/4 t. salt
1/4 t. pepper
8 strips bacon, cooked
  and crumbled**

Place avocados in food processor (or mash in mixing bowl). Add mayonnaise and green onion; blend. Add lemon juice, salt and pepper. Blend. Scrape into serving bowl. Cover; chill.

Just before serving, stir in all but 2 T. crumbled bacon. Garnish with remaining bacon.

## Beaumonde Dip
Add color with fresh vegetables for dipping                    Serves 8

**1-1/3 c. mayonnaise
1-1/2 c. sour cream
6 oz. dried beef
2 T. parsley, chopped
2 T. onion, chopped
2 t. dill weed
2 t. Beaumonde
  seasoning
1 medium loaf rye bread**

The day before serving, mix all ingredients, except bread. Chill. Cut top slice from bread loaf and hollow out, leaving a 1-inch shell. Cut scooped-out bread into cubes for dipping. Wrap cubes and shell tightly until serving. To serve, fill shell with dip and arrange bread cubes around the loaf.

## Chutney Dip
Pretty served in pineapple half                    Serves 8

**8 oz. cream cheese
1/4 c. mango chutney
1/4 t. dry mustard
1 t. curry powder
1/4 c. toasted almonds**

Blend cream cheese, chutney, mustard and curry powder. Cover and chill 4 hours or overnight. To serve, sprinkle with almonds and surround with crisp crackers.

## Curry Dip
Overnight chilling brings out the flavor                    Serves 8

**2 c. mayonnaise
1/2 c. sour cream
2 T. curry powder
2 cloves garlic, crushed
4 t. sugar
1 t. salt
2 t. fresh lemon juice
1/4 c. parsley, chopped**

Mix all ingredients. Cover and chill overnight. Serve with raw vegetables.

## Mrs. Blott's Cucumber Dip

Especially easy in a food processor                    Serves 6

1/4 c. green onion
1/4 c. radishes
1/4 c. cucumber,
  unpeeled
1/4 c. green pepper
1 clove garlic
1 c. sour cream
1/2 c. mayonnaise
1 T. sugar
1 t. salt
1/8 t. pepper
1—3-oz. pkg. cream
  cheese, softened

Mince onions, radishes, cucumber, green pepper and garlic. Mix with sour cream, mayonnaise, sugar, salt, pepper and cream cheese. Chill.

Serve with crisp crackers.

## Green Grape Dip

Bet you can't eat just one                    Serves 4

1 can deviled ham
1 t. dill weed
1 c. sour cream
1 c. seedless green grapes

In a small, shallow dish, spread deviled ham thinly. Mix dill weed with sour cream and spread over ham. Add green grapes on top of sour cream.

Serve with potato chips.

## Avocado Pinwheel

Looks smashing — and so easy!                    Serves 12

1 T. unflavored gelatin
1/4 c. cold water
1 c. mashed avocado
1 T. lemon juice
1—6-oz. pkg. dry Italian
  salad dressing
2 c. sour cream
3 T. chopped parsley
6 drops hot pepper sauce
2 drops green food coloring

Garnish:
cooked shrimp, chopped
cucumber, chopped
black olives, chopped
green onions, chopped
caviar
tomato bits
grated cheese

Oil a shallow 9-1/2-inch round baking tin. In a small pan, soften gelatin in water 5 minutes; then heat gelatin to boiling. Pour gelatin into blender or food processor; add remaining ingredients. Process until smooth. Pour into prepared tin. Refrigerate several hours until firm. May be prepared 2 days ahead.

To serve, unmold onto large tray. Arrange garnishes in concentric circles atop mold, beginning at outer edge and varying colors as you move toward center. Surround with crackers.

## Stuffed Camembert
Easy and elegant                                    Serves 8

1 whole Camembert
  cheese
1/2 c. butter, softened
1/4 t. salt
1/8 t. paprika
1/2 c. whipping cream
1/2 c. slivered almonds,
  toasted
seedless green grapes
crackers

Slice top from Camembert. Carefully hollow out cheese, leaving bottom and sides 1/4-inch thick. In a food processor, puree the removed cheese, butter, salt, paprika and cream. When mixture is smooth and fluffy, pile it into the shell. Press almonds over cheese to cover. Surround with grapes and serve with crackers.

## Cheese Chips
Easy to keep on hand                              Makes 5 dozen

1/2 c. butter
1 c. flour
8 oz. sharp cheddar
  cheese, grated
4 drops hot pepper sauce
2 T. dry onion soup
  mix

Have all ingredients at room temperature. Mix all thoroughly by hand or in food processor.

Chill mixture in refrigerator for 1 hour. On plastic wrap, form chilled mixture into 1-1/4-inch diameter rolls. Place wrapped rolls in refrigerator (will keep 1-2 weeks) or freeze.

To serve, cut rolls into thin round slices and place on ungreased non-stick baking sheet. Bake at 400° for 5-8 minutes, until golden and crisp.

## Roquefort Shrimp
For sophisticated tastes                            Serves 12

2 lb. large raw shrimp
  (about 36)
8 oz. Roquefort cheese
2—3-oz. pkg. cream
  cheese
Worcestershire sauce

Plunge shrimp into a large kettle of boiling salted water. Cook until pink, about 3 minutes. Cool slightly; remove shells and veins. Cut pockets along the vein lines to hold a filling.

Mix Roquefort with cream cheese; blend well and add Worcestershire to taste. Pack filling into shrimp pockets; chill at least 2 hours.

Serve with toothpicks.

## Finger Salad

Drain and serve in glass bowl with toothpicks                Serves 8-10

1-1/2 c. vegetable oil
2/3 c. vinegar
2-1/2 t. salt
1 t. pepper
1-1/2 t. garlic salt
1-1/2 t. sugar
8 carrots
8 stalks celery
2 cans pitted black olives
2 jars stuffed green
  olives
1 head cauliflower, in
  florets
2 cans tiny artichoke
  hearts
1 pint cherry tomatoes
fresh or canned
  mushrooms

Combine oil, vinegar, salt, pepper, garlic salt and sugar in large bowl. Cut up vegetables and add to dressing. Marinate at least 24 hours, covered and refrigerated, stirring several times. Will keep one week in refrigerator. Other vegetables may be added as desired.

## Cold Vegetable Pizza

Great for tailgate brunches                Serves 8-12

2 cans refrigerated
  crescent rolls
3—8-oz. pkg. cream
  cheese, softened
1 c. mayonnaise
1-1/2 t. onion powder
1/2 t. Worcestershire
  sauce
1-1/2 t. dillweed
dash garlic salt
3 c. chopped vegetables
  (radishes, green
  peppers, mushrooms,
  carrots, green
  onions, celery)
1/4 c. chopped green
  and/or black olives
2 c. shredded Monterey
  Jack or cheddar cheese
1/2 c. alfalfa sprouts
12 cherry tomatoes,
  halved

Lay out rolls to cover a greased 11 x 17-inch pan. Pinch edges together. Bake at 400° for 8 minutes. Cool.

In large mixing bowl, blend cream cheese, mayonnaise and seasonings. Spread half cream cheese mixture over cooled crust. Add vegetables and olives to remaining cheese mix and gently stir until blended. Carefully spread over cream cheese mix on crust. Sprinkle cheese over all. Cover with plastic wrap; chill 3-4 hours.

Just before serving, sprinkle alfalfa sprouts over cheese. Carefully cut pizza into 24 squares. Place cherry tomato half in center of each.

## Shrimp Mousse
Pretty and delicious on crackers                                    Serves 8

1-1/2 T. unflavored
   gelatin
1/2 c. cold water
1—10-oz. can tomato
   soup
1—8-oz. pkg. cream
   cheese, softened
1 c. mayonnaise
2—4-oz. cans shrimp,
   drained
1 c. chopped celery
6 green onions, chopped
   fine

Dissolve gelatin in cold water. Heat undiluted soup to boiling and stir in gelatin. Add cream cheese and mayonnaise and mix well. Add shrimp, celery, and onions. Pour into oiled mold, and refrigerate 4 hours or overnight.

## Lox and Cream Cheese Mold
A whole breakfast for four                                    Serves 8

1/2 lb. lox, diced
2—8-oz. pkg. cream
   cheese
1 cucumber, peeled and
   chopped
6 green onions, minced
cherry tomatoes
8 bagels

Combine all ingredients. Press into oiled fish-shaped mold. Chill until firm. Unmold and garnish with cherry tomatoes. Serve as spread on bagels.

## Spicy Nuts
Makes a nice hostess gift                                    Serves 8-12

1 egg white
1 T. water
2 c. walnut or pecan
   halves
1/2 c. sugar
1 t. cinnamon
3/4 t. salt
1/4 t. ground cloves
1/4 t. ground nutmeg

In medium bowl, beat egg white and water until foamy and double in volume. Stir in nuts. In small bowl, mix remaining ingredients. Sprinkle over nuts and mix thoroughly. Spread on greased baking sheet.

Bake at 300° for 30 minutes. Spread nuts on greased sheet of aluminum foil to cool completely. Break cooled nuts apart. Pack into jar or tin. Store in refrigerator or freeze.

## Curried Pecans
These are addictive!                                    Makes 4 cups

1 lb. pecan halves
1/2 c. butter
1/4 c. vegetable oil
2 T. brown sugar
2 T. curry powder
1 T. ground ginger
1 T. mango chutney
salt to taste

Toast pecans on a baking sheet at 350° for 10 minutes. Remove from oven (do not turn oven off) and place pecans in bowl.

In a skillet, melt butter; stir in oil, brown sugar, curry, ginger and chutney. Pour mixture over pecans and stir to coat.

Line baking sheet with paper towels; spread pecans on baking sheet in a single layer; place in oven. Turn oven off and let pecans warm 10 minutes. Remove from oven; salt lightly and cool.

Store in covered container in refrigerator.

## Zucchini Cups
Another idea for the endless zucchini crop              Serves 10

4—6-inch-long
  zucchini
1-1/2 T. mayonnaise
1-1/2 T. sour cream
2 t. finely chopped
  parsley
salt & pepper to taste
1 t. Dijon mustard
1 t. Worchestershire
  sauce
1/4 t. celery salt
1 lb. crabmeat, flaked

Scrub zucchini and trim ends flat. Cut into 1-inch pieces. With a melon baller or small spoon, scoop out the insides of zucchini without removing bottom to form cups.

Combine all ingredients except crabmeat. Blend thoroughly. Gently fold crabmeat into mixture.

Stuff zucchini cups with crab mixture. Chill. Serve cold.

## Asparagus Foldovers
A great side dish with ham                                    Serves 12

**24 pieces of white bread**
**1 package instant**
   **hollandaise sauce**
**3/4 c. Parmesan cheese**
**24 fresh asparagus**
   **spears, cooked**
   **and cooled**
**melted butter**
**1/4 c. Parmesan cheese**

Trim crusts from bread and roll each piece flat. Spread each with hollandaise sauce made according to package directions. Then, using the 3/4 cup Parmesan cheese, sprinkle each with cheese.

Fold each over an asparagus spear, insert a wooden pick and brush with butter. Sprinkle remaining 1/4 cup Parmesan cheese over all. Bake at 400° for 12 minutes until golden.

## Bacon Crisps
Perfect accompaniment to Bloody Marys                         Serves 6-8

**1 egg, beaten**
**1/4 t. chili powder**
**3-4 drops hot pepper**
   **sauce**
**1-2 T. water**
**1/2-1 c. Parmesan cheese**
**8 slices bacon, cut in**
   **thirds**

In a shallow dish, mix egg with seasonings and water. Place Parmesan cheese in another shallow dish. Dip bacon in egg mixture, then cheese. Cover both sides of bacon. Place on broiler pan.

Bake at 350° for 15-20 minutes until golden brown. Remove from pan and serve immediately.

## Artichoke Cheese Dip
Serve warm with wheat crackers                                Serves 12

**1 c. mayonnaise**
**1 c. grated Parmesan**
   **cheese**
**2 c. shredded Mozzarella**
   **cheese**
**2—8-oz. cans artichoke**
   **hearts, drained and**
   **chopped in quarters**
**1/2-1 t. garlic powder**
**paprika**

In a 1-1/2-qt. casserole dish, combine the mayonnaise, cheeses, artichoke hearts and garlic powder. Sprinkle with paprika. Bake at 350° for 25 minutes.

## Cheese Dunk

Dip can also be heated over simmering water                    Serves 6-8

5 green onions, sliced
2—5-oz. jars cheese
  spread
1—8-oz. pkg. cream
  cheese
6 slices bacon, cooked
  and crumbled

In micro-proof bowl, place onions, cheese spread and cream cheese. Heat in microwave on high for 1-1/2 minutes. Remove. Add bacon crumbles. Mix well. Heat 30 seconds on high. Stir well.

Serve warm with crudites (cauliflower, carrots, fresh mushrooms, zucchini sticks) or hearty crackers.

## Japanese Chicken Wings

Special picnic fare!                                           Serves 16

3 lb. chicken wings
garlic/parsley salt
1 egg
2 t. water
cornstarch
5 T. peanut oil
1/2 c. sugar
1/2 c. Japanese rice
  vinegar
1/2 c. chicken broth
3 T. Japanese soy sauce
3 T. ketchup

Cut each chicken wing into 3 pieces at joint; discard wing tip or use to make chicken broth. Soak wings in cold salted water for 30 minutes. Drain; sprinkle with garlic/parsley salt and let stand for 30 minutes.

Beat egg with water. Dip each wing into egg, then roll in cornstarch. Saute wings in hot peanut oil until golden. Place in one layer in a large, flat baking dish.

Mix sugar, vinegar, chicken broth, soy sauce and ketchup. Pour over chicken. Bake at 350° for 30-40 minutes. Serve hot or cold.

May be made ahead and refrigerated until baking.

## Swiss Cheese Bread

Hearty and delicious — people love it!                        Serves 6-8

1 loaf French or Italian
  bread
1 lb. Swiss cheese, thinly
  sliced
1 c. butter, melted
2 T. minced onion
1 T. poppyseed
1 t. seasoned salt
1—4-oz. can mushrooms
1 T. dry mustard
1 T. lemon juice

Slice bread loaf partly through, diagonally in both directions, making little diamonds. Stuff slices of cheese in openings. Place loaf of bread on foil on cookie sheet. Mix remaining ingredients and pour mixture over bread. Seal foil tightly around loaf.

Bake at 350° for 45-60 minutes. Check several times to be sure bottom is not browning too quickly.

## Fried Camembert

Fruit drinks are a nice complement to this                    Serves 4

1—8-oz. round ripe
  Camembert
2 T. flour
1 egg, beaten
1 T. milk
1 c. dry breadcrumbs
1/4 c. melted butter

Cut Camembert in half horizontally, forming 2 thin rounds. Do not remove rind. Dredge rounds in flour. Combine egg and milk. Dip cheese into egg mixture, then into bread crumbs. Repeat dipping process.

Cook in butter over medium heat about 1 minute on each side until brown and crisp. Serve immediately with French bread slices.

## Cantonese Ribs

Heat over the hibachi for an Oriental brunch             Serves 8-12

4-5 lbs. spareribs, cut in
  half horizontally
Sauce:
1 c. orange marmalade
1 c. soy sauce
1 t. ginger
3 cloves garlic, crushed
salt and pepper

Combine sauce ingredients and pour over ribs. Bake at 350° for one hour, uncovered. Baste with sauce frequently. Cut into individual riblets (after baking).

May be frozen. Ribs may also be partially roasted, then degreased, before sauce is added.

## Mushroom Croustades

Make and freeze crumbs from extra bread             Makes 2 dozen

1 loaf firm square bread,
3 T. minced green
  onions
4 T. melted butter
8 oz. mushrooms, minced
2 T. flour
1 c. heavy cream
1/2 t. salt
1/8 t. cayenne pepper
2 t. parsley
3 t. chives
2 T. lemon juice

Using round cookie cutter, cut a circle of bread from each slice. Press circles into greased muffin tins. Bake croustades at 400° for 7 minutes until browned. Cool in pans.

For filling, saute green onions in butter. Add minced mushrooms and cook for 10-15 minutes until moisture is gone. Remove from heat and add flour, stirring until well blended. Add cream, bring to boil and simmer for 2 minutes. Remove from heat and add salt, cayenne pepper, parsley, chives and lemon juice. Mix well and cool. Fill baked croustade cups. Can be frozen at this stage. Bake at 350° for 10 minutes, until bubbly.

## Mushroom Sandwiches
Garnish tray with curly parsley or lettuce                    Makes 75

1 lb. mushrooms,
  chopped
1 small onion,
  chopped
1 clove garlic,
  minced
1/2 c. butter
3 T. flour
2 loaves thin white
  sandwich bread
1 c. melted butter

Saute mushrooms, onion and garlic clove in 1/2 c. butter. Add flour (enough to hold mixture together). Set aside.

Remove crusts from bread. Roll bread with rolling pin to flatten. Spread 1 slice of flattened bread with mushroom mixture. Cover with another slice of bread. Brush top of sandwich with melted butter. Slice sandwich into 4 triangles. Repeat with remaining mixture and bread.

Place buttered triangles on a buttered cookie sheet and bake at 400° for 10 minutes, until browned.

## Spinach Squares
Even spinach-haters love these                    Serves 12

4 T. butter, softened
3 eggs
1 c. milk
1 lb. Monterey Jack
  cheese, grated
1 c. flour
1 t. salt
1 t. baking powder
2—10-oz. pkg. frozen
  spinach, thawed and
  squeezed dry

In a 9 x 13-inch pan, spread butter, then mix remaining ingredients in order in a large mixing bowl. Spread in pan and bake at 350° for 35 minutes. Cool. Cut into small squares and serve.

To freeze, put squares on a baking sheet and freeze. When frozen, put into plastic bag to store. When frozen, warm at 325° for 12-15 minutes.

## Spinach-In-The-Rye
No other centerpiece is needed                    Serves 8

2—10-oz. pkg. frozen
  spinach, cooked,
  and squeezed dry
1 c. sour cream
1 c. mayonnaise
1/2 t. seasoned salt
4 green onions, sliced
1-1/2 c. cubed cooked
  ham
salt and pepper
1 firm round loaf
  rye bread

Combine all ingredients except bread. Slice top off bread. Carefully hollow out bread leaving 1-inch shell. Pour spinach mixture into bread shell. Chill well.

To serve warm, bake at 350° for 30 minutes, covered lightly with foil.

Slice into large wedges. Serve with vegetable dippers and rye crackers arranged colorfully around bread.

## Hot Stuffed Mushrooms
Couldn't be easier                                     Serves 10

1 lb. mushrooms
1/2 lb. Italian sausage,
  crumbled
grated Parmesan cheese

Wash mushrooms and remove and discard stems. Stuff mushroom caps with sausage. Sprinkle cheese on top. Bake on a flat baking pan (with edge to catch the grease) at 350° for 10-15 minutes.

## Mexican Bean Dip
Can be made in microwave                               Serves 6-8

1 lb. ground beef
1 pkg. taco sauce mix
1/4 c. chopped onion
1/4 c. chopped green
  pepper
1—8-oz. can tomato
  sauce
1 T. prepared mustard
1/2 t. chili powder
1—16-oz. can refried
  beans
5 oz. grated cheddar cheese

Topping:
1/2 t. chili powder
1 c. sour cream
5 oz. grated cheddar cheese

Brown ground beef in skillet. Drain fat. Add taco mix, onion and green pepper. Cook until tender. Add tomato sauce, mustard, chili powder and refried beans. Mix well and put into 2-quart casserole dish. Top with cheese. Bake at 350° for 30 minutes. Mix additional 1/2 t. chili powder, sour cream and additional cheese. Spread over casserole. Serve with plain tortilla chips.

## Ripe and Rye Appetizers
Great for teens — let them do the cooking               Makes 36

1—4 oz. pkg. sliced
  smoked beef,
  cut up
1 c. grated cheddar
  cheese
1 can pitted ripe olives,
  drained and sliced
1 c. mayonnaise
1—8-1/2-oz. pkg. rye
  crackers

Combine beef, cheese, olives and mayonnaise and spread on crackers. Bake at 375° for 5-7 minutes, or bake in microwave 45 seconds on high.

## Chicken Strudel
Complicated — but worth it for the compliments          Serves 6-8

8 oz. mushrooms, sliced
3 chicken breast halves,
   boned, skinned and
   thinly sliced
3/4 c. water
1/2 t. salt
pinch of pepper
1/2 bay leaf
2 T. minced onions
1/4 c. vermouth or
   dry white wine
4 T. butter
1/3 c. flour
1/4 c. milk
2 egg yolks
1/2 c. whipping cream
1/2 c. grated Swiss
   cheese
1 T. pimiento
1/4 c. chopped parsley
1/2 lb. phyllo dough
   leaves
1/2 c. butter, melted
1/2 c. dry bread crumbs

In a saucepan, place mushrooms, chicken, water, salt, pepper, bay leaf and onions. Bring to a boil, and simmer 10 minutes. Remove mushrooms and meat with a slotted spoon and place in bowl. Boil down the cooking liquid to 1/2 cup. Remove from heat, add wine, and set aside.

In a separate saucepan, melt butter, add flour, and stir constantly over medium heat for 2 minutes. Slowly add cooking liquid and milk; stir with a wire whisk until thick and smooth. Remove from heat.

Slowly stir in egg yolks, whipping cream and cheese. Add chopped pimiento and parsley. Then add chicken and mushrooms, stir well and correct seasoning.

On a dry kitchen towel, lay 1 phyllo sheet, brush lightly with melted butter, sprinkle with 1 tablespoon dry bread crumbs, top with another phyllo sheet, brush again with melted butter and sprinkle with bread crumbs. Repeat until 1/2 lb. phyllo leaves are used.

Pour chicken mixture in a band lengthwise down center of prepared phyllo sheets. Roll sheets up as you would a jelly roll. Carefully transfer roll to a greased baking sheet, seam side down, and brush top with remaining melted butter. With a sharp knife divide roll into 6 or 8 portions, cutting halfway though the roll. Bake at 375° for 35 minutes until golden.

To serve, cut roll into small serving pieces. Serve hot.

## Sesame Scallops
Also good cooked over charcoal                                    Serves 6

1/4 c. butter
1 T. lemon juice
salt and pepper
1 lb. scallops
8 slices bacon
3 T. sesame seeds

Melt butter and mix with lemon juice. Season with salt and pepper and place scallops in this mixture. Cut bacon into slices large enough to wrap around scallops. Place sesame seeds in dish.

Preheat broiler to medium. Wrap bacon around scallop. Secure with a toothpick and roll bacon in sesame seeds. Place on greased oven tray and broil about 5 inches from heat until bacon is crisp, about 5 minutes.

## Shrimp Balls
Serve in a large seashell                                    Makes 4 dozen

2—3-oz. pkg. cream
   cheese, softened
1-1/2 t. prepared mustard
1 t. lemon juice
1 t. onion, grated
1/8 t. pepper
1/8 t. salt
1 c. chopped cooked
   shrimp
2/3 c. chopped, salted
   mixed nuts

Blend all ingredients except mixed nuts. Chill. Shape into 1-inch diameter balls. Roll balls in nuts. Chill until serving.

## Spicy Shrimp Spread
Try this as an entree over rice                                    Serves 8

1-1/2 T. butter
1/2 c. chopped onion
1/2 c. chopped green
   pepper
1—19-oz. can tomatoes,
   well-drained
1/3 c. crushed saltine
   crackers
1/2 t. salt
1/8 t. pepper
1/4 t. hot pepper sauce
1/8 t. nutmeg
1/8 t. thyme
1/8 t. mace
2—4-1/2-oz. cans tiny shrimp,
   rinsed and drained
1 hard cooked egg, chopped

In a small skillet, melt butter and saute onion and green pepper until soft. Add tomatoes, crackers and seasonings. Simmer 15 minutes. Stir in shrimp. Place mixture in a small ovenproof dish and bake 15 minutes at 350°. Sprinkle with hard-cooked egg. Serve warm on crackers. May be frozen and reheated.

## Hot Corned Beef Spread

Serve with vegetable dippers or hearty crackers                    Serves 8

4-5 green onions, sliced
1/4 lb. fresh mushrooms,
   sliced
1 T. butter
1—8-oz. pkg. cream
   cheese, softened
1 t. Worcestershire sauce
2 T. mayonnaise
2/3 c. shredded corned
   beef
1/4 c. toasted almonds
parsley flakes

In medium saucepan, saute onions and mushrooms in butter for 2-3 minutes. Add cream cheese, Worcestershire, and mayonnaise, and stir over low heat until smooth and well-blended. Stir in corned beef and heat through. Pour mixture into serving dish. Garnish with toasted almonds and parsley flakes.

## Crab Tarts

These versatile shells can take sweet or savory fillings       Makes 2 dozen

Pastry:
1/2 c. butter
1—3-oz. pkg. cream
   cheese
1 c. flour

Filling:
1—6-oz. pkg. frozen crab
   meat
1 T. lemon juice
2 medium scallions,
   finely chopped
1/4 c. celery, finely
   chopped
3 drops hot pepper sauce
1/2 t. Worcestershire
   sauce
1/8 t. seasoned salt
1/2 c. grated cheddar
   cheese

Mix pastry ingredients until a smooth dough forms. Divide mixture among 24 miniature muffin tins, pressing on bottom and sides. Bake at 350° for 12-15 minutes. Do not remove from tins.

Mix filling ingredients and divide among the 24 pastry shells. Bake at 350° for 15 minutes, until filling bubbles. Serve hot.

May be prepared ahead and refrigerated or frozen before the second baking.

## Butterflied Shrimp
Serve with fried rice for a main dish          Serves 4-6

1 lb. large, raw shrimp
  (about 24)
1 egg, slightly beaten
1/4 t. salt
1/4 t. pepper
1/2 c. fine dry bread
  crumbs
1/2 c. melted butter
1/4 c. lime or lemon
  juice
lime wedges

Remove shells, tails and veins from shrimp and slit back side, cutting almost all the way through so they can be laid flat.

Dip shrimp in mixture of egg, salt and pepper, then in bread crumbs to coat each side.

Thread each shrimp on a single, long, thin bamboo skewer. Insert point of skewer at the tail and impale its full length so that the point just shows at the head of the shrimp. Refrigerate.

Cook over hot coals, basting with mixture of butter and lime or lemon juice. Serve with lime wedges.

## Chinese Sausage Balls
Inexpensive and easy          Serves 8-12

1 lb. lean bulk pork
  sausage
1 egg
1/3 c. dry crumb stuffing
  mix
1—10-oz. bottle sweet
  and sour sauce
1/2 c. white wine

In a bowl, combine sausage, egg and stuffing mix to form mixture that holds together well. Form into small balls. Place in large baking pan and bake at 350° until brown, about 30 minutes.

Drain off fat. Combine sauce and wine. Pour over meatballs, stirring well to coat completely. Bake another 15-20 minutes and serve.

## Mini-Quichettes
Substitute bacon, ham or crab for shrimp          Makes 2 dozen

1/2 c. butter
3 oz. cream cheese
1 c. flour
4 oz. small shrimp,
  cooked
1 medium onion,
  chopped
1/2 c. grated Swiss cheese
2 eggs, lightly beaten
1/2 c. milk
1/8 t. nutmeg
1/8 t. pepper

Mix butter, cream cheese and flour. Form into ball and wrap with plastic wrap. Chill 30 minutes. Press the dough onto bottom and sides of 24 small muffin cups.

Layer the shrimp, onion, and cheese in the cups. Combine eggs, milk, nutmeg and pepper and pour over shrimp.

Bake at 450° for 10 minutes; reduce heat to 350° and bake 15 minutes. Serve immediately.

## Oysters Supreme

Can be a main course for brunch, too                              Serves 4

1—10-oz. pkg. frozen
  chopped spinach
2 T. butter
2 T. chopped onion
2 t. lemon juice
salt and pepper
dash of nutmeg
2 English muffins
12 large oysters
4 slices bacon

Cook spinach according to package directions; drain well. In a skillet, melt butter, add onion and cook until soft but not browned. Add spinach, lemon juice, salt, pepper and nutmeg. Mix lightly. Split and toast English muffins. Divide spinach mixture over muffin halves. Place 3 oysters on each.

Cut bacon slices in half, and fry until nearly done. Criss-cross two bacon strips over each muffin half. Broil until bacon is crisp and edges of oysters are curled. Cut into quarters and serve immediately.

## Beef Balls in Paprika Sauce

Leftover sauce makes good Beef Stroganoff                         Serves 8

4 T. butter
2-1/2 c. thinly sliced
  onions
1 T. paprika
1-1/2 lb. ground beef
1/3 c. fine dry bread
  crumbs
1 egg, beaten
1/2 c. ice water
2 T. ketchup
1-1/2 t. salt
1/4 t. pepper
1 clove garlic, minced
1/2 c. flour
1-1/2 c. beef broth
3/4 c. sour cream
2 T. minced parsley

In small skillet, melt 2 T. butter and add onions. Saute 15 minutes, covered, stirring occasionally. Stir in paprika.

Mix together the beef, bread crumbs, egg, water, ketchup, salt, pepper and garlic. Shape into 1-inch balls. Roll balls in flour, reserving 1-1/2 T. flour. Melt remaining 2 T. butter in large skillet and brown meatballs, shaking skillet to turn. Remove meatballs.

Blend 1-1/2 T. flour in the fat remaining in skillet. Add beef broth and cook over medium heat, stirring constantly, until mixture boils. Add meat balls and paprika sauce and cook over low heat 20 minutes, stirring constantly.

Stir in sour cream and parsley. Serve hot from chafing dish.

## Sauerkraut Balls
Make ahead for baking at the last minute                    Serves 8

**8 oz. bulk pork sausage, crumbled**
**1/4 c. onion, finely chopped**
**1—14-oz. can sauerkraut, drained and snipped**
**2 T. dry bread crumbs**
**1—3-oz. pkg. cream cheese, softened**
**2 T. parsley**
**1 T. prepared mustard**
**1/4 t. garlic salt**
**1/4 t. pepper**
**1/4 c. flour**
**2 eggs, well beaten**
**1/4 c. milk**
**1 c. bread crumbs**
**oil for deep frying**

In a skillet, saute sausage with onion until browned. Drain. Add sauerkraut and 2 T. bread crumbs.

Combine cream cheese, parsley, mustard, garlic salt and pepper; stir into sauerkraut mixture. Chill. Shape into small balls and coat with flour. Beat milk with eggs. Dip balls into egg-milk mixture and roll in bread crumbs.

Heat oil to 375°; deep fry meatballs until brown. Bake at 375° for 15-20 minutes.

## Shrimp Toast
Nice as a side dish with eggs, too                    Serves 8-12

**2 green onions**
**8 water chestnuts**
**1 lb. shrimp, peeled and deveined**
**1 egg, beaten**
**1 t. salt**
**1/8 t. white pepper**
**1 T. vegetable oil**
**2 T. sherry**
**1 T. cornstarch**
**8 slices thin white bread, crusts removed**
**sesame seed or paprika**
**oil for deep frying**

**Sauce:**
**1 T. soy sauce**
**1 T. chicken broth**
**1 T. sherry**
**1 green onion, minced**

In food processor, mince onions and water chestnuts; remove. Process shrimp until almost a paste. In processor, mix well water chestnuts, onion, shrimp, egg, salt, white pepper, oil, sherry and cornstarch.

Cut each bread slice in half diagonally to form 4 triangles. Spread shrimp paste generously on bread. Sprinkle with sesame seeds and/or paprika, if desired.

Heat oil to 375° or until it turns bread golden brown in 30-40 seconds. Cook bread, shrimp-side down, 30 seconds. Turn and cook other side 30 seconds. Drain on paper towel. Keep warm in oven until all are fried.

Cook 3-5 pieces at a time, allowing oil to reheat between each batch.

Serve with dipping sauce made by mixing soy sauce, chicken broth, sherry and onion.

## MUSIC

these large baskets sit on our back porch.
i've had the guitar for twenty years, its a martin, and
has a good sound.
when i'm having trouble with a painting, i sometimes pick
up my old friend and plunk on it while i study the problem

day november 17 1987 sunny, windy, cold                                    tom heflin

*Breads*

# Apple Coffeecake
Nice for an informal coffee

Makes 1 coffeecake

1/2 c. sugar
1/2 c. chopped nuts
2 t. cinnamon
1/2 c. butter, softened
1-1/2 c. sugar
2 eggs
1 t. vanilla
2 c. flour
1 t. baking powder
1 t. soda
1/2 t. salt
1 c. sour cream
4 large cooking apples,
    pared, cored and
    thinly sliced

In a small bowl, mix sugar, nuts and cinnamon. In a mixing bowl, cream butter; add sugar, eggs and vanilla; beat well.

Sift dry ingredients together and slowly add to batter alternately with sour cream.

Spread half of batter in a greased 9 x 13-inch pan. Top with apples and half of nut mixture. Spread evenly with remaining batter and rest of nut mixture.

Bake 40 minutes at 375°.

# Apricot Coffeecake
Complicated but delicious

Makes 2 large coffeecakes

**Dough:**
1 c. butter, melted
    and cooled
3 eggs
1 c. sour cream
1/2 c. milk, heated to
    lukewarm (110°)
2 pkg. dry yeast
5 c. flour
1/2 c. sugar
1 t. salt

**Filling:**
1—6-oz. pkg. dried
apricots
1 c. sugar
1 c. water
1/4 c. brown sugar
1/2 t. cinnamon
1/4 t. nutmeg
melted butter
1 c. chopped pecans

**Glaze:**
2 c. powdered sugar
2-3 T. hot milk

In a medium bowl, beat together butter, eggs and sour cream. Dissolve yeast in warm milk and add to egg mixture. Sift flour, sugar and salt into a large bowl and blend in yeast mixture. Mix well. Cover and refrigerate 24 hours.

For filling, simmer apricots, 1 c. sugar and water until tender, about 15 minutes. Cool; place in blender with brown sugar, cinnamon and nutmeg. Blend until smooth.

Divide dough into 2 balls. On a lightly floured surface, roll each ball into a 20 x 12-inch strip. Brush strips with melted butter, and spread with most of apricot mixture (reserve 4 T.). Sprinkle with pecans. Roll, jelly-roll style, from the long side, and coil each into a greased and floured 10-inch round pan. Let rise, covered, until double.

Bake at 350° for 30 minutes, until browned. Remove from pans and cool well on racks. When cooled, combine glaze ingredients and drizzle over cakes. Dab remaining apricot mixture over cakes. These freeze well.

## Candybar Coffeecake
A sweet way to start the day                                    Serves 12

2 c. flour
1 c. brown sugar
1/2 c. sugar
1/2 c. butter
1 c. buttermilk
1 t. baking soda
1 egg
1 t. vanilla
3/4 c. chopped Heath
   candy bars (3 bars)

In a large bowl, stir together flour and sugars. Cut in butter to make a crumbly mixture. Take out 1/2 cup of mixture for topping. To remaining mixture, add buttermilk, soda, egg and vanilla and mix well.

Pour into a greased 9 x 13-inch pan. Mix reserved flour mixture with candy bars. Sprinkle over batter in pan. Bake at 350° for 30 minutes. Cool. Cut into generous squares to serve. May be made one day ahead. Freezes well.

## Chocolate Chip Coffee Ring
Put a candle in the center for a birthday breakfast        Makes 1 coffeecake

1 c. sugar
1/2 c. butter
2 c. flour
1 c. sour cream
2 eggs
1 t. baking powder
1 t. baking soda
1 t. vanilla
1/2 c. chocolate chips

Topping:
1/2 c. flour
1/2 c. brown sugar
1-1/2 t. unsweetened
   cocoa
1/4 c. butter, softened
1/2 c. chopped walnuts
1/2 c. chocolate chips

In a large bowl, beat sugar and butter 5 minutes at medium speed. Beat in flour, sour cream, eggs, baking powder, soda and vanilla. Beat 3 minutes. Stir in chocolate chips.

Pour batter into a greased and floured 9-inch tube pan.

Mix all topping ingredients until crumbly. Spread topping over batter in pan.

Bake at 350° for 1 hour. Cool well. Remove from pan and serve as coffeecake or dessert.

## Christmas Coffeecake
Start a family tradition with this treat          Makes 1 coffeecake

1 c. margarine, softened
2 c. sugar
2 eggs
1 t. vanilla
1/2 t. almond extract
2 t. baking powder
1/4 t. salt
3 c. flour
1—13-oz. can evaporated
　milk
1 c. chopped walnuts
15 maraschino cherries
　(red and green),
　quartered

Topping:
maraschino cherries
1 T. butter
3/4 c. powdered sugar
2 T. boiling water

In a large bowl, beat margarine and sugar 3 minutes. Beat in eggs and extracts. Sift together dry ingredients; add to sugar mixture alternately with milk, beating well after each addition. Stir in nuts and cherries just until blended.

Pour into a greased and floured 9-inch springform tube pan. Bake at 350° for 60-70 minutes, until a toothpick inserted in center comes out clean.

Cool; then remove from pan. Decorate cake with halved cherries. Mix butter, powdered sugar and water to make a thin glaze. Pour quickly over top of decorated coffeecake.

## Honey Bun Coffeecake
Sweet enough to be dessert          Makes 1 coffeecake

1/2 c. butter
1-1/3 c. flour
3 T. cold water
1 c. hot water
1/2 c. butter
1 c. flour
4 eggs
1/2 c. honey
1 t. vanilla

Icing:
1 c. powdered sugar
1/2 t. vanilla
3 T. cream
1/4 c. chopped pecans

In a bowl or food processor, mix 1/2 c. butter and 1-1/3 c. flour until crumbly. Add 3 T. cold water and stir until dough forms. Press onto ungreased baking sheet to form a 10-inch circle. Set aside.

In saucepan, bring hot water and butter to boil. Add 1 c. flour all at once and mix over low heat until mixture forms a ball. Remove from heat. Beat in eggs, one at a time, and add honey and vanilla. Beat until mixture is glossy. Pour batter over prepared crust.

Bake at 400° for 30 minutes. Cool slightly.

Mix powdered sugar, vanilla and cream, and spread over coffeecake. Sprinkle with pecans.

# Cranberry Ring
A festive holiday bread

Makes 2 coffeecakes

**Dough:**
4 c. flour
1/2 c. sugar
1 t. salt
1 c. milk
1/2 c. butter
1 pkg. dry yeast
1/4 c. warm water (110°)
1 egg

**Filling:**
1 c. ground fresh
   cranberries
1/2 c. ground fresh
   orange (unpeeled)
3/4 c. dark brown sugar

**Glaze:**
1/2 c. powdered sugar
1 T. orange juice

Dough: In mixing bowl, combine 1-1/4 c. flour, sugar and salt. In saucepan, heat milk and butter just until barely warm (120°). Dissolve yeast in water. Add milk mixture and yeast to flour mixture in bowl. Beat at medium speed 2 minutes. Beat in 1 egg. Gradually add enough of remaining flour to make a stiff batter.

Cover bowl tightly and refrigerate until well chilled — up to 3 days.

Filling: Mix all ingredients in saucepan and heat to boiling. Reduce heat and simmer 5 minutes. Cool.

To assemble, divide dough into 2 balls. Roll each on a well-floured board into a 9 x 16-inch rectangle. Spread each with half of filling. Roll up from long side.

Form roll into a ring on a greased baking sheet. Seal seam and cut slits two-thirds through outer side of ring, 1-inch apart. Turn each section on its side. Repeat with second roll. Cover rings and let rise until double, about 1 hour.

Bake at 375° for 20 minutes until browned. Remove and cool on racks. When cool, mix together glaze ingredients and drizzle over rings.

May be served warm or cold. Freezes well.

## Oatmeal Cake

For dessert, add raisins or chocolate chips                    Serves 16

1-1/2 c. boiling water
1 c. oatmeal
1/2 c. butter
1 c. brown sugar
1 c. white sugar
2 eggs
1-1/2 c. flour
1/2 t. cinnamon
1 t. soda
1/2 t. nutmeg

Topping:
1/2 c. butter, softened
1 c. brown sugar
1/2 c. chopped nuts
1/2 c. fine flaked
  coconut

Grease and flour 9 x 13-inch pan. Pour 1-1/2 c. boiling water over 1 c. oatmeal. Let stand 20 minutes. Cream butter, brown sugar, white sugar and eggs. Sift together flour, cinnamon, soda and salt. Blend dry ingredients into butter mixture. Stir in oatmeal. Pour into prepared pan.

Bake 30 minutes at 350°.

Mix together all topping ingredients. Frost warm cake with mixture, and place under broiler just until bubbly.

Serve warm or cold, as bread or dessert.

## Raisin-Praline Coffeecake

An excellent dessert with ice cream              Makes 1 coffeecake

1-1/2 c. dark seedless
  raisins
1/2 c. shortening
3/4 c. sugar
1 t. vanilla
3 eggs
2 c. sifted flour
1 t. baking powder
1 t. baking soda
1 t. salt
1 c. sour cream

Topping:
1 c. packed brown sugar
2 t. cinnamon
1/3 c. butter
3/4 c. coarsely chopped
  pecans

Chop raisins lightly. Beat shortening, sugar and vanilla together until fluffy. Beat in eggs, one at a time. Stir in raisins. Sift flour with baking powder, soda and salt. Add to raisin mixture alternately with sour cream.

Spread half the batter in a greased and floured 9-inch tube pan. Mix topping ingredients and sprinkle half over batter in pan. Repeat layers.

Bake at 350° for 60 minutes or until cake tests done. Cool 10 minutes; then remove to cool on rack. Serve warm or cold.

## *River Room Coffeecake*

Served in the YMCA River Room, overlooking
the beautiful Rock River                              Serves 16

2/3 c. margarine,
  softened
2 c. sugar
2 eggs
3 c. flour
2 t. baking soda
1 t. salt
1-3/4 c. milk
4 c. sliced pared apples

Topping:
3/4 c. flour
3/4 c. brown sugar
1 t. cinnamon
4 T. margarine

In a large bowl, beat together margarine, sugar and eggs. In a separate bowl, mix flour, baking soda and salt. Add dry ingredients to egg mixture alternately with milk. Beat until smooth.

Mix together all topping ingredients. Pour half of batter into a greased 9 x 13-inch baking pan. Sprinkle with half of topping. Spread with remaining batter. Place apple slices evenly over batter. Sprinkle with remaining topping.

Bake at 350° for 1 hour (325° for a glass pan). Cool well in pan. Cut into squares for serving.

Note: Chopped pecans or any desired sliced fruit may be substituted for apples.

## *Swedish Sausage Cake*

Serve in very thin slices                              Serves 8-10

2 c. brown sugar, packed
1 c. fresh pork sausage
  (mild)
1 c. black walnuts,
  chopped
1 t. allspice
1 t. nutmeg
1 t. cinnamon
1 c. raisins
1 t. baking soda
1-1/2 c. strong brewed
  coffee
3 c. flour

Line 10-cup tube pan with greased brown paper. Blend brown sugar, sausage, nuts, spices and raisins. Add soda to coffee; then add to sausage mixture. Add the flour. Mix well. Pour mixture into tube pan. Bake 1 hour at 325° or until toothpick inserted in center comes out clean. When cool, wrap well to keep moist.

## Sweet Yeast Dough
Multiple rewards for the time invested          Makes 3-4 coffeecakes

2/3 c. shortening
1 c. sugar
1-1/2 t. salt
1 c. mashed potatoes
1 c. milk, warmed
1 pkg. dry yeast
1 c. lukewarm water
   (110°)
2 eggs
7 c. flour

In a large bowl, mix shortening, sugar, salt, potatoes and milk. Let stand until barely lukewarm. Dissolve yeast in water. Add yeast and eggs to milk mixture. Add 3 c. flour and beat until very smooth. Stir in remaining flour to make a thick, slightly sticky dough. Place in a large bowl, cover tightly, and place in refrigerator overnight.

Next morning, dough will have risen and be ready for shaping. Dough will be sticky, and easier to shape if cold. After shaping, dough will take several hours to warm and begin rising.

Use this dough to make Cinnamon Rolls, Caramel Bubble Ring, Black Raspberry Braid, Apricot Quick-Braid, or your favorite coffeecake or sweet dinner rolls.

## Cinnamon Rolls
An all-time, all-American favorite          Makes 20 rolls

1/4 Sweet Yeast Dough
   (see above)
1/4 c. butter, melted
sugar
cinnamon
chopped nuts or raisins,
   optional

Roll dough on floured surface to a 20 x 12-inch rectangle. Brush dough with melted butter. Sprinkle with sugar, cinnamon and nuts or raisins. Roll up from long side and pinch seam to seal. Cut roll into 1-inch slices. Place about 1 inch apart in greased 13 x 9-inch baking pan. Let rise until double, about 2 hours.

Bake at 350° for 15-20 minutes. Remove from pan immediately and cool on rack. Rolls may be frosted with powdered sugar icing.

## Caramel Bubble Ring
Good baked without the sugar topping, too          Makes 1 coffeecake

1/3 Sweet Yeast Dough
  (page 73)
1/2 c. butter, melted
1/3 c. brown sugar
2 T. sugar
1/2 t. cinnamon
1/3 c. chopped nuts

Divide dough into 24 pieces. Roll each into a small ball. Dip balls in butter. Mix brown sugar, sugar, cinnamon and nuts in a small bowl. Roll each dough ball in sugar mixture and pile evenly in a well-greased 12-cup tube pan. Let rise until double, 2-3 hours.

Bake at 350° for 30-35 minutes. Immediately invert onto tray and remove pan, scraping any remaining sugar from pan onto top of ring. Cool well. To serve, pull chunks from ring rather than slicing.

## Black Raspberry Braid
Chocolate icing makes this even better          Makes 1 coffeecake

1/3 Sweet Yeast Dough
  (page 73)
1/2 c. black raspberry
  preserves (seedless)
1/2 c. chopped nuts
1/2 c. sugar
1/4 c. flour
3 T. butter, softened
2 t. unsweetened cocoa
1/2 c. light raisins
  soaked in sherry

Divide dough into 3 balls. Roll each on a floured surface into a 16 x 5-inch rectangle. Spread preserves lengthwise down center of each rectangle. Mix remaining ingredients and sprinkle evenly over preserves. Bring edges of dough to center, enclosing filling, to form 3 long ropes. Pinch seams and ends to seal. Braid the three ropes together and tuck ends under. Place on greased baking sheet. Let rise to double, 2-3 hours.

Bake at 350° for 30 minutes. Remove from pan and cool on rack. Ice as desired, or top with additional preserves.

## Apricot Quick-Braid
Perfect accompaniment to ham and eggs     Makes 1 coffeecake

**1/3 Sweet Yeast Dough**
  **(page 73)**
**3 T. butter, melted**
**3 oz. cream cheese,**
  **softened**
**4 T. apricot preserves**
**1/2 t. cinnamon**
**1/2 t. nutmeg**

Roll dough on a floured surface to a 15 x 13-inch rectangle. Brush with butter to within 1 inch of edges. Beat together cream cheese, preserves, cinnamon and nutmeg. Spread filling in a 2-inch band down length of rectangle.

Make cuts 2 inches apart on each side, from edge to filling. Overlap strips alternately over filling to resemble braid. Place on greased baking sheet and let rise to double, about 2 hours.

Bake at 350° for 30 minutes. Remove and cool on rack. Ice if desired, or sprinkle with powdered sugar. Serve warm or cooled.

## Apple Cider Doughnuts
Best served warm with cider     Makes 3 dozen

**2 eggs**
**1 c. sugar**
**2 T. margarine, softened**
**3/4 c. apple cider**
**3-1/2 c. flour**
**4 t. baking powder**
**1/2 t. salt**
**1/4 t. nutmeg**
**1/2 t. cinnamon**
**oil for deep frying**

**Coating:**
**1 c. sugar**
**2 T. cinnamon**

Mix all ingredients except oil. Turn out onto floured board. Roll 1/2-inch thick. Cut with doughnut cutter. Fry 4 at a time in oil heated to 375°, turning once, until doughnuts are golden brown. Drain on paper towels.

For coating, mix sugar and cinnamon in a paper bag. Shake doughnuts in bag, a few at a time.

## Chocolate Doughnuts
Easier than you think                                          Makes 18

2 c. flour
1-1/2 t. baking powder
1/4 t. baking soda
1/2 t. salt
1 t. cinnamon
2—3-5/8-oz. pkg.
    chocolate pudding mix
    (not instant)
2 eggs
2 T. vegetable oil
1/2 c. milk
oil for deep frying

Mix all dry ingredients in large bowl. Stir in eggs, oil and milk. Knead dough on floured board until smooth. Roll dough 1/2-inch thick. Cut with doughnut cutter.

Fry doughnuts and "holes" a few at a time, in oil heated to 375°. Fry 2-3 minutes on each side, turning only once. Drain on paper towels. Cool.

## Beignets
Serve for a New Orleans style brunch              Makes 4-1/2 dozen

1-1/2 c. warm water
    (110°)
1 pkg. dry yeast
1/2 c. sugar
1 t. salt
2 eggs, at room
    temperature
1 c. evaporated milk
7 c. flour
1/4 c. vegetable oil
oil for deep frying
powdered sugar

In a large bowl, sprinkle yeast over water. Stir until dissolved. Beat in sugar, salt, eggs and evaporated milk. Gradually beat in 4 cups flour and the oil. Add remaining flour gradually and beat until a smooth dough forms. Cover bowl and refrigerate overnight.

Roll dough on a floured board to 1/4-inch thickness. Cut into rectangles 2-1/2 x 3-1/2-inches.

Heat oil in deep fryer to 360°. Fry 4 rectangles at a time for 2-3 minutes. Drain on paper towels.

Keep beignets warm in a 200°-oven until serving. Just before serving, sprinkle with powdered sugar.

## Doughnut Drops
Kids enjoy helping to make these                    Makes 2-3 dozen

**oil for deep frying**
**1-1/2 c. flour**
**1/3 c. sugar**
**2 t. baking powder**
**1/2 t. salt**
**1/2 t. nutmeg**
**1/2 c. milk**
**2 T. vegetable oil**
**1/2 t. vanilla**
**1 egg**

**Coating:**
**1/2 c. sugar**
**1 t. cinnamon**

Heat cooking oil in a deep fryer to 375°.

In a large bowl, combine dry ingredients. Add remaining ingredients and stir with fork just until moistened.

Drop dough by teaspoonsful into hot oil. Fry 1-1/2 minutes on each side, until golden. Drain on paper towels.

Mix sugar and cinnamon for coating in a plastic bag. Drop warm doughnuts into bag and shake to coat evenly. Serve warm.

## Popovers
Pair these with homemade strawberry butter (page 162)          Serves 8

**1-1/2 c. flour**
**1/2 t. salt**
**4 eggs**
**1-1/2 c. milk**
**1 T. unsalted butter,**
  **melted**
**4 t. unsalted butter**

Oil 8 custard or popover cups. Preheat oven to 450° and set cups in lower third of oven while making batter.

In a food processor or blender, combine flour, salt, eggs, milk and melted butter. Process about 1 minute.

Place 1/2 t. butter in each cup and return to oven until butter is bubbly. Fill each cup half full with batter. Bake 20 minutes. Reduce heat to 350° and bake 15-20 minutes, until golden. Remove from cups and serve immediately.

Batter may be prepared and refrigerated overnight before using.

## Butterhorns
Canned fillings are also delicious·in these                     Makes 4 dozen

3-1/2 c. flour
4 T. sugar
1 t. salt
1/2 c. butter
1/2 c. margarine
1—1/2-oz. cake yeast
1 c. milk, heated to
   lukewarm (110°)
3 egg yolks, beaten
softened butter
sugar
cinnamon

In a large bowl, mix flour, sugar and salt. Cut in butter and margarine until mixture resembles cornmeal. In a separate bowl, mix yeast with milk and egg yolks. Add yeast to flour mixture and beat until smooth. Cover bowl and refrigerate overnight. (Dough will keep, refrigerated, up to 3 days.)

To make rolls, divide chilled dough into 4 equal balls. Roll each into a circle about 14 inches in diameter. Spread circles with softened butter and sprinkle with sugar and cinnamon. Cut each circle into 12 wedges. Starting at wide end, roll up each wedge and place on lightly greased baking sheet.

Let rise until light, about 2 hours. Bake at 375° for 12-15 minutes. If desired, frost with favorite icing and sprinkle with nuts.

## Taffy Apple Rolls
Don't plan to have any left over!                     Makes 3 dozen

2 pkg. dry yeast
1/2 c. warm water (110°)
1/3 c. sugar
2 t. salt
1 c. milk, scalded
1 egg
5—5-1/2 c. flour
1/2 c. vegetable oil
3/4 c. grated apple
1 c. chopped nuts
1 c. brown sugar
1/2 c. butter
1/2 c. light corn syrup

Mix yeast and water in small bowl. In mixing bowl, mix sugar, salt and milk; cool to lukewarm. Stir yeast and egg into milk mixture. Add 2 cups flour and beat until smooth. Stir in oil, apple and enough remaining flour to form a thick, soft dough. Knead 8-10 minutes. Cover dough and let rise 1-1/2 hours, until double.

Grease 36 muffin cups. Divide nuts evenly among cups. In a saucepan, combine brown sugar, butter and corn syrup; bring to boil. Pour syrup over nuts.

Cut dough into 36 equal pieces, form into balls, and place one in each prepared muffin cup. Cover loosely with tea towel and let rise in warm place until almost double, about 45 minutes. Bake at 375° for 20 minutes. Invert pans onto sheets of foil and let rest 10 minutes before removing pans. Cool rolls completely before serving.

## Kids' Karamel Rolls
An easy "old favorite"                                       Makes 1 dozen

**frozen dough for 12
  rolls**
**1/2 c. chopped pecans**
**1—3-5/8-oz. pkg.
  butterscotch pudding**
**1/2 c. brown sugar**
**1/2 t. cinnamon**
**4 T. butter, melted**

Assemble dish the night before serving:
In a well-greased 12-cup tube pan, arrange frozen rolls evenly. Sprinkle with remaining ingredients, in order listed. Let pan sit, uncovered, at room temperature overnight.

Next morning, bake at 350° for 25-30 minutes. Immediately invert pan onto serving plate and cool rolls slightly. Serve warm.

## Poppy Seed Loaves
Alternate slices with different fillings on a tray          Makes 4 loaves

**1 pkg. dry yeast**
**1 t. sugar**
**1/2 c. lukewarm water
  (110°)**
**1 c. lukewarm milk**
**1/3 c. margarine, melted
  and cooled**
**1/3 c. sugar**
**2 t. salt**
**1 egg**
**5 c. flour**
**2 cans prepared
  poppyseed filling**

In a large bowl, mix yeast, 1 t. sugar and water. Let stand 5 minutes. Stir in milk, margarine, sugar, salt and egg. Gradually beat in flour to make a soft dough. Knead 8-10 minutes until dough is smooth and elastic. Place in greased bowl, turn over, and cover. Let dough rise in warm place about 1 hour, until double.

Punch down dough and divide into 4 equal pieces. Roll each into a 14 x 12-inch rectangle. Spread each with 1/2 can filling. Starting on long side, roll up dough jelly-roll fashion. Pinch seam and ends to seal well. Place rolls on 2 greased baking sheets, cover with tea towels and let rise 1 hour, until nearly double.

Bake at 350° for 30-35 minutes. Immediately remove from pans and cool on racks. Let cool completely before slicing.

Any flavor canned filling or preserves may be used.

# Golden Raisin Buns
Similar to cream puffs                                    Makes 24-30

1 c. hot water
1/2 c. butter
1 t. sugar
1/4 t. salt
1 c. flour
4 eggs
1/2 c. golden raisins

Frosting:
1 T. butter
1-1/2 T. milk
1 c. powdered sugar
1/2 t. lemon juice
1/2 t. vanilla

In a large saucepan, combine water, butter, sugar and salt. Bring to boil. Add flour all at once, then beat with wooden spoon over low heat for 1 minute, until mixture forms thick, smooth dough. Remove from heat and continue to beat 2 minutes.

Add eggs one at a time, beating well after each. Beat in raisins.

Drop dough by tablespoons onto a greased baking sheet, spacing 2 inches apart. Bake at 350° for 30 minutes, until puffed and golden. Remove from sheet and cool on racks.

For frosting, heat butter and milk until warm. Mix all ingredients and spread on tops of cooled buns.

# Pineapple Whole Wheat Rolls
Subtle pineapple flavor in a moist dinner roll            Makes 15

1—8-oz. can crushed
  pineapple
1 c. unbleached flour
1 pkg. dry yeast
1/3 c. milk
4 T. brown sugar
3 T. vegetable oil
1/2 t. salt
2-1/4 c. whole wheat
  flour
1/4 c. honey
1/4 c. butter, melted

Drain pineapple, reserving 1/3 cup juice. In a mixing bowl, combine unbleached flour and yeast. Heat pineapple juice, milk, brown sugar, oil and salt just until lukewarm; add to yeast mixture. Beat on high speed for 3 minutes. Stir in pineapple and enough whole wheat flour to form a soft dough. Knead 5 minutes. Place in greased bowl; cover and let rise 1 hour.

Punch dough down. Divide dough into thirds. Shape each third into 15 equal balls. Place 3 balls in each of 15 greased muffin cups. Let rise until nearly double, about 40 minutes. Bake at 375° for 15 minutes. Immediately remove from pans. Let cool 30 minutes.

Mix honey and melted butter in a small bowl. Dip tops of warm rolls in mixture and serve immediately.

## Peanut Butter Twists
A hurry-up treat for morning coffee                    Makes 12

1/3 c. peanut butter
1/4 c. honey
1/4 c. brown sugar
1/4 c. nuts
1/2 t. cinnamon
1—8-oz. can refrigerated
  crescent rolls

Glaze:
1/3 c. powdered sugar
4 t. peanut butter
1-1/2 t. honey
5 t. milk
3 T. chopped peanuts

In small bowl, combine peanut butter and honey. In separate bowl, mix brown sugar, nuts and cinnamon.

Unroll dough and press together to form rectangle; roll to 16 x 10 inches. Spread dough with peanut butter mixture; sprinkle with sugar mixture.

Fold in half to form 16 x 5-inch rectangle; seal edges. Cut dough crosswise into 12 strips. Twist each strip twice and place on ungreased baking sheet.

Bake at 375° for 10-12 minutes, until browned. Mix all glaze ingredients and drizzle over warm rolls (or reserve peanuts to sprinkle over glaze). Serve immediately.

## Herbed Pinwheel Rolls
Vary the filling with different herbs or cheese                    Makes 16

1 pkg. dry yeast
1/4 c. lukewarm water
  (110°)
1 c. milk, warmed
1 T. butter, softened
1 T. sugar
1 t. salt
3-1/2 c. flour
1/2 c. onion
2 T. butter
2 t. dill weed
2 t. chopped parsley
1 t. crushed savory
2 T. butter, melted

Dissolve yeast in water in large bowl. Add milk, 1 T. soft butter, sugar and salt. Add flour gradually and beat to form a soft dough. Knead 10 minutes. Place in greased bowl, cover, and let rise until double, 1-1/2 hours.

Punch down dough and roll to 16 x 11-inch rectangle. Saute onion in 2 T. butter and spread over dough. Mix dill weed, parsley and savory and sprinkle over onion. Roll dough from long side into tight roll. Slice into 1-inch pieces and arrange in greased 10-inch round baking pan. Brush tops of rolls with melted butter. Let rise until double, about 45 minutes.

Bake at 375° for 30 minutes. Serve warm.

## Parmesan Round Bread

Wonderful addition to an Italian meal                    Makes 1 large loaf

2 c. warm water (110°)
2 pkg. dry yeast
2 T. sugar
2 t. salt
2 T. margarine, softened
1/2 c. plus 1 T. freshly
   grated Parmesan
   cheese
1-1/2 T. dried oregano
4-1/2 c. flour

In a large bowl, sprinkle yeast over water and stir to dissolve. Add sugar, salt, margarine, 1/2 c. cheese and oregano. Add 3 c. flour and beat until smooth. Gradually beat in remaining flour to form a soft dough.

Cover and let rise in a warm place for 45 minutes, until doubled and bubbly.

Preheat oven to 375°. While oven is heating, beat dough with a wooden spoon for 25 strokes; then turn it into a greased, round 2-qt. casserole dish. Sprinkle with remaining cheese.

Bake at 375° for 55 minutes. Serve hot. Can be made ahead and reheated in microwave or oven.

## Herbed Cheese Bread

Toast and top with creamed shrimp                    Makes 2 loaves

1 c. milk
4 T. butter
1 pkg. dry yeast
1/2 c. lukewarm water
   (110°)
1 t. sugar
4 c. flour
2/3 c. grated extra sharp
   cheddar cheese
2 T. minced parsley
1 T. chopped chives
2 T. chopped dillweed
1 T. salt

Scald milk; pour into mixing bowl. Add butter; cool to lukewarm. In a small bowl, mix yeast, water and sugar; add to milk. Beat in 2 cups flour, mixing until smooth. Add cheese, herbs, remaining flour and salt. Knead 10 minutes until dough is shiny and smooth with a blistered surface. Place dough in greased bowl; cover and let rise 1-1/2 hours, until doubled. Punch down, divide in half, and form 2 loaves. Place in 2 well-greased 8 x 5-inch loaf pans. Cover lightly and let rise until almost doubled, about 45 minutes.

Bake 40 minutes at 375°. Immediately remove bread from pans and cool on racks.

This bread is best served toasted, and makes delicious croutons.

## Cheese Casserole Bread
Best baked and eaten the same day                    Makes 2 loaves

5—5-1/2 c. flour
3 T. sugar
1 T. salt
2 pkg. dry yeast
1 c. milk
1 c. water
2 T. margarine
1-1/2 c. grated sharp
  cheddar cheese
1/4 c. grated Parmesan
  cheese
1 egg

In a large bowl, mix 2 c. flour, sugar, salt and yeast. Combine milk, water and margarine in saucepan and heat until lukewarm (115°). Gradually add milk mixture to dry ingredients and beat 2 minutes at medium speed. Add cheeses, egg and 1/2 c. flour. Beat 2 minutes at high speed. Beat in remaining flour to form a stiff batter. Do not knead. Cover and let rise 50 minutes, until double.

Stir batter down and beat on medium speed about 1/2 minute. Divide batter between 2 greased 1-qt. casserole dishes. Bake at 375° for 40-50 minutes. Remove from dishes and cool on racks. Serve warm, cut into wedges. Freezes well.

## English Muffin Bread
Best when toasted                                    Makes 2 loaves

5-1/2 c. flour
1 c. bran buds
2 pkg. dry yeast
1 T. sugar
2 t. salt
1/4 t. baking soda
2 c. milk
1/2 c. water
cornmeal

In large bowl, combine 2-1/2 cups flour, bran, yeast, sugar, salt and baking soda.

Combine milk and water in saucepan; heat until liquids are warm (120°). Add liquid gradually to dry ingredients and stir well. Stir in remaining flour to make a stiff batter. Spoon into two 8 x 5-inch loaf pans which have been greased and coated with cornmeal. Sprinkle tops with additional cornmeal. Cover; let rise in a warm place about 45 minutes until doubled.

Bake at 400° for 25 minutes. Immediately remove from pans and cool on racks. Keeps well refrigerated or frozen.

## Panettone
Classic Italian holiday bread

Makes 2 loaves

5-1/2 c. flour
2 pkg. dry yeast
1 c. milk
1/2 c. honey
1/2 c. butter
1 t. salt
3 eggs
1 t. vanilla
1/2 t. grated lemon peel
1/2 c. light raisins
1/2 c. dried currants
1/4 c. candied citron,
   chopped
3 t. anise seed, crushed
1 egg, beaten
1 T. water

In mixing bowl, combine 2 cups flour and yeast. In saucepan, heat milk, honey, butter and salt just until lukewarm. Add to dry mixture. Beat in 3 eggs; beat 3 minutes at high speed. Add vanilla, lemon peel, raisins, currants, citron and anise seed. Stir in remaining flour to make a soft dough. Knead 5 minutes. Place in greased bowl, cover and let rise until double, 1-1/2 hours.

Punch down dough and divide in half. Shape into 2 round loaves and place on greased baking sheets. Cut a cross 1/2-inch deep in top of each loaf. Cover loosely; let rise to double, about 1 hour.

Brush loaves with mixture of egg and water. Bake at 350° for 35 minutes. Cool on racks.

Loaves may also be baked in well-greased coffee cans. Handle with care when removing from cans as loaves are fragile when hot.

## Oatmeal Bread
A nutritious, basic yeast bread

Makes 2 loaves

2 c. boiling water
1 c. quick-cooking
   oatmeal
2 T. shortening
1/2 c. dark molasses
2 t. salt
1 pkg. dry yeast
1/2 c. warm water
   (110°)
6-1/2 c. flour
2 T. melted butter

In large mixing bowl, mix boiling water, oatmeal and shortening. Cool to lukewarm. Add molasses and salt. In a small bowl, dissolve yeast in warm water. Add to oatmeal mixture. Gradually stir in flour to make a soft dough. Knead 8 minutes, adding more flour if needed, until dough is smooth and no longer sticky.

Place dough in greased bowl, cover, and let rise 1-1/2 hours, until doubled. Punch down, divide in half, and form 2 loaves. Place in 2 greased 9 x 5-inch loaf pans; cover loosely with tea towels, and let rise 1 hour until dough is 1 inch above pan. Bake at 350° for 50 minutes.

Immediately remove from pans, brush tops of loaves with melted butter, and cool on racks.

## Sauerkraut Bread

Makes out-of-this-world Reuben sandwiches                    Makes 1 loaf

**1 pkg. dry yeast**
**3/4 c. lukewarm water**
   **(110°)**
**1/2 c. instant mashed**
   **potato flakes**
**3 T. dark brown sugar**
**1 t. salt**
**1/2 t. caraway seed**
**2 T. vegetable oil**
**1—8-oz. can sauerkraut,**
   **drained and chopped**
**1 c. whole wheat flour**
**2-1/2 c. all-purpose flour**

Dissolve yeast in warm water. Stir in potato flakes, sugar, salt, caraway seed, oil and sauerkraut. Beat in whole wheat flour. Gradually add flour to make a firm dough. Knead 6-8 minutes, until smooth. Place dough in greased bowl, cover, and let rise until double, about 1 hour.

Punch down dough; let rest 10 minutes. Form into loaf and place in greased 9 x 5-inch loaf pan. Cover lightly. Let rise until double, about 45 minutes.

Bake at 350° for 50-60 minutes. Cover top lightly with foil after 30 minutes of baking. When loaf sounds hollow when topped, remove and cool on rack. Serve warm.

## Gerri's Swedish Rye Bread

A blue-ribbon winner at the Illinois State Fair               Makes 2 loaves

**2 c. warm water**
**1/2 c. dark brown sugar**
**3 T. molasses**
**1 pkg. dry yeast**
**2-1/4 c. rye flour**
**1 t. salt**
**1 t. caraway seed**
**1 t. anise seed**
**1 T vegetable oil**
**4 c. all-purpose flour**

In a warmed bowl, mix water, brown sugar and molasses. Stir in yeast. Cover and set in a warm place 20 minutes. Then beat in rye flour until almost smooth. Cover and again set in a warm place 20 minutes, until dough is spongy.

Beat in remaining ingredients, using only enough flour to form a moderately firm dough. Knead 8-10 minutes, until smooth and elastic. Place dough in greased bowl, cover, and let rise 1 hour, until doubled.

Punch down dough and divide into 2 pieces. Let rest 10 minutes, covered. Shape into 2 loaves and place in greased 9 x 5-inch loaf pans. Grease tops of loaves. Let rise 1 hour, until double.

Bake at 350° for 45 minutes. If loaves brown too fast, cover lightly with aluminum foil during last 15 minutes of baking time. Remove bread from pans immediately and cool on racks. Freezes well.

## French Loaves
A classic to star on any menu                               Makes 3 loaves

2—1/2-oz. cakes
  compressed yeast
2 T. sugar
1 T. salt
2-1/2 c. warm water
  (110°)
6-7 c. unbleached flour
cornmeal
1 egg
1 T. milk

Mix yeast, sugar and salt until mixture liquifies. Add water and 3 c. flour. Beat until smooth. Add enough of remaining flour to make a firm dough. Knead until smooth and no longer sticky, about 6 minutes. Place in greased bowl. Turn, cover, and let rise until doubled, about 1 hour.

Punch down and turn dough over. Let rise again until doubled, about 30 minutes. Turn onto a floured board and divide into 3 balls. Cover, let rest 5 minutes. Shape into long loaves and place on baking sheets which have been sprinkled with cornmeal. Let rise until almost doubled, about 50 minutes.

Mix egg and milk; brush this mixture on loaves, being careful not to let it drip. Slash tops of loaves. Let them rest 5 minutes.

Bake for 30 minutes at 350°. Cool on racks.

## Apple Bread
Add 1/2 c. cheddar to batter for a different flavor         Makes 1-2 loaves

1/2 c. butter
1 c. sugar
2 eggs
1 t. vanilla
1/2 t. salt
1 t. baking soda
2 T. sour milk
2 c. finely diced apples
2 c. flour

Topping:
2 T. butter
2 T. flour
2 T. sugar
1 t. cinnamon

Cream together butter and sugar. Beat in eggs, vanilla, and salt. Dissolve soda in milk and add. Stir in apples and flour. Pour into greased and floured 9 x 5-inch loaf pan.

Mix together all topping ingredients until crumbly. Sprinkle evenly over batter in pan.

Bake at 325° for 1 hour 10 minutes. Remove from oven and cool 10 minutes in pan. Remove from pan and cool on rack.

For 2 smaller loaves, prepare two 7 x 3-inch loaf pans. Bake at 325° for 55 minutes.

## Apricot Bread
Nice with whipped cream cheese                    Makes 1 loaf

1-1/2 c. dried apricots
1 c. water
2-1/2 c. sifted flour
2 t. baking powder
1/2 t. baking soda
1/2 t. salt
1/2 c. sugar
1/2 c. chopped pecans
1 egg, well beaten
1 c. sour milk or
  buttermilk
2 T. melted margarine

Grease one 9 x 5-inch loaf pan. Cook apricots in water 10 minutes until soft. Drain apricots, cool, and chop finely. Sift together dry ingredients and stir in nuts. Stir in egg, milk and margarine all at once. Fold in apricots.

Pour into prepared pan and let stand 20 minutes before baking. Bake at 350° for 65-70 minutes. Cool in pans 10 minutes, then remove and cool on rack.

## Minted Honey Banana Bread
An unexpected flavor treat                    Makes 1 loaf

2 ripe bananas
1/4 t. peppermint extract
3 T. honey
2 T. butter, softened
1/2 c. sugar
2 eggs
1/4 t. salt
2 c. flour
1 t. baking powder
1 t. baking soda

In a large bowl or food processor, mash the bananas well. Add extract, honey, butter, sugar and eggs. Beat or process for 2-3 minutes. Sift together the dry ingredients and fold gently into banana mixture. Pour into a well-greased 9 x 5-inch loaf pan.

Bake at 350° for 45 minutes. Do not over-bake. Cool in pan 10 minutes; then remove and cool on rack. Freezes well.

## That's-Not-All-Banana Bread
Delicious new twist on an all-time favorite                    Makes 2 large loaves

1/2 c. mayonnaise
1 c. sugar
3 eggs, beaten
3 ripe bananas, mashed
2 c. flour
1 t. baking soda
1/2 t. salt
3 T. flour
1/2 c. chopped pecans
1/2 c. miniature
  chocolate chips
1/2 c. drained
  maraschino cherries,
  chopped

In a mixing bowl, cream together mayonnaise and sugar. Beat in eggs and bananas. Stir in 2 c. flour, soda and salt. In a small bowl, mix 3 T. flour with nuts, chocolate chips and cherries. Fold this mixture into the batter.

Pour batter into two greased and floured 9 x 5-inch loaf pans. Bake at 350° for 1 hour. Cool 10 minutes in pans; then remove and cool on racks. Freezes well.

## *Blueberry-Orange Nut Bread*
Bread is easier to remove if pan is lined with foil          Makes 1 loaf

3 eggs
1/2 c. milk
1/2 c. butter, melted
   and cooled
1 T. grated orange peel
2/3 c. orange juice
3 c. flour
3/4 c. sugar
3 t. baking powder
1/4 t. baking soda
1 t. salt
1 c. blueberries
1/2 c. chopped nuts

In a large bowl, beat together eggs, milk, butter, orange peel and juice. Mix together dry ingredients and stir into egg mixture just until moistened. Fold in blueberries and nuts.

Pour batter into a well-greased 9 x 5-inch loaf pan. Bake at 350° for 60-70 minutes. Cool 10 minutes in pan. Remove and cool on rack. Wrap tightly in foil and keep overnight before slicing.

To make 2 smaller loaves, bake at 350° for 50 minutes.

## *Brown Bread in a Can*
Spread with soft cream cheese and favorite preserves          Makes 4 small loaves

2 c. buttermilk
2 c. All-Bran cereal
2 t. baking soda
2 eggs, beaten
2 c. dark raisins
2 c. brown sugar
2 c. chopped pecans
2 c. flour
1/2 t. salt

In a large mixing bowl, mix buttermilk, cereal and soda; let stand 30 minutes. Add remaining ingredients and mix well.

Generously grease four 19-oz. cans (soup cans work well). Fill each can 2/3 full with batter. Bake at 350° for 1 hour.

Remove from oven and allow to cool on a rack for 10 minutes. Use a sharp knife to loosen each loaf from pan. Gently shake loaves from cans and allow to cool completely. To serve, slice into thin circles.

## *Maple Pecan Bread*
Much better than the average nut bread          Makes 1 loaf

2 c. flour
3/4 c. sugar
1 T. baking powder
1/2 t. salt
1/2 c. chopped pecans
1 c. milk
2 eggs
1/4 c. vegetable oil
1/4 c. maple-blended
   syrup
1/2 t. vanilla

Sift dry ingredients into a large bowl. Stir in pecans. Add remaining ingredients and stir only until thoroughly blended.

Pour batter into a greased 9 x 5-inch loaf pan. Bake at 350° for 55-60 minutes. Cool 10 minutes; then remove from pan and cool on rack. Wrap cooled bread and store one day before slicing. May be frozen.

To serve, slice thinly and spread with cream cheese or soft butter.

## Lemon Bread

Refreshing with seafood                                    Makes 1 loaf

3/4 c. butter
1-1/2 c. sugar
3 eggs
2-1/4 c. flour
1/4 t. baking soda
3/4 c. buttermilk
grated rind of one lemon

Glaze:
juice of two lemons
3/4 c. sugar

In mixing bowl, cream butter and sugar. Beat in eggs, one at a time, mixing well. Beat in remaining ingredients until well blended.

Pour into a well-greased 9 x 5-inch loaf pan. Bake at 325° for 50-60 minutes.

While loaf is baking, mix glaze ingredients together and let stand. When loaf is removed from oven, use a wooden skewer to poke holes through bread. Immediately pour glaze over loaf. Allow to stand until cool and glaze is absorbed before removing from pan. Freezes well.

## Orange In and Out Bread

A tart and colorful loaf                                    Makes 1 loaf

1 T. frozen orange juice
   concentrate, thawed
1 c. sugar
2 eggs
1/2 c. butter, softened
1/2 c. milk
1-1/2 c. flour
2 t. baking powder
1/2 t. salt
1/3 c. frozen orange juice
   concentrate, thawed

In mixer bowl or food processor, mix 1 T. orange juice concentrate, sugar, eggs, butter and milk. Stir in flour, baking powder and salt until batter is smooth. Pour into greased 9 x 5-inch loaf pan.

Bake at 350° for 55 minutes. Remove from oven and loosen bread from sides of pan. Immediately spoon 1/3 c. orange juice concentrate over bread, letting it run down sides. Cool in pan 15 minutes, then remove loaf and cool on rack.

## Pecan-Carrot Bread

Sweet and very moist                                    Makes 1 loaf

2 c. flour
1-1/2 c. sugar
2 t. baking soda
2 t. cinnamon
1/2 t. salt
3-1/2 oz. flaked coconut
3/4 c. chopped pecans
1/2 c. raisins
2 c. grated raw carrots
1 c. peanut oil
3 eggs
2 t. vanilla

In a large bowl, mix all ingredients, in order, with a wooden spoon. (Or, grate pecans and carrots in food processor and add remaining ingredients. Mix with steel blade 20 seconds.) Pour into a greased and floured 9 x 5-inch loaf pan. Let stand 20 minutes.

Bake at 350° for 1 hour 40 minutes. Cool in pan 5 minutes before removing loaf to cool on rack. Freezes well.

## Pineapple Bread

Best served the day after baking                    Makes 1 loaf

1/2 c. butter, softened
1-1/3 c. sugar
3 egg yolks
2-1/4 c. sifted cake flour
3 t. baking powder
1/2 t. salt
1 c. whipping cream
1/2 c. milk
3 egg whites, beaten stiff
1 c. chopped nuts
1/4 c. drained crushed
  pineapple

In mixing bowl, beat butter and sugar until light. Beat in egg yolks. Sift dry ingredients together, and add to sugar mixture alternately with cream and milk. Gently fold in egg whites, nuts and pineapple. Pour batter into greased and floured 9 x 5-inch loaf pan.

Bake at 350° for 50 minutes. Remove from pan and cool on rack.

## Poppy Seed Quick Bread

Different, with a lovely texture                    Makes 2 loaves

3 eggs
2/3 c. vegetable oil
1-1/4 c. evaporated milk
1-1/2 t. vanilla
2-1/4 c. flour
1-1/2 c. sugar
4-1/2 t. baking powder
1/2 c. poppy seeds

In a mixing bowl, lightly beat eggs. Beat in oil, milk and vanilla. Stir in remaining ingredients and blend gently. Pour batter into 2 greased and floured 9 x 5-inch loaf pans.

Bake at 325° for 50 minutes. Cool 10 minutes; then remove from pans. Cool well and wrap in plastic wrap. Will stay moist for serving the next day. Freezes well.

## Pumpkin Cherry Bread

Perfect for Thanksgiving morning                    Makes 1 loaf

2 eggs
1 c. cooked pumpkin
1/2 c. vegetable oil
1/3 c. juice from
  maraschino cherries
1-1/4 c. sugar
1/2 t. nutmeg
1/4 t. salt
1/2 t. cinnamon
1-1/2 c. flour
1 t. baking soda
1/2 c. maraschino
  cherries, chopped
1/2 c. chopped nuts

In a large bowl, combine eggs, oil, pumpkin and cherry juice. Sift dry ingredients together and beat into pumpkin mixture. Stir in cherries and nuts. Pour into greased and floured 9 x 5-inch loaf pan. Bake at 350° for 1 hour.

Cool loaf in pan 10 minutes; then remove and cool on rack. When cooled, wrap tightly in foil. Freezes well.

## Rhubarb Bread
A family favorite                                  Makes 2 loaves

1-1/2 c. brown sugar
2/3 c. vegetable oil
1 egg
1 c. sour milk (1 T.
   lemon juice plus
   1 c. milk)
1 t. vanilla
1 t. salt
1 t. baking soda
2-1/2 c. flour
1-1/2 c. chopped rhubarb
1/2 c. chopped nuts

Topping:
1/2 c. sugar
1 T. butter

Mix ingredients well in order given. Pour into 2 well-greased 9 x 5-inch bread pans.

Mix topping ingredients and sprinkle over dough in pans. Bake at 325° for 40-50 minutes.

Cool bread in pans 10 minutes; then remove and cool on racks.

## Southern Spoon Bread
Good with sausage entrees                                  Serves 6

3 c. milk
1 c. water-ground
   cornmeal
3 eggs, beaten
3 t. baking powder
1/2 t. salt
2 T. butter, melted

In a large saucepan, stir together 2 cups milk and cornmeal. Bring to a boil. Add remaining milk and other ingredients. Mix well.

Pour batter into a 2-quart casserole dish and bake at 325° for 30 minutes. Serve immediately in the baking dish, with lots of butter.

## Strawberry Bread
Lovely on a tea tray                                  Makes 2 loaves

3 c. flour
1 t. baking soda
1 t. salt
3 t. cinnamon
2 c. sugar
2 c. thawed frozen
   strawberries
   (do not drain)
4 eggs, beaten
1-1/4 c. cooking oil
1-1/4 c. chopped nuts

Sift dry ingredients together. In a large bowl, mix remaining ingredients. Stir in flour mixture just until well blended.

Grease and flour two 9 x 5-inch loaf pans. Pour in batter, smoothing top. Bake at 350° for 1 hour. Cool in pans 10 minutes; then remove from pans and cool on rack.

For 4 small loaves, decrease baking time to 50 minutes.

## Apple Muffins
Easy to keep on hand for after-school treats          Makes 18

1-1/2 c. brown sugar
2/3 c. vegetable oil
1 egg
1 c. buttermilk
1 t. baking soda
1 t. salt
1 t. vanilla
1/2 t. nutmeg
2-1/2 c. flour
1-3/4 c. peeled, grated apple

Topping:
1/3 c. sugar
1 T. butter

In a mixing bowl, combine brown sugar, oil and egg. Add buttermilk, soda, salt, vanilla and nutmeg. Stir in flour just until blended. Fold in apple.

Divide batter among 18 paper-lined muffin pans. Mix topping ingredients and sprinkle over batter.

Bake at 325° for 30 minutes. Remove from pans immediately and cool. These freeze well.

## Blueberry Tea Muffins
Always irresistible          Makes 2 dozen

2/3 c. sugar
1/2 c. vegetable
   shortening
1 c. milk
1 egg
1 t. finely grated lemon
   peel
2 c. flour
2 t. baking powder
1/2 t. salt
1 c. blueberries, rinsed
   and dried

In a large bowl, beat together sugar, shortening, milk, egg and lemon peel. Sift together dry ingredients and mix gently into sugar mixture. Fold in blueberries.

Grease 24 tiny muffin cups. Divide batter among them. Bake at 375° for 20 minutes. Immediately remove muffins from pans and cool slightly on racks.

Best when served warm with butter. These freeze well.

## Bran Muffins

As good now as when grandmother baked them          Makes 6 dozen

5-1/2 c. bran and
   raisin cereal
3 c. sugar
5 c. flour
5 t. baking soda
2 t. salt
4 c. buttermilk
1 c. vegetable oil
4 eggs, beaten

In a large bowl with tight-fitting cover, combine cereal, sugar, flour, soda and salt. Stir in remaining ingredients and mix well. Cover and refrigerate.

To bake, fill greased (or paper-lined) muffin tins three-fourths full of batter. Bake at 400° for 12-15 minutes. Serve warm.

Batter will keep 6 weeks in refrigerator so bake only what is needed, or bake all and freeze. Reheat to serve. When filling tins, blueberries, raisins or dates may be added.

## Buttermilk Date Muffins

Good the next day, split and toasted          Makes 1 dozen

1 c. buttermilk
1 c. quick-cooking
   oatmeal
1/2 c. brown sugar
8 oz. dates, chopped
1 c. chopped walnuts
1 egg, beaten
1/4 c. vegetable oil
1 c. flour
2 t. baking powder
1/2 t. baking soda
1/2 t. salt

In a large bowl, mix buttermilk with oats, sugar, dates and nuts. Stir in egg and oil. Sift dry ingredients together and mix in just until moistened.

Line 12 muffin tins with paper and divide among them.

Bake at 375° for 20 minutes. Immediately remove muffins from pan. Serve warm.

Raisins may be substituted for dates. If using raisins, add 1/2 t. cinnamon and 1/4 t. ground cloves.

## Honey-Wheat Muffins

A family breakfast favorite          Makes 1 dozen

1 c. unbleached flour
1/2 c. whole wheat flour
2 T. baking powder
1/2 t. salt
1 egg
1/2 c. milk
1/2 c. honey
1/4 c. vegetable oil
1/2 t. grated lemon peel

In a large bowl, mix dry ingredients. Make a well in dry ingredients and add egg, milk, honey, oil, and lemon peel. Stir only until moistened. Pour into 12 paper-lined muffin tins. Bake at 375° for 20 minutes. Immediately remove from tin and cool muffins on rack.

Serve warm with butter. These freeze well.

## Orange-Walnut Muffins
Spread with orange juice-flavored cream cheese          Makes 1 dozen

2 c. flour
1/4 c. sugar
3 t. baking powder
1/2 t. salt
2 T. grated orange peel
1/3 c. chopped walnuts
1 c. milk
1/3 c. vegetable oil
1 egg, slightly beaten

In a large bowl, mix flour, sugar, baking powder, salt, orange peel and walnuts. In a separate bowl, mix milk, oil and egg. Pour milk mixture into center of flour mixture. Stir quickly with fork until moistened; batter will be lumpy.

Divide batter among 12 well-greased muffin cups. Bake at 400° for 20-25 minutes, until toothpick inserted in center of one muffin comes out clean. Immediately remove muffins from pan. Serve hot.

May be frozen.

## Pecan-Bran Muffins
Unsalted butter and honey make a perfect topping          Makes 1 dozen

1/2 c. chopped pecans
1/2 c. brown sugar
1 c. flour
1 c. bran flakes
1 T. brown sugar
3/4 t. baking soda
1/2 t. cinnamon
1/8 t. salt
1 T. grated orange peel
1 c. buttermilk
1 egg
1/2 c. honey
2 T. vegetable oil
1 c. dark raisins or
    currants

Mix pecans and 1/2 cup brown sugar in small bowl. Divide mixture among 12 well-buttered muffin pans.

Mix flour, bran flakes, 1 T. brown sugar, baking soda, cinnamon, salt and orange peel in a large bowl. In a separate bowl, mix remaining ingredients. Stir buttermilk mixture into flour mixture just until moistened; do not overmix.

Divide batter among prepared muffin pans. Bake at 350° for 15-20 minutes until browned. Immediately turn muffins out onto rack set over a large platter. Cool slightly. Serve muffins warm.

## EGG BASKET

i found this old beat up basket in emmerts barn.
emmert told me that when he was a boy they used this
basket to gather eggs.
i love things that have the worn patina of years of service.
i left the basket outside one evening. next morning it
was beautifully touched with new fallen snow.

*thursday december 29, 1983 sunny, windy cold -6°*                    tom heflin

# Soups

## Berry Soup
Refreshing with highly seasoned foods                                    Serves 6

**2 c. fresh strawberries**
**1 c. fresh raspberries**
**2 c. ice water**
**1/2 c. sugar**
**1/2 c. sour cream**
**1/2 c. rosé wine**
**sour cream for garnish**

Reserve 6 strawberries for garnish. Blend berries with water; strain through fine sieve. Return juice to blender and add sugar, sour cream and wine. Blend well. Chill.

Serve very cold, garnished with a dollop of sour cream and a whole strawberry.

## Cold Cherry Soup
Float a colorful blossom in each bowl                                    Serves 8

**3 c. cold water**
**2/3 c. sugar**
**1 cinnamon stick**
**32 oz. pitted sour red cherries**
**2 T. cornstarch**
**1 c. whipping cream**
**8 oz. plain yogurt**
**1/2 c. red wine**

In a 2-quart saucepan, combine water, sugar and cinnamon stick. Bring to a boil, partially cover, and reduce heat. Simmer for 15 minutes.

Drain cherry liquid into a small bowl. Stir in cornstarch until dissolved. Remove sugar syrup from heat and remove cinnamon stick. Stir in cornstarch. Cook over low heat 5 minutes, stirring often.

Remove from heat and stir in cream, yogurt and wine. Add cherries. Pour into glass or stainless steel bowl and refrigerate until chilled.

## Iced Cherry Soup
For a crowd, serve in a glass punch bowl                                  Serves 6

**1—2-lb. can sour pitted cherries**
**5-1/2 c. water**
**1/2 c. sugar**
**1/2 lemon, thinly sliced**
**1 stick cinnamon**
**3 T. cornstarch**
**1/2 t. salt**
**1/2 t. almond extract**
**1/2 t. red food coloring**
**1 c. sour cream**

Mash cherries slightly. Combine 5 cups water with sugar, lemon and cinnamon. Cover and cook slowly 30 minutes. Remove lemon and cinnamon stick.

Dissolve cornstarch in remaining 1/2 cup water; add to cherry mixture with salt, almond extract and coloring. Cook until soup clears and begins to thicken. Serve cold with generous mounds of sour cream.

## Avocado Soup in the Shell
Perfect for summer—no cooking needed                    Serves 4-6

2 large or 3 small
 avocados
1-1/4 c. chicken broth,
 chilled
1 small scallion, chopped
1 egg
2 T. lemon juice
pinch of chili powder
1 tomato or 1 lemon for
 garnish
4-6 parsley sprigs

Cut avocados in half lengthwise. Remove pits and scoop out pulp, keeping shells intact. Beat or blend all ingredients until smooth.

Fill shells with soup, garnishing each with lemon or tomato slice and parsley sprig.

## Gazpacho
Store in a juice container for easy serving                    Serves 8-10

2—28-oz. cans tomatoes
2 T. red wine vinegar
1/4 t. dry mustard
1/2 t. salt
1/4 t. freshly ground
 pepper
1/4 t. sugar
1 cucumber, peeled,
 seeded and diced
1 green pepper, diced
3 T. minced onion
3 ribs celery, diced
2 T. sweet pickle relish
4 drops hot pepper sauce

Drain tomatoes; reserve juice. In blender, combine tomatoes, vinegar, mustard, salt, pepper, and sugar; blend until tomatoes are in small bits. In large container, combine with tomato juice, cucumber, green pepper, onion, celery and relish. Stir in hot pepper sauce. Refrigerate several hours. Serve well chilled.

## Avocado Vichyssoise
Especially good served cold with bits of bacon crumbled on top    Serves 8

1 lb. potatoes,
 peeled and sliced
2 leeks, white part only,
 washed and thinly sliced
1 medium onion,
 thinly sliced
4 c. chicken stock
1/8 t. pepper
1/8 t. garlic powder
1 c. whipping cream
2 avocados, peeled
 and mashed

In a large saucepan, combine potatoes, leeks, and onion. Add chicken stock, pepper and garlic; cook until vegetables are tender. Puree the mixture in blender or processor. Return to saucepan, add cream, and heat soup thoroughly, but *do not* let it boil. Add avocados, stirring into hot soup.

Serve the soup hot or well chilled. Do not freeze.

## Leek Soup
For a hot variation, add carrots and onions with potatoes          Serves 4

2 T. butter
3 T. water
3 leeks, sliced
2 potatoes, sliced
4 c. chicken broth
salt & pepper
1 c. half and half cream
2 T. chives, chopped

Simmer butter, water and leeks 5 minutes. Add potatoes and chicken broth. Simmer 15-20 minutes. Puree mixture in blender, half at a time. Add salt and pepper to taste. Stir in cream. Heat or chill. To serve, garnish with chives.

## Vegetable Vichyssoise
May add broccoli or watercress          Serves 12

1/3 c. butter
4 leeks, sliced
   (white part only)
1 medium onion, sliced
5 medium potatoes, diced
4 c. chicken stock
1 T. salt
3 c. milk
2 c. half and half cream
chopped chives

In a large pot, melt butter. Add leeks and onions; saute until golden. Add potatoes, chicken stock and salt: boil until potatoes are tender. Puree in blender or food processor. Add milk and half and half. Cool and refrigerate until well chilled. Sprinkle with chopped chives when served.

## Cold Squash Soup
Just as tasty served hot          Serves 8

1/4 c. butter
1 c. chopped onion
1 carrot, chopped
1 stalk celery, chopped
3 c. chicken broth
2 c. beef broth
1-1/2 lb. yellow summer
   squash, diced
1 baking potato, peeled
   and diced
3/4 c. whipping cream
1-1/2 T. Dijon mustard
1/2 t. freshly grated
   nutmeg
salt and pepper
carrots and chives for
   garnish

Melt butter in large saucepan. Add onion, carrot and celery; saute 10 minutes over low heat. Stir in chicken broth, beef broth, squash and potato; bring to boil. Simmer over low heat, covered, until vegetables are tender, about 30 minutes.

In a blender or processor, puree soup until smooth. Strain if extra smoothness is desired. Stir in cream, mustard and nutmeg. Check seasonings, adding salt and pepper if needed. Cover and chill.

To serve, garnish each bowl with grated carrots and chives.

## Cream of Cucumber Soup

Straining is the key to this smooth-textured soup                Serves 6

1-1/2 lb. cucumber
  (3 medium), peeled
1/2 c. onion, minced
3 T. butter
6 c. chicken broth
1-1/2 t. white wine
  vinegar
3/4 t. dill weed
4 T. quick-cooking farina
salt and pepper
1/2 c. sour cream

Cut and reserve 18 paper-thin slices of cucumber. Cut remaining cucumber into 1/2-inch chunks (about 4-1/2 c.).

Saute onion in butter until tender. Add cucumber chunks, chicken broth, vinegar and dill weed to butter and onions. Bring to a boil. Stir in farina. Simmer, partially covered, 20-25 minutes.

Puree in blender. Strain to remove cucumber seeds. Return soup to pan; thin with more broth if necessary. Season carefully with salt and pepper. Soup may be made ahead, to this point, and frozen.

To serve hot, bring to simmer just before serving and beat in sour cream. To serve cold, let cool and stir in sour cream and a little more salt. Cover and chill until ready to serve.

Garnish with cucumber slices floating on a drop of sour cream.

## Cream of Broccoli-Leek Soup

Fresh broccoli florets make an attractive garnish                Serves 8-10

1-1/2 lb. broccoli,
  chopped
3/4 lb. leeks, sliced
1/2 c. butter
2 medium potatoes,
  peeled and cubed
10 c. chicken stock
1 c. whipping cream
1/2 t. salt
1/4 t. white pepper

Reserve broccoli florets. In a large soup pot, saute the broccoli stems and leeks in butter for 3-5 minutes. Add the broccoli florets and saute the mixture for 3-5 minutes more. Add potatoes and chicken stock. Bring liquid to a boil and cook 20 minutes, or until vegetables are tender.

Puree in blender or food processor until smooth. Transfer to large saucepan; stir in cream, salt and pepper. Heat just to boiling point and serve in heated bowls.

Soup may be made ahead and reheated. Freezes well before addition of the cream.

## Zucchini Soup
May be cooked in microwave

Serves 8

3 c. chopped zucchini
4 slices bacon, cut in
   squares
1 clove garlic, sliced
1 onion, quartered
1/2 t. basil
1 t. seasoned salt
1/4 t. pepper
2 T. parsley
2 c. chicken broth
1/2 c. grated Swiss cheese
   for garnish

Mix all ingredients except cheese in a large kettle. Bring to boil; reduce heat and simmer until vegetables are tender. Cool.

Blend soup in blender or food processor until smooth. Serve hot or cold, garnished with Swiss cheese. Freezes well.

## Cream of Spinach Soup
A good basic technique for any cream soup

Serves 6

10 oz. fresh spinach
3 T. butter
3 T. flour
1/2 c. chopped onion
3 c. chicken stock
1/2 t. salt
1/4 t. pepper
1 c. whipping cream

Steam spinach over boiling water until soft. In a saucepan, melt butter; stir in flour and cook, stirring, until bubbly. Add onions and cook 3 minutes. Stir in spinach and chicken stock; simmer 20 minutes.

Transfer soup to blender; puree until very smooth. Season with salt and pepper. Return soup to saucepan; stir in cream. Heat until steaming. Serve hot.

## Cream of Peanut Soup
Perfect for tailgating

Serves 8-10

1/4 c. butter
1 c. very finely chopped
   celery
1/3 c. very finely
   chopped onion
1/3 c. very finely
   chopped carrot
1 T. flour
1 c. chunk-style
   peanut butter
3—13-oz. cans chicken
   broth
1 t. sugar
2 c. cream or whole milk

In butter, saute celery, onion and carrots for 5 minutes. Add flour and peanut butter. Stir until peanut butter is melted. Stir in gradually chicken broth and sugar. Simmer 10 minutes. Stir in cream. Heat and serve.

## Watercress Soup

Garnish with watercress leaves                                    Serves 6

4 c. cleaned, trimmed
   watercress
1/2 c. chopped onion
3 T. flour
2 T. butter
1/2 t. salt
1/4 t. pepper
1/2 t. Beau Monde
   seasoning
2—11-oz. cans chicken
   broth
1 c. half and half cream

Saute onions in butter 5 minutes. Blend in flour, salt, pepper and Beau Monde. Add broth slowly, stirring constantly. Add watercress and simmer 5 minutes. Remove from heat.

Blend in blender, a cup at a time, for 1 minute. Return to pan; add cream. Serve hot, or chill and serve ice-cold.

## Beer Cheese Soup

Serve in mugs with carrot-stick stirrers                          Serves 6-8

1/2 c. butter
1/2 c. celery, diced
1/2 c. carrots, diced
1/2 c. onion, diced
1/2 c. flour
1/2 t. dry mustard
5 c. chicken stock
3/4 c. grated cheddar cheese
2 T. grated Parmesan cheese
1-1/2 c. beer
salt and pepper

Saute vegetables in butter until tender but not browned. Blend in flour, dry mustard and chicken stock and cook 5 minutes. Add cheeses and beer. Simmer for 10 minutes. Season with salt and pepper.

## Cream of Cheese Soup

A great food processor recipe                                     Serves 6

1 carrot, peeled
1 stalk celery
1/2 small onion
1 c. boiling water
1/2 t. salt
1/4 c. butter
1/2 c. flour
2 c. milk
2 c. chicken broth
8 oz. sharp cheddar
   cheese, grated

In a food processor or blender, finely chop the carrot, celery and onion. Cook in boiling water with the salt until tender, about 5 minutes. Do not drain. Melt butter in a saucepan. Add flour; cook and stir 2 minutes. Add milk and chicken broth; cook and stir until thickened.

Add cheese and stir until melted. Add vegetables and cooking water. Cook, stirring constantly, over low heat until smooth. Serve hot.

# Scalloped Potato Soup

Serve as a first course or main dish — Serves 4

4 medium potatoes,
  peeled & cubed
1 t. salt
1 c. chopped onion
4 T. margarine
4 T. flour
salt and pepper
4 c. milk
1-1/2 c. chopped ham
3 c. shredded American
  cheese

Cook potatoes in small amount of boiling salted water until tender, about 15 minutes. Drain, reserving water. Add enough water to the reserved liquid to measure 1 cup.

In large saucepan, saute onion in margarine until tender. Blend in flour, salt and pepper to taste. Add potato water and milk. Cook and stir until mixture thickens and bubbles. Add chopped ham, potatoes and cheese. Stir until cheese is completely melted. Serve hot.

# Roquefort Soup

Uniquely flavored and very rich — Serves 8-10

1/2 c. butter
1 large head white
  cabbage, chopped
1 medium head
  cauliflower,
  coarsely chopped
6 c. chicken broth
1 c. whipping cream
1/4 c. blue or Roquefort
  cheese
salt and pepper
buttered croutons

Melt butter in 4-quart saucepan. Add cabbage; stir to coat well and cook uncovered over low heat until soft, stirring occasionally with wooden spoon. Add cauliflower and chicken broth; bring to boil over high heat. Reduce heat, cover and simmer 15 to 30 minutes, until vegetables are tender.

In blender or mixing bowl, mix cream and cheese. Stir into soup. Season to taste and garnish with croutons. If desired, soup may be pureed in blender in small batches. Reheat and serve.

# Viennese Barley Soup

Flavorful addition to a German-style brunch — Serves 4-6

3 T. butter
1/2 c. medium barley
1 stalk celery, minced
2 T. onion, minced
1 T. flour
6 c. chicken broth,
  heated
1/2 c. whipping cream
salt and pepper

In large saucepan, heat butter until melted. Add barley, celery and onion and saute until tender. Stir in flour. Gradually add hot broth and simmer, covered, 1 hour, stirring occasionally until barley is tender. Remove from heat. Stir in cream and serve immediately.

## Chicken Velvet Soup
Rich and delicious                                                    Serves 10

5 lb. chicken
10 c. cold water
3/4 c. butter
3/4 c. flour
1 c. milk, warmed
1 c. whipping cream,
  warmed
2 t. salt
1/8 t. white pepper
chopped parsley for
  garnish

In a large kettle, combine chicken and water. Bring to boil and skim surface for 10 minutes. Lower heat and simmer, covered, until chicken is tender and pulls away from bones. Cool chicken in its broth, then remove and debone. Chop meat into bite-size pieces. Strain broth.

In a large saucepan, melt butter and stir in flour. Cook until bubbly. Stir in 2 cups hot chicken broth, milk and cream. Simmer, stirring constantly, 10 minutes. Add 4 cups chicken broth, 1-1/2 c. chopped chicken, salt and pepper. Heat and serve, garnished with parsley.

## Cauliflower Soup on Egg
With fruit, this makes a complete brunch                          Serves 4-6

1 medium head very white
  cauliflower
2 c. chicken stock
2 c. milk
4 T. butter
2 T. flour
salt
1 egg per person,
  poached
freshly grated nutmeg
4 t. parsley
8-12 slices bread
1/4 c. butter

Cut the stalk from the cauliflower and divide the head into small, fingertip-size florets. In a saucepan, poach florets in boiling chicken stock about 7 minutes, until cooked but still firm. Remove with slotted spoon. Add milk to cauliflower stock and bring to a boil.

In a second pan, melt 4 T. butter; stir in flour and cook 2 minutes. Gradually whisk in liquid from saucepan and simmer for 5 minutes. Strain; add cauliflower and salt to taste and reheat gently.

Put one poached egg onto each plate and pour soup over. Garnish with nutmeg and parsley. Serve with croutons arranged around edge of plates.

To make croutons, remove crusts from bread (2 slices per person). Cut diagonally. Place on cookie sheet in 400° oven for about 5 minutes to dry out. Saute in skillet in 1/4 c. melted butter, turning once.

## Lamb-Barley Soup
Make a kettle full and freeze some                     Serves 6-8

1 lb. lamb shoulder,
  cubed
1/2 c. chopped onion
2-3 T. vegetable oil
3 c. beef stock or
  bouillon
1—35-oz. can whole
  tomatoes
1—8-oz. can tomato
  sauce
2 T. brown sugar
1/2 c. barley
1/2 t. rosemary
salt and pepper
1/4 c. parsley, finely
  chopped

Cook lamb cubes and onion in oil in large soup pot until lamb is browned. Pour off fat. Add stock, tomatoes, tomato sauce, brown sugar, barley, rosemary, salt and pepper.

Heat to boil; reduce heat. Simmer, covered, over low heat for 35 minutes. Add chopped parsley; heat 10 minutes more. Serve hot.

## Parmesan Corn Chowder
Any smoked meats may be added                     Serves 8

2 c. boiling water
1/2 c. chopped potatoes
1/2 c. carrot slices
1/2 c. chopped celery
1/4 c. chopped onion
1-1/2 t. salt
1/4 t. pepper
1/4 c. butter or margarine
1/4 c. flour
2 c. milk
1 c. Parmesan cheese,
  grated
1—17-oz. can creamed
  corn

Bring water to boil; add potatoes, carrots, celery, onion, salt and pepper. Cover and simmer 10 minutes. Do not drain.

Make white sauce out of butter or margarine, flour and milk. Add cheese, stirring until melted. Add corn and undrained vegetables. Heat, but do not boil. Season to taste.

## Peasant Soup
A meal with fresh bread and salad                                    Serves 8-10

1/2 lb. Polish Kielbasa
  sausage, diced
1 c. chopped onion
2 T. vegetable oil
1 lb. cooked roast beef,
  diced
1—16-oz. can whole
  tomatoes, cut up
1—1-lb. can sauerkraut,
  rinsed and squeezed dry
4 c. beef broth
2 c. water
1 t. caraway seed
1/2 t. dill weed

In large saucepan, saute sausage and onions in vegetable oil until lightly browned. Add remaining ingredients and simmer over low heat for 1-1/2 hours. Serve hot.

## Potage Oriental
From *Chez Gerlinde*, French cuisine in a charming atmosphere   Serves 8-10

12 c. chicken stock
3 cloves garlic, minced
3 T. soy sauce
2-3 T. diced fresh ginger
3 bunches green onions,
  minced
3 large green peppers,
  minced
6 white turnips, chopped
4 large carrots, chopped
4 celery stalks, chopped
6 oz. shrimp, cooked
1 c. ham, minced
6 oz. crabmeat, flaked
salt and pepper

Bring chicken stock to a boil and simmer. Add garlic, soy sauce, ginger and green onions; simmer 10 minutes. Add the green peppers, turnips, carrots and celery; simmer 15 minutes. Just before serving, add the shrimp, ham, crabmeat and season as desired; heat through. Serve immediately.

## Chill-Chasing Tomato Soup
A south-of-the-border specialty                    Serves 4

1 T. butter
1 small onion, chopped
1 small green pepper,
   chopped
2—10-oz. cans tomato
   bisque soup
1 soup can milk
1 soup can water
1-2 t. Mexican hot sauce
4 slices bacon, cooked
   crisp and crumbled
croutons
1-1/2 c. grated Colby
   cheese
grated Parmesan cheese

Saute onions and pepper in butter in medium saucepan. Slowly stir in soup. Blend in milk and water. Bring to boil.

Remove from heat. Stir in hot sauce. Pour into 4 ovenproof soup bowls and set on baking sheet. Sprinkle bacon, croutons and Colby evenly on each. Sprinkle a bit of Parmesan on each. Place under broiler 4-5 minutes or until cheese melts and bubbles. Serve immediately.

## Bellamy's Crabmeat Bisque
From Chef John Dargo of *Bellamy's*,
specializing in dining for the discerning taste        Serves 8-10

1/2 c. chopped onion
1/2 c. chopped celery
1/2 c. chopped carrot
2 T. vegetable oil
1/2 c. tomato paste
4 c. fish stock or court
   bouillon
1/4 t. thyme
1/2 t. dried basil
1-2 t. salt
white pepper to taste
1/2 c. quick-cooking oats
1 c. whipping cream
1/4 c. sherry
1 c. crabmeat
plain whipped cream
   (optional)
red caviar (optional)

Saute all vegetables in casserole in oil until tender, about 4-5 minutes. Add tomato paste and fish stock, stirring to blend. Add seasonings and bring to a boil. Stir in oats. Cook for 1-1/2 hours; strain.

Return stock to pan; add cream, sherry, and crabmeat and heat through.

Serve immediately. (Chef Dargo recommends garnishing each serving with one teaspoon of plain whipped cream and a sprinkle of red caviar.)

## Crab Bisque
Unique, elegant ... and easy                                    Serves 4-6

1/2 c. unsalted butter
8 tomatoes, peeled,
   seeded & quartered
4 t. sugar
1/2 t. pepper
2—7-oz. cans King crab,
   undrained
2 T. dry white wine
6 c. half and half cream
2 t. dill weed
freshly ground black
   pepper

In large saucepan, brown butter. Add tomatoes, sugar and pepper and simmer 15 minutes. Add crabmeat and juice. Stir in wine and simmer 2 minutes, just to heat crab. In a separate saucepan, heat cream almost to boiling. Combine with crab mixture and serve immediately, garnished with dill weed and pepper.

## Bookbinder Soup
From David Salamone and *The Mayflower*,
where dining is always a rewarding experience        Serves 16-20

1 lb. chopped clams
16 c. water
3 c. fresh seafood pieces
   (snapper, whitefish,
   cod, etc.)
2 c. chopped celery
1 c. chopped carrots
1 c. chopped onion
1 T. beef base
1 t. salt
1 t. marjoram
1 t. seasoned salt
1 t. Worcestershire
   sauce
1/4 t. pepper
1—12-oz. can tomato
   puree
roux as needed (melted
   butter and flour)
1/4 c. cocktail sherry

Bring clam meat and seafood to boil in water; boil 15 minutes. Add celery, carrots, onions, and seasonings. Allow to boil over low heat for about 30 minutes. Add tomato puree and cook an additional 30 minutes. Thicken to desired consistency with roux. Add more seasonings to taste. Add cocktail sherry before serving.

## Cioppino
Serve with sour dough bread                                          Serves 4

1 T. cooking oil
1/2 green pepper, cut
  into 1/2-inch squares
2 T. finely chopped
  onion
1 clove garlic, minced
1—16-oz. can tomatoes,
  cut up
1—8-oz. can tomato
  sauce
1/2 c. dry white or red
  wine
3 T. snipped parsley
1 chicken bouillon cube
1/2 t. salt
1/4 t. dried oregano
1/4 t. dried basil
  (crushed)
dash pepper
1 lb. fresh or frozen fish
  fillets, in 1-inch pieces
12 oz. raw shrimp,
  shelled
1—7-1/2-oz. can minced
  clams

In a 3-quart saucepan, cook green pepper, onion and garlic in hot oil until onion is tender but not brown. Add undrained tomatoes, tomato sauce, wine, parsley, bouillon cube, salt, oregano, basil and pepper. Heat, cover and simmer 20 minutes. Add fish, shrimp (or crab) and undrained clams. Bring just to boiling. Reduce heat, cover and simmer 5-7 minutes or until fish are done. Serve immediately.

## Salmon-Corn Chowder
Very easy for stovetop or microwave                        Serves 7-8

1—15-1/2-oz. can salmon
3/4 c. chopped celery
3/4 c. chopped onion
2 T. butter
1—10-oz. can cream of
  potato soup
1—10-oz. can cream of
  celery soup
2 c. milk
1—17-oz. can whole
  kernel corn, undrained
1/4 t. thyme

Flake salmon; do not drain. Set aside.

In a large saucepan, saute celery and onion in butter until tender. Stir in salmon and remaining ingredients; heat well over medium heat. Serve immediately.

## Red Salmon Bisque

May substitute cooked white fish for salmon                    Serves 4-6

2 T. finely chopped
  onion
1/2 c. finely chopped
  carrot
1/2 c. finely chopped
  celery
1/4 c. butter
1/2 c. flour
1 c. chicken broth
1/2 c. clam juice
1/2 c. half & half cream
2 c. milk
1 lb. salmon, poached
  and cut into chunks
salt, pepper & garlic salt
  to taste
1/4 c. dry white wine

Saute onion, carrot and celery in butter until tender. Stir in flour slowly to thicken, stirring constantly over medium heat. Add chicken broth, clam juice and half and half; lower heat.

Stirring gently, add milk and salmon chunks. Season to taste with salt, pepper and garlic salt. Add wine and stir gently to blend. Heat well to serve.

## Shrimp-Scallop Soup

A food processor will speed preparation time                    Serves 8

1/4 lb. bacon, diced
6 T. butter
1-1/2 c. onion, chopped
1 stalk celery, diced
1 leek (white only),
  diced
1-1/2 c. mushrooms, thinly
  sliced
1 lb. tomatoes, peeled,
  seeded and chopped
3 c. bottled clam juice
3 c. water
1 t. salt
1/2 t. pepper
1/2 t. thyme
6 sprigs parsley
1-1/2 lb. potatoes, peeled
  and diced
1/2 lb. shrimp, peeled
  cleaned and diced
1 lb. scallops, washed
  and diced
2 c. half and half cream

In a large saucepan or crockpot, lightly brown bacon. Add butter, onion, celery, leek, mushrooms and tomatoes. Simmer 5 minutes, stirring often. Add clam juice, water, salt, pepper, thyme and parsley. Bring to a boil and cook, covered, over low heat 30 minutes. Add potatoes; cook 20 minutes. Add shrimp and scallops; heat 10 minutes. Remove and discard parsley. Stir in cream. Adjust seasonings; heat over low heat just to warm cream. Serve hot.

To make ahead, remove soup from heat after potatoes have cooked. Refrigerate until needed. Reheat soup before adding seafood; then proceed as indicated in recipe.

## ROOM AND BOARD

last fall this old tom cat would come around our back
door looking for food. he was gaunt and wild.
when my daughter would open the door to give him
something to eat, he would run for the woods.
eventually beth gained his trust.
when the cold days of winter came the cat moved in to
stay. now he acts like he owns the place.

tuesday january 10, 1984 sunny, cold.

*Salads*

## Baskets of Spinach-Strawberry Salad

Baskets are best made and served the same day.      Serves 8

1 qt. fresh strawberries,
  hulled
1 large bag fresh spinach,
  stems removed
1/2 c. sugar
1-1/2 t. minced onion
1/4 t. Worcestershire
  sauce
1/4 t. paprika
1/4 c. cider vinegar
1/2 c. vegetable oil
2 T. sesame seed
1 T. poppy seed
peanut oil
8 egg roll wrappers

Chill strawberries and spinach. For dressing, mix sugar, onion, Worcestershire, paprika and vinegar in blender. With blender running, slowly add vegetable oil. Stir in sesame seed and poppy seed. Chill dressing.

For salad baskets, heat a 3-inch depth of peanut oil to 375° in a deep fryer. Plunge one egg roll wrapper into hot oil and immediately press down on its center with a soup ladle. Keep the ladle in place until "basket" is nicely browned. Remove and drain upside down on paper towels. Repeat process with remaining wrappers.

To serve, toss spinach and strawberries with dressing. Divide salad among the "baskets".

## Sacramento Fruit Bowl

Serve in a hollowed-out pineapple or melon "basket"      Serves 12

2 c. water
1-1/2 c. sugar
3 T. lemon juice
2 T. anise seeds
1/2 t. salt
1 small pineapple, cubed
1 small honeydew melon,
  cubed
1 small cantaloupe
  cubed
2 oranges, in sections
2 large nectarines,
  unpeeled, cut into
  wedges
2 large purple plums,
  cut into wedges
1/2 lb. green grapes,
  seedless, halved
2 kiwi fruit, peeled,
  sliced

Prepare very early in the day or one day ahead. In a 2-quart saucepan over medium heat, boil water, sugar, lemon juice, anise seeds and salt for 15 minutes or until mixture becomes a light syrup. Refrigerate until syrup is cool.

Combine all fruits except kiwi in large bowl or clear compote. Strain chilled syrup over fruit. Cover and refrigerate until well chilled, stirring occasionally.

When ready to serve, gently stir kiwi slices into fruit mixture.

## Stuffed Pear Salad
Both salad and dressing can be made ahead and refrigerated        Serves 8

2—3-oz. pkg. cream
  cheese
1—8-oz. can crushed
  pineapple, drained
1/2 c. crushed ginger
  snaps
1 T. mayonnaise
1—28-oz. can pear
  halves, drained
salad greens

Dressing:
1/3 c. lemon juice
1/3 c. vegetable oil
2 T. honey
1/4 t. salt

Mix cream cheese, pineapple, ginger snaps and mayonnaise. Stuff mixture into pear halves. Arrange on salad greens. Chill.

Mix all dressing ingredients. Spoon dressing over pears when served.

## Fruit Salad with Yogurt Dressing
Try this for a fresh taste during winter        Serves 8

3 sliced bananas
2 red apples, cut in
  chunks
2 pears, cut in chunks
1/2 c. chopped pecans
1/2 c. golden raisins
1/3 c. flaked coconut

Dressing:
1 c. plain yogurt
1/2 t. cinnamon
1 T. honey
dash white pepper

Combine fruit with coconut in large bowl.

Combine dressing ingredients and pour over fruit.

Toss lightly. Chill no more than 3 hours before serving.

## Champagne Frozen Fruit
Garnish with mint leaves or stemmed cherry                Serves 12

1—6-oz. can frozen
  orange juice
1—6-oz. can frozen pink
  lemonade
1—15-oz. can crushed
  pineapple with juice
1—15-oz. can fruit
  cocktail with juice
4 large bananas
2—10-oz. pkg. frozen
  strawberries
2 cans lemon-lime soda

Mix juices and fruits together in large bowl. Divide among lined muffin tins. Freeze. To serve, remove paper, put frozen fruit cup in champagne glass and pour lemon-lime soda over frozen fruit.

## Frozen Fruit Salad
Easy enough for children to make                Serves 9

1 large can crushed
  pineapple
1—10-oz. pkg. frozen
  strawberries, thawed
1—21-oz. can apricot or
  peach pie filling
1/2 c. sugar
1 c. whipping cream,
  whipped

Mix all ingredients together and pour into 9 x 9-inch pan. Freeze several hours. Cut into squares and serve each on lettuce leaf. Keeps well in freezer if covered.

## Spiced Peaches
Stuff with preserves and use to garnish pork or beef                Serves 8

1—29-oz. can peach
  halves, drained
1-1/2 c. honey
1/2 c. vinegar
4—3-inch cinnamon
  sticks
4 whole cloves

Place peach halves in quart jar. Heat remaining ingredients to boiling; pour over peaches and cool. Refrigerate at least 8 hours, or overnight.

## Apricot Ring Mold
Bright fruit colors offset the creamy mold                    Serves 8-10

2 envelopes unflavored
  gelatin
1/2 c. sugar
pinch salt
2 c. apricot nectar
3/4 c. water
1 c. white wine
1 c. sour cream
fresh fruit: melon balls,
  strawberries, pineapple
  chunks

In saucepan, combine gelatin, sugar, salt, apricot nectar and water. Cook and stir over low heat until gelatin dissolves. Stir in wine and remove pan from heat. Gradually whisk in sour cream until smooth. Pour into 5-1/2-cup ring mold. Chill until set. Unmold and fill ring with fresh fruit.

## Spiced Jellied Apricot Salad
For a festive look, add cherries and pineapple                Serves 6-8

3/4 c. apricot syrup (from
  canned apricots)
1/4 c. vinegar
1/2 c. sugar
12 cloves
1 stick cinnamon
12 canned apricot halves,
  drained
1—3-oz. pkg. orange
  gelatin

Combine apricot juice, vinegar, sugar, cloves and cinnamon. Bring to boil. Add apricots; simmer 10 minutes. Remove apricots from syrup; strain syrup. Add enough hot water to make 1 pint. Dissolve gelatin in hot liquid. Chill until slightly thickened; arrange apricots in oiled 6-cup ring mold; pour gelatin mixture over. Chill at least 4 hours.

## Molded Cranberry Salad
Goes very well with chicken or turkey divan                   Serves 10-12

1—6-oz. pkg. cherry or
  raspberry gelatin
1c. boiling water
1—16-oz. can whole
  cranberry sauce
1—20-oz. can crushed
  pineapple
1—4-oz. can mandarin
  oranges, drained
1 c. chopped celery
1/2 c. chopped pecans

Dissolve gelatin in boiling water. Stir in remaining ingredients. Pour into 6-cup mold. Refrigerate at least 4 hours. Unmold on lettuce leaves.

## Cranberry Fluff

Serve with one of the chicken breast recipes                    Serves 8

2 c. raw cranberries
3 c. miniature
  marshmallows
3/4 c. sugar
2 c. diced unpared tart
  apples
1/2 c. seedless green
  grapes
1/2 c. chopped pecans
1/4 t. salt
1 c. whipping cream,
  whipped

Combine cranberries, marshmallows and sugar; cover and chill overnight. Add apples, green grapes, nuts, and salt. Fold whipped cream into cranberry mixture; chill several hours.

## Orange Sherbet Salad

Deep green leaves make an attractive garnish                    Serves 10

1—6-oz. pkg. orange
  gelatin
1 c. boiling water
1 pt. orange sherbet
1—11-oz. can mandarin
  oranges, drained
1—10-oz. can crushed
  pineapple
1 c. whipping cream,
  whipped

Dissolve gelatin in boiling water. Add sherbet and stir well. Add oranges and pineapple and fold in whipped cream. Pour into a 2-quart mold that has been rinsed with cold water and sprayed with vegetable oil. Refrigerate. To serve, unmold on serving platter.

## Molded Spinach Salad

Easy make-ahead for adult tastes                    Serves 12

2 c. boiling water
2—3-oz. pkg. lemon
  gelatin
1 c. cold water
3 T. vinegar
1 c. mayonnaise
salt and pepper
1—10-oz. pkg. chopped
  frozen spinach, thawed
1-1/2 c. cottage cheese
2/3 c. chopped celery
3 T. chopped green
  onion

Dissolve lemon gelatin in boiling water. Add cold water, vinegar, mayonnaise, salt and pepper to taste. Refrigerate until partially set. Gently fold in spinach, cottage cheese, celery and green onion. Pour into an oiled 2-quart mold or 8 x 12-inch dish. Refrigerate until set. Unmold or cut into squares.

## Strawberry-Rhubarb Mold

Tangy and a bit different                                 Serves 12

1—8-oz. can crushed
  pineapple
1—16-oz. pkg. frozen
  strawberries
1—10-oz. pkg. frozen
  rhubarb
3/4 c. sugar
2—3-oz. pkg. strawberry
  gelatin
2 c. boiling water
1 c. juice from fruit

Drain pineapple and reserve juice. Defrost strawberries; drain and reserve juice. Cook rhubarb according to directions on package; sweeten with sugar. Put through strainer and keep juice. Dissolve gelatin in boiling water; add cup of mixed fruit juice. Chill for 45 minutes.

Mix together pineapple, strawberries and rhubarb. Add to gelatin and put into 6-cup mold that has been lightly oiled. Refrigerate until set.

## Russian Raspberry Cream

Fresh berries or peaches make attractive garnish        Serves 6

1—3-oz. pkg. raspberry
  gelatin
1 c. boiling water
1 T. lemon juice
1—10-oz. pkg. frozen
  whole raspberries,
  thawed and drained
1/2 c. half and half cream
1/4 c. sugar
1/2 envelope unflavored
  gelatin (1/2 T.)
1/4 c. cold water
1/2 c. sour cream
1/2 t. vanilla

Dissolve raspberry gelatin in boiling water. Stir in lemon juice and raspberries and pour into a 4-cup ring mold. Refrigerate until barely firm. Heat cream and sugar in a saucepan. Soften unflavored gelatin in one-fourth cup cold water and add to warm cream mixture; stir until dissolved. Add sour cream and vanilla. Beat well. Pour slowly over chilled red layer. Refrigerate until firm. Unmold onto a serving platter and garnish as desired.

## Artichoke/Asparagus Tossed Salad
Wine makes a flavorful contribution to this dressing     Serves 6-8

1—14-oz. can artichoke
  hearts, drained and
  chilled
1 lb. fresh asparagus,
  cooked and chilled
4 c. torn mixed salad
  greens

Burgundy Vinaigrette
  Dressing:
1/2 c. salad oil
1/2 c. white vinegar
2 T. Burgundy wine
1/2 t. sugar
1/4 t. Worcestershire
  sauce
1/4 t. salt
1/4 t. coarsely ground
  pepper
1/4 t. salad herbs
1/4 t. minced garlic
2-3 drops hot pepper
  sauce

Cut artichoke hearts into halves or quarters and asparagus spears into 1-inch pieces. Combine with salad greens in bowl. Add dressing and toss until greens are well coated.

For dressing, combine all ingredients in jar with close-fitting cover and shake well. Refrigerate. Shake well before using.

## Bean 'N Bacon Salad
Nice change from the standard tossed salad     Serves 6

2—15-oz. cans whole
  green beans, drained
1/2 c. chopped onion
1/3 c. salad oil
1/4 c. vinegar
1/2 t. salt
1/4 t. pepper
4 hard-cooked eggs,
  chopped
1/4 c. mayonnaise
1 t. prepared mustard
2 t. vinegar
1/4 t. salt
4 slices bacon, fried and
  crumbled
salad greens
paprika

Combine beans, onion, oil, 1/4 cup vinegar, salt and pepper. Toss lightly. Cover and chill. Mix eggs, mayonnaise, mustard, 2 t. vinegar and salt. Just before serving, drain bean mixture and toss with bacon. Mound on crisp greens; top with egg mixture and spinkle with paprika.

# Salade Marie-Helene
From *Chez Gerlinde*, serving fine French cuisine          Serves 8-10

6 ripe pears, pared,
  cubed
lemon juice
3 avocados, cut with
  small end of melon
  scoop
1 muskmelon, cut with
  small end of melon
  scoop
1 honeydew melon, cut
  with small end of
  melon scoop
1 can hearts of palm,
  sliced
1 lb. prosciutto, cut in
  1/2-inch slices, then in
  julienne strips
1-1/2—2 cups blue cheese,
  broken in pieces
several avocados, sliced,
  for garnish

Vinaigrette:
4 T. wine vinegar
2 T. lemon juice
1-1/2 t. salt
3/4 c. salad oil
3 T. minced parsley
1 t. chopped capers
1 T. minced shallots
1 T. minced chervil
salt, pepper, and cayenne
  to taste
pinch of sugar

Pare and cube pears; sprinkle with lemon juice. Combine with balls of avocado, melons, hearts of palm, and prosciutto in large bowl. Toss gently to mix. Combine ingredients for vinaigrette and set aside.

To serve, center a scoop of melon mixture on plate lined with lettuce and 6 avocado slices, 3 on each side of melon mixture, to give the appearance of a flower opening. Sprinkle each salad with a generous amount of blue cheese. Top with several tablespoons of Vinaigrette. Pass the remaining Vinaigrette.

## Avocado Romanoff

From *Jungle Jim's*, where chef Thomas Sullivan
specializes in preparing seafood                    Serves 1

1 ripe avocado
8 oz. crabmeat
2 green onions
1 T. mayonnaise
1/3 t. horseradish
1/2 t. lemon juice
black pepper
celery salt
Bibb or Romaine lettuce
   leaves
caviar (optional)

Open avocado and cut each half into 3 wedges. Chop crabmeat and green onions together; mix together with mayonnaise, horseradish, lemon juice, fresh-ground pepper and celery salt to taste. Arrange avocado slices on lettuce leaves. Fill cavity with crabmeat mixture. Top each avocado with caviar, such as black lumpfish, if desired.

## Artichoke Salad

Creamy dressing is also good on cabbage              Serves 4-6

1—14-oz. can artichoke
   hearts, drained and
   halved
2 c. thinly sliced
   mushrooms
1-1/3 c. snow peas, cut
   into 1/2-inch pieces
1/2 c. sliced blanched
   almonds, toasted
   lightly
soft-leafed lettuce

Dressing:
1/4 c. red wine vinegar
1/4 c. vegetable oil
2 t. Dijon mustard
1 t. minced garlic
1 t. dried dill
1 t. salt
1 t. pepper
1 c. half and half cream

Mix artichokes, mushrooms and snow peas. Toss the vegetables with the dressing and almonds and serve the salad on plates lined with soft-leafed lettuce.

For dressing, combine all ingedients except cream; add cream in a slow stream, whisking until the dressing is well combined.

## Caesar Salad

Add pimiento or red peppers for a pretty variation                    Serves 6

1 head Romaine lettuce
1/2 c. grated Parmesan
   cheese
1 c. garlic-flavored
   croutons

Dressing:
1 clove crushed garlic
1 T. wine vinegar
1 T. dry mustard
4 T. tarragon vinegar
1 T. Worchestershire
   sauce
3/4 c. vegetable oil
1 raw egg
1 tin anchovies, drained
1/2 t. salt
1/4 t. pepper

Mix dressing ingredients with wire whisk.

Place greens in salad bowl; sprinkle with Parmesan and croutons. Add dressing and toss before serving.

## Blumenkohl Salat Bunt

Cauliflower Floret Salad                    Serves 6-8

1 small head cauliflower
1 c. milk
1/4 c. water
1 t. sugar
1 t. paprika
salt and pepper
1—16-oz. pkg. frozen
   peas and carrots

Marinade:
1 small onion, chopped
1 small clove garlic,
   minced
salt
dillweed
chives or tops of green
   onions
1 T. wine vinegar
1/2 c. mayonnaise
1/4 c. plain yogurt

Cut cauliflower in small florets; cook in mixture of milk and water, salt, pepper, sugar and paprika for 15 minutes. Add peas and carrots; heat again, then drain and cool.

Marinade: Mix all ingredients and season to taste. Add vegetables and let stand for 30 minutes at room temperature.

## Cauliflower/Bacon Salad

Salad should be tossed just before serving                    Serves 12

1 lb. bacon, cooked and
  crumbled
1 head cauliflower,
  separated
1-2 heads lettuce, torn
1 medium onion,
  chopped

Dressing:
1 c. mayonnaise
1/4 c. Parmesan cheese
1/4 c. sugar

Mix bacon and vegetables. Make dressing by mixing all ingredients. Toss dressing with salad; serve immediately.

## Celery Vinaigrette

Easy to make ahead any time of year                    Serves 6-8

1/2 c. vegetable oil
1/3 c. pitted ripe olives,
  sliced
1/4 c. sliced stuffed
  olives
3 T. vinegar
2 T. chopped celery
  leaves
2 T. chopped parsley
1 t. fennel seed
1 clove garlic, crushed
4 c. thinly sliced celery
Boston lettuce

Combine all ingredients except celery and lettuce. Add dressing to celery and toss lightly. Chill for 2 hours and serve atop lettuce.

## *Layered Coleslaw*

Salad may be frozen successfully if
vegetables are grated instead of sliced                    Serves 8

1 head cabbage, thinly
  sliced
1 large green pepper,
  sliced in rings
2 medium onions, thinly
  sliced
1 c. sugar
1 t. dry mustard
2 t. sugar
1 T. salt
1 t. celery seed
1 c. white vinegar
3/4 c. salad oil
1 c. cherry tomatoes,
  halved

In a large straight-sided glass bowl, make layers of thinly sliced cabbage, green pepper rings, onion slices. Sprinkle 1 cup sugar over top. In saucepan, combine mustard, 2 t. sugar, salt, celery seed, vinegar and oil. Mix well. Bring to a full boil, stirring constantly. Pour over slaw. Cover and refrigerate for at least 4 hours. To serve, add tomatoes; toss salad well.

## *Frozen Cucumber Relish*

Great way to save your garden's abundance          Makes 2 cups dressing

cucumbers
onions
salt
1-1/2 t. celery seed
1 c. sugar
1 c. salad oil
1 c. white vinegar

Peel and slice thinly equal amounts of cucumber and onions. Layer and sprinkle each layer with salt. Cover, put on a weight and let set for 2 hours. Drain well. Taste. If too salty, rinse with water.

Combine celery seed, sugar, salad oil and vinegar. Stir until sugar is completely dissolved. Put drained cucumbers and onions in container; cover with dressing and freeze. Freeze only in container size that can be eaten at one time. Serve while still slightly frozen.

## Cucumber/Tomato Delights
Wonderful summertime coolers—and also nice at Christmas          Serves 4

1/4 c. mayonnaise
1/4 t. ground thyme
1/4 t. curry powder
1 chopped green onion,
    including greens
1 cucumber, peeled,
    scored lengthwise with
    a sharp fork, sliced
    thin (16 slices)
4 slices homemade-type
    white bread, crusts
    trimmed
seasoned salt
8 cherry tomatoes

Mix mayonnaise, thyme, curry and onion in small dish. Cover; refrigerate at least one hour or overnight. Prepare cucumber, dry and refrigerate until ready to use.

Just before serving, spread each slice of bread with mayonnaise mixture, then cut each slice into four squares. Place a slice of cucumber on each bread square. Sprinkle the 16 cucumber slices with seasoned salt. Cut cherry tomatoes in half and place one on the center of each cucumber, cut side down. Secure with a toothpick if you wish, though this is not essential. Do not assemble these more than a few minutes before they are to be served, because they tend to become soggy. Do not stack. Have plenty on hand.

## Endive Salad with Oranges
Chicory may be substituted for endive          Serves 4

2 large Belgian endive
1 orange, seedless
1/2 c. whipping cream
1 T. mustard
salt and pepper

Remove outer leaves of endive using only those that are white. Cut leaves in half, along center; place on platter. Peel oranges, removing inner white skin. Shred peels and cook in water for 5 minutes to eliminate any bitterness. Dry and cool. Mix cream with mustard, salt and pepper and pour this marinade over endive. Sprinkle with shredded orange peels. Slice remainder of orange and garnish salad with orange slices.

## Gazpacho Salad with Asparagus

Tangy taste treat                                                    Serves 8

2 envelopes unflavored
  gelatin
1—18-oz. can tomato
  juice
1/3 c. wine vinegar
1 t. salt
dash hot pepper sauce
2 medium tomatoes,
  peeled and diced
1 large cucumber, peeled
  and diced
1 green pepper, diced
1/4 c. finely chopped red
  onion
1 T. chopped chives
2 lb. asparagus, cooked
lemon wedges

In a saucepan, sprinkle gelatin over 1/2 cup of the tomato juice. Dissolve over low heat and add vinegar, salt, hot pepper sauce and the remaining juice. Chill until consistency of egg white. Fold in tomatoes, cucumber, pepper, onion and chives. Pour into a 6-cup mold that has been rinsed with cold water and sprayed with vegetable oil. To serve, unmold on a large platter and garnish with asparagus and lemon wedges.

## Salad of Hearts

Just right for a Valentine brunch                                    Serves 6

2—8-1/2 oz. cans
  artichoke hearts or
  hearts of palm, or
  combination, drained

Marinade:
1/2 c. olive oil
2 T. wine vinegar
1 T. fresh lemon juice
1 t. salt
dash pepper
1 clove garlic, minced
1 t. chopped chives
2 T. chopped pimiento
2 T. chopped green
  pepper
dash paprika

Combine ingredients for marinade and pour over artichoke hearts and/or hearts of palm in shallow glass dish. Refrigerate 2 hours or more. To serve: Remove artichokes and hearts of palm from marinade with slotted spoon. Place on bibb lettuce.

## Mushroom and Watercress Salad

May add hearts of palm and serve on individual plates    Serves 6-8

**Salad:**
1 lb. mushrooms
6 T. lemon juice
1 T. minced chives
1 T. chopped parsley
1 t. dried tarragon
1 small bunch watercress

**Dressing:**
1/2 c. bottled Italian
   dressing
1/4 c. finely chopped
   pimiento
1/2 t. salt
1/8 t. pepper
1-1/2 T. sugar
2 t. prepared mustard

Wash and dry mushrooms; thinly slice into large bowl; sprinkle with lemon juice, chives, parsley and tarragon. Stir gently; refrigerate covered for 1 hour. Meanwhile, combine dressing ingredients in bowl. Stir well; refrigerate, covered, 1 hour. To serve, toss mushrooms with dressing. Arrange on top of watercress on large serving plate.

## Poppy Seed Salad

The secret: Have salad ingredients very cold    Serves 10-12

1 head Romaine lettuce
1 head iceberg lettuce
1 red onion, sliced
1—4-oz. can mandarin
   oranges, drained
1 pomegranate, sliced

**Dressing:**
1/2 medium onion,
   chopped
1 c. sugar
1/2 c. white vinegar
2 t. dry mustard
1-1/2 t. salt
1-1/2 t. salad oil
2 t. poppy seed

In blender, combine onion, sugar, vinegar, dry mustard and salt. Mix at low speed until all sugar dissolves. Drizzle salad oil into blender slowly and mix at medium speed until dressing is thick and glossy. Stir in poppy seed.

Line clear glass serving bowl with Romaine lettuce leaves. In center, place broken iceberg lettuce leaves, remaining Romaine, purple onion, mandarin oranges and pomegranate. Add dressing and serve.

## Sesame Lettuce Salad

Salad dressing may be served separately                     Serves 6

**Dressing:**
2 T. sesame seeds
1/2 c. mayonnaise or
   salad dressing
1/2 c. French salad
   dressing
2 T. grated Parmesan
   cheese
1 T. sugar
1 T. vinegar
1/2 t. salt

**Salad:**
1 small head lettuce,
   torn up
1/2 c. chopped green
   pepper
2 green onions, sliced
1—11-oz. can mandarin
   orange sections,
   drained
1/2 medium cucumber,
   sliced

In skillet, toast sesame seeds until lightly browned, set aside. Combine mayonnaise, French dressing, cheese, sugar, vinegar, and salt; add sesame seeds.

Combine lettuce, green pepper and onions. Arrange lettuce mixture, orange sections and cucumber in salad bowl. Pour salad dressing on top. Toss lightly to serve.

## Sunrise Salad

May also add sliced ripe avocado                     Serves 6-8

1/4 lb. crumbled blue
   cheese
3/4 t. salad oil
1 t. grated lemon peel
3 T. lemon juice
1 c. sour cream
1/2 t. seasoned salt
6 navel oranges, peeled
   and cut into bite-sized
   pieces
6 c. assorted salad
   greens, such as
   Romaine, iceberg, bibb
   or red-leaf lettuce

Combine blue cheese, oil, lemon peel and juice. In a small deep bowl, beat with electric mixer until smooth. Add sour cream and salt; mix well. Cover and chill at least one hour to mellow the flavors. Place orange sections and salad greens in a large bowl. Add dressing and toss lightly just before serving.

## Mexican Chef's Salad
Garnish with whole chips and avocado slices     Serves 8

1 lb. ground beef
1—15-oz. can kidney
  beans, drained
1/4 t. salt
1 onion, chopped
4 tomatoes, chopped
1 head lettuce, chopped
4 oz. grated cheddar cheese
8 oz. French or thousand island dressing
2 drops hot pepper sauce
1—6-oz. bag corn or tortilla chips, crushed
1 large avocado, peeled and cubed

Brown ground beef; drain. Add kidney beans and salt. Simmer 10 minutes. In large salad bowl mix onion, tomatoes, lettuce, cheese, salad dressing, hot sauce, crushed chips and avocado. Toss until well mixed. Top with meat mixture. Serve immediately.

## Italian Pasta Salad
May be stuffed into large hollowed-out tomatoes     Serves 8

**Fennel Dressing:**
3 T. red wine vinegar
1 t. chopped garlic
1 t. dried marjoram
salt
freshly ground pepper
1/2 c. extra virgin olive
  oil
2 t. fennel seed

**Salad:**
1-1/4 lb. broccoli, cut
  into 1-inch pieces
1/2 t. salt
2 red bell peppers, cut in
  julienne strips
1/2 lb. corkscrew-
  shaped pasta
1 lb. Italian sweet
  sausage
4 T. water
3 T. dry white wine
2/3 c. mayonnaise
  (preferably homemade,
  page 140)

For dressing, combine in blender vinegar, garlic, marjoram, salt and pepper to taste. With blender running, slowly add olive oil. Stir in fennel seed.

Place broccoli and salt in a large pot of boiling water; cook, uncovered, 3-5 minutes until broccoli is crisp-tender. Drain, rinse in cold water, and dry on paper towels. Toss broccoli with 1/4 c. Fennel Dressing and set aside.

Toss red pepper strips in 2 T. Fennel Dressing; set aside.

Cook pasta in boiling salted water just until tender, about 7-10 minutes. Drain; toss immediately with 4 T. Fennel Dressing; set aside.

In frying pan, place sausage, water and wine; cook uncovered, 5 minutes over high heat. Reduce heat and simmer 15 minutes, turning sausage often until cooked through. Remove sausage; slice 1/2 inch thick; toss with remaining Fennel Dressing.

In a large bowl, toss broccoli, red pepper, pasta and sausage; stir in mayonnaise. Serve warm or at room temperature.

## Salmon Mold with Cucumber Sauce

A classic when chilled in a fish-shaped mold                    Serves 4-6

1—15-1/2-oz. can red
  salmon
1 t. salt
1-1/2 T. sugar
1 T. flour
2 egg yolks
1-1/2 T. melted butter
3/4 c. milk
1/4 c. vinegar
2 T. cold water
3/4 T. unflavored gelatin

Cucumber Sauce:
1/2 c. heavy cream
1/2 t. salt
1/2 t. pepper
2 T. vinegar
1 cucumber, finely
  chopped

Rinse salmon thoroughly with hot water and separate flakes. Mix salt, sugar and flour. Add egg yolks, butter, milk and vinegar to flour mixture. Cook butter and flour mixture over boiling water, stirring constantly until thickened. Add gelatin which has been soaked in cold water. Stir and strain mixture. Add salmon. Put in greased mold and chill. Serve with cucumber sauce.

For sauce, beat cream until stiff. Add salt and pepper. Gradually add vinegar while continuing beating. Fold in cucumber. Pour over unmolded salad, or serve on the side.

## Shrimp Salad

Served in its own bowl                    Serves 4

2 grapefruit
1 green apple
1—4-oz. can mandarin
  oranges
1—8-oz. pkg. frozen
  cooked shrimp
6 oz. natural-flavor
  yogurt
2 T. mayonnaise
1 t. lemon juice
salt and pepper
parsley

Wash grapefruit and cut into halves. Remove fruit and reserve for another use; set aside grapefruit "bowls". Wash apple and cut into small pieces. Drain the mandarin segments. Wash shrimp briefly under cold water and mix apple, orange sections and shrimp.

Make a sauce from yogurt, mayonnaise, salt and pepper and lemon juice.

Mix sauce with fruit and shrimp combination and refrigerate for 1 hour. Just before serving, fill grapefruit halves with salad and decorate with parsley.

## Fresh Spinach Salad
May be served chilled or at room temperature                    Serves 8

1 pkg. fresh spinach
1—6-oz. can water
  chestnuts, sliced
1 can bean sprouts,
  drained
4 hard-boiled eggs, finely
  chopped
8 slices bacon, fried and
  crumbled

Dressing:
1 c. oil
3/4 c. sugar
1/3 c. catsup
1/4 c. vinegar
1 T. Worcestershire
  sauce
1 medium onion,
  chopped
2 t. salt

Combine dressing ingredients in blender; blend until fully mixed. Lightly toss spinach, water chestnuts, bean sprouts, eggs and bacon. Add dressing.

## Salmon Mold
May be served as appetizer with crackers                    Serves 6

1—10-oz. can tomato
  soup
1—8-oz. pkg. cream
  cheese
2 envelopes (2 T.) plain
  gelatin
1/2 c. cold water
1—16-oz. can salmon,
  drained
1 c. diced green pepper
1 c. diced celery
1 small onion, grated
1 c. mayonnaise
salad greens

Heat soup in saucepan; blend in cream cheese, mixing thoroughly. Soften gelatin in water; add to soup mixture, stirring to dissolve. Add remaining ingredients; mix well. Pour into lightly oiled 6-cup mold. Chill several hours or until firm. Unmold on greens and serve.

## Tortellini Salad

Perfect packable for a picnic                                    Serves 4-6

1 lb. frozen meat-filled
   tortellini
1 T. salt
1 T. olive oil
1-1/2 t. Dijon-style
   mustard
1/3 c. red wine vinegar
salt and pepper
1-1/3 c. olive oil
1 T. minced fresh parsley
1 T. snipped fresh dill
2 t. dried basil
6 oz. ham, shredded
1 large jar pimiento, cut
   in julienne strips
1 c. thin-sliced scallions
1/3 c. pine nuts, toasted
1-1/2 T. grated Parmesan
   cheese

Bring 6 quarts of water to boil with 1 T. each salt and olive oil. Add meat-filled tortellini and cook 5 minutes, stirring occasionally. Drain in large colander; refresh under cold running water and drain well.

In large serving bowl, combine mustard, red wine vinegar, salt and pepper to taste; add 1-1/3 c. olive oil in a stream, beating the dressing until it is well combined. Stir in parsley, dill, basil and pasta. Add ham, pimiento, scallions, pine nuts and cheese; toss gently. Chill one hour before serving.

## Turkey Salad Sublime

Serve in lettuce cups or on melon slices                         Serves 8

3 c. diced cooked turkey
1 can sliced water
   chestnuts
1/2 c. sliced stuffed
   olives
1 c. diced celery
2 c. red seedless Emperor
   grapes
1 c. pitted light cherries,
   drained
1 hard-cooked egg,
   diced
1 t. salt
1/2 c. French dressing
1 c. mayonnaise
1/2 c. whipping cream,
   whipped
1/2 t. curry powder

Marinate turkey, water chestnuts, olives, celery, fruit, egg and salt in French dressing for at least 1 hour. Fold mayonnaise, curry powder and whipped cream into mixture. Chill thoroughly.

## Chicken Almond Salad
May also be served in cantaloupe halves                    Serves 8-10

4 c. cooked chicken,
  diced
1-1/2 c. celery, diced
3 T. lemon juice
1-1/2 c. seedless white
  grapes
1—3-oz. pkg. almonds,
  toasted
2 small green onions,
  sliced (white portion
  only)
3 hard-boiled eggs,
  chopped
1 t. celery seed
3/4 t. seasoned salt
3/4 t. salt
1/8 t. pepper
3/4 c. salad dressing
3/4 c. mayonnaise
1/4 c. half and half
  cream
8-10 pineapple rings, or
  2 cantaloupes
lettuce

Combine chicken, celery and lemon juice; chill for 1 hour. Add grapes, almonds, onions, eggs. Combine remaining ingredients. Add to chicken mixture.

Serve on lettuce and top with pineapple ring, or top with cantaloupe slices. Garnish with paprika and parsley.

## Chicken-Artichoke-Rice Salad
Hearty main course to make ahead                             Serves 8

1 c. artichoke hearts,
  sliced
1—4-oz. jar pimientos,
  chopped
2 c. chopped celery
1 c. chopped green
  pepper
1 pkg. dry Italian salad
  dressing, prepared
2—6-oz. pkg. long grain
  and wild rice
4 whole chicken
  breasts, cooked and
  diced
1 c. mayonnaise
1 lb. mushrooms, sliced
1 head lettuce

Marinate artichokes, pimientos, celery and green pepper in Italian dressing overnight. Using 1/2 cup less water for each package, cook rice as directed on package. Combine rice, chicken and mayonnaise. Add sliced mushrooms and marinated mixture. Chill. Serve on lettuce cups.

## Hot Chicken Nest

From *Bellamy's*, one of Rockford's finest restaurants          Serves 1

1-1/4 c. spinach leaves
1 hard-cooked egg,
  grated
1/4 c. fresh mushrooms,
  sliced
2 slices bacon, cooked
  and crumbled
1 small tomato, sliced
1 slice red onion,
  separated into rings
1—4-oz. chicken breast,
  cooked, boned

Bacon dressing:
2 T. bacon drippings
1/4 c. cider vinegar
1/2 t. sugar
salt and pepper

Place spinach leaves in large salad bowl. Add egg, mushrooms, and bacon bits. Stand tomato and onion slices on sides of the bowl. Julienne the cooked chicken breast and place over the spinach leaves.

For dressing, mix all ingredients well. Pour 3 oz. hot bacon dressing over chicken. Serve immediately.

## Hot Chicken Salad

From *The Pie Shell*, where Dorine Muller and staff
prepare delicious, home-cooked favorites          Serves 8-10

1 c. chopped celery
1 T. butter
2 c. white meat of
  chicken, cut up
1 c. cooked rice
1—10-oz. can cream of
  chicken soup
1 t. minced onion
1 t. lemon juice
1 t. salt
3/4 c. mayonnaise
1/2 c. water chestnuts,
  sliced
1 c. crushed cornflakes
1/2 c. sliced almonds

Saute celery in butter. Mix remaining ingredients, except cornflakes and almonds, with celery. Place in greased casserole. Sprinkle cornflakes and almonds over top. Bake at 350° for 30 minutes.

## Oriental Chicken Salad
Serve in hollowed-out pineapple half                          Serves 6

1 large chicken breast
1 c. water
1/4 c. white wine
1/4 t. powdered ginger
1/4 t. celery salt
1 c. celery, chopped
3 green onions, chopped
1/2 c. drained crushed
   pineapple (save juice)
1/3 c. walnut pieces
1 small can peeled, sliced
   water chestnuts
1/2 t. paprika
1/2 t. salt
1/2 t. white pepper
mayonnaise

Dressing:
1/4 c. pineapple juice
3/4 c. mayonnaise
1 t. rum extract
   (optional)

Cook chicken in water, white wine, ginger and celery salt until tender. Cool and dice.

Mix chicken with other ingredients, adding just enough mayonnaise to bind.

Before serving, mix dressing ingredients and pour over top. Chill 1 hour. Toss and serve.

## Marmalade Dressing for Fruit
Delicious served over orange and grapefruit wedges            Serves 6

1/2 c. mayonnaise
1/4 c. orange marmalade
1 T. powdered sugar
1/2 t. poppy seeds

Blend mayonnaise, marmalade and powdered sugar in a bowl. Mix well. Add poppy seeds. Refrigerate until needed.

## Fruit Salad Dressing
Fruit brandy may be added for "spark"                         Makes 1 cup

1/2 c. sugar
2 T. cornstarch
3/4 c. water
juice and rind of one
   lemon
juice and rind of one
   orange

Mix sugar and cornstarch in saucepan; add water, shredded rinds and juices. Cook over low heat, stirring constantly, until thick. Cool. Chill until serving.

Combine with any combination of mixed fresh fruit.

## Orange Fruit Salad Dressing

Could be served as a dip for fresh fruit                    Makes 2-3 cups

1/3 c. sugar
2 eggs
3 T. cornstarch
1/4 t. salt
1-1/2 c. milk
1-1/2 t. vanilla
1 c. whipping cream,
   whipped
7-8 T. Triple Sec

Prepare pudding by combining sugar, eggs, cornstarch and salt. Gradually blend in milk. Cook over medium heat, stirring constantly, until mixture thickens. Cook 2 to 3 minutes more. Add vanilla. Cover with plastic film and chill.

Fold whipping cream and Triple Sec into cooled pudding: refrigerate. Serve with assorted fresh fruits as a salad dressing.

## Homemade Mayonnaise

So easy and good, you'll never go back to store-bought        Makes 2 cups

2 eggs
1 T. fresh lemon juice
2 t. sugar
1/2 t. salt
1/8 t. white pepper
1 t. Dijon mustard
1-1/2 c. vegetable oil

In blender or food processor, mix all ingredients except oil. With motor running, **very slowly** add oil. When half has been added, the mixture will begin to thicken. Gradually add remaining oil and process until thick. Taste and adjust seasoning. Use immediately or refrigerate in a covered jar. Will keep 2 to 3 weeks.

## Herb Mayonnaise

Any of your favorite herbs may be used                     Makes 1-1/2 cups

1 c. mayonnaise
   (homemade preferred)
1/2 c. sour cream
1/2 T. lemon juice
1/4 t. salt
1/4 t. paprika
1 T. dried mixed herbs
1 T. onion juice
1 clove garlic, minced
1 T. chive, chopped
1/8 t. curry powder
1/2 t. Worcestershire
   sauce

Mix all ingredients and chill 24 hours before serving.

## Buttermilk-Dill Dressing

Better than the bottled variety                           Makes 2 cups

1 c. mayonnaise
1 c. buttermilk or 1/2 c.
  buttermilk and 1/2 c.
  sour cream
1 T. onion flakes,
  minced
1 T. parsley flakes
1-1/2 T. dill weed
1 t. seasoned salt
1 dash Worcestershire
  sauce

Mix all ingredients and refrigerate. Let stand several hours before serving.

## Sweet Homemade Dressing

Excellent over garden-fresh tomatoes                      Makes 1 cup

1/2 c. plain yogurt
1/2 c. cucumber, peeled
  and chopped
1 T. sugar
1 T. vegetable oil
1/2 t. onion powder
1/2 t. salt
1/8 t. garlic powder
1/8 t. pepper
1 T. red wine vinegar

Mix all ingredients except vinegar in a bowl. Slowly add the vinegar. Refrigerate for 4 hours before serving.

## Pepper Dressing

Sour cream may be substituted for buttermilk              Makes 3 cups

2 c. mayonnaise
1/4 c. milk
1/4 c. buttermilk
1/4 c. water
2 T. Parmesan cheese,
  freshly grated
1 T. fresh ground pepper
1 t. lemon juice
2 t. green onion, finely
  chopped
1 t. garlic salt

Whisk all ingredients together. Chill for 24 hours before serving.

## Sweet Cream Dressing

Pour over bibb lettuce                                                      Makes 1 cup

1—5-1/3-oz. can
  evaporated milk
5 T. sugar
3 T. white vinegar

Stir sugar in milk until completely dissolved. Slowly add vinegar, constantly stirring, until thickened. May be served at room temperature, but better chilled.

## French Dressing

Exceptional with blue cheese added                          Makes 1 quart

1 c. sugar
1 c. ketchup
1 t. garlic powder
1 t. pepper
1 t. salt
1/2 c. vinegar
2 c. vegetable oil

Blend all ingredients except oil in blender or food processor. Add oil slowly, blending continuously until thickened. Keeps for several weeks in refrigerator.

## WAITING FOR SPRING

the front porch of my farm studio.

in the spring, when its warm, i often sit on this chair
and watch the sun go down.

when the bats begin to zig-zag across the sky and the
night birds begin to call, i return to my basel.

esday december 20, 1983 sunny, cold 3:00                    tom heflin

# Pancakes, Waffles & Crepes

## Feather Pancakes
Couldn't be easier                                    Serves 4

1 c. cream style cottage
   cheese
6 eggs
1/4 c. vegetable oil
1/4 c. milk
1/2 c. flour
1/2 t. vanilla

In blender container, combine all ingredients in order listed. Blend until smooth. Bake on hot griddle or in waffle iron until golden brown. Serve with butter and warmed syrup or preserves.


## Dutch Baby Pancake
Follow across chart for the amount you wish

| Pan Size | Butter | Eggs | Milk | Flour |
|----------|--------|------|------|-------|
| 2-3 qt. | 1/4 c. | 3 | 3/4 c. | 3/4 c. |
| 3-4 qt. | 1/3 c. | 4 | 1 c. | 1 c. |
| 4-4-1/2 qt. | 1/2 c. | 5 | 1-1/4 c. | 1-1/4 c. |
| 5 qt. | 1/2 c. | 6 | 1-1/2 c. | 1-1/2 c |

Heat oven to 425°. Melt butter in casserole dish in oven. Meanwhile, mix remaining ingredients for 3-4 minutes in blender. Pour into dish and bake 20-35 minutes, until puffed, browned, and almost set in center. Serve immediately.

Toppings: Serve with sour cream and fruit; or butter and syrup; or preserves of your choice. Or, heat canned pie filling for topping.


## Southern Rice Pancakes
Best with warmed syrup or honey                        Serves 4

3/4 c. flour
1/4 c. sugar
1/2 t. salt
1/4 t. nutmeg
1/4 t. cinnamon
1-1/2 t. baking powder
3/4 c. milk
1 egg, well beaten
2 T. melted butter
1 c. cooked cooled rice

Sift all dry ingredients together and place in a bowl. Add milk, egg and butter all at one time; mix until well blended; stir in cooked rice. Pour 1/4 c. batter onto a hot lightly greased griddle and allow to bake until brown underneath. Turn and bake until golden brown.

## Low-Calorie Pancakes

Good with fresh or low-sugar canned fruit          Makes 20-25 pancakes

1 c. low-fat cottage
   cheese
6 large eggs
1/2 c. sifted flour
1/4 c. oil
1/4 c. skim milk
1 t. vanilla

Blend all ingredients in blender for one minute. Bake on hot griddle, using 3 T. batter for each pancake. Serve immediately.

## Mom's Buckwheat Pancakes

Ground Kasha may be substituted for buckwheat flour          Serves 6

3 eggs
1-3/4 c. buttermilk
1-3/4 c. buckwheat flour
3/4 c. rolled oats
1 T. sugar
1-1/2 t. baking powder
1 t. baking soda
1 t. cinnamon
1/8 t. salt
1/4 c. butter or
   margarine, melted
1 T. honey
1 t. vanilla
1 t. almond extract
butter (optional)
maple syrup (optional)

In a large bowl, stir eggs into buttermilk. In medium bowl, mix flour, oats, sugar, baking powder, baking soda, cinnamon and salt. Slowly stir flour mixture into buttermilk mixture. Stir in butter, honey, vanilla and almond extracts. Bake pancakes on greased griddle 3 minutes on each side until browned. Serve warm with butter and warm maple syrup, if desired.

## Blueberry-Cinnamon Pancakes

Unthawed frozen blueberries may be used for a year-round treat          Serves 4

1-1/2 c. flour
1 T. sugar
2 t. baking powder
1/2 t. baking soda
1/2 t. salt
1/4 t. cinnamon
2 eggs, slightly beaten
2 T. vegetable oil
1 c. buttermilk
1/4 c. sherry
3/4 c. fresh blueberries,
   rinsed and dried
1/4 c. chopped pecans

In large mixing bowl, combine dry ingredients. In small mixing bowl, combine eggs, oil, buttermilk, and sherry. Stir into dry ingredients; add blueberries and pecans. Stir gently. Spoon batter onto hot, greased griddle or large frying pan using 2 heaping T. for each pancake. Turn when bubbles cover pancakes. Cook until well browned. Serve immediately with butter and syrup.

## Swedish Pancakes
Omit the sugar and you have crepe batter                    Serves 4

4 eggs, well beaten
1/3 t. salt
2 T. sugar
1/2 c. flour
1 c. milk
1/3 c. melted butter
lingonberries

Mix all ingredients in blender. Use 1/4 c. batter per pancake. Bake on ungreased skillet (copper-bottomed skillet is best). Butter pancakes; top with lingonberries; roll up. Serve hot. Pancakes, unbuttered, may be wrapped and frozen for several weeks.

## Sweet Apple Pancake
Cheddar cheese is a nice accompaniment                    Serves 4

4 large Golden Delicious
    apples
5 T. butter (do not
    substitute)
1 t. cinnamon
1/4 t. nutmeg
1/3 c. sugar

Batter:
1/3 c. flour
1/3 c. milk
1/2 t. baking powder
1/8 t. salt
4 eggs, separated
1/3 c. sugar

Peel, core and slice apples thinly. In a large skillet, melt butter. Stir in cinnamon, nutmeg, sugar and apples. Cook over low heat about 8 minutes, until apples are almost tender. Remove from heat.

In a large bowl, mix flour, milk, baking powder, salt and egg yolks just until blended. Beat egg whites with sugar until soft peaks form. Fold whites into flour mixture gently.

Pour batter gently over apples in skillet. Bake at 400° for 20 minutes until pancake is puffed and center tests done when a toothpick is inserted.

Loosen edge of pancake from pan and invert over deep serving plate. Serve immediately.

## Bacon Pancake
To double, bake one hour in 9 x 13-inch pan                    Serves 4

4 slices bacon
3 eggs, well beaten
2 c. milk
1 c. flour
2 T. sugar
1/2 t. salt

Cook bacon until crisp in a 9-inch ovenproof skillet. Remove bacon and crumble; return to skillet. Combine eggs and milk; add sifted dry ingredients; beat until smooth. Pour over bacon and drippings; bake at 375° for 40 minutes.

## High-Rise Apple Pancake
Even more spectacular served flaming                    Serves 4-6

1/4 c. butter
6 c. peeled apple slices
1/4 c. sugar
1/2 t. cinnamon
2 eggs
1/2 c. flour
1/2 c. milk
1/4 t. salt
1 T. butter
1 c. strawberry preserves

Melt butter in a large skillet; add apple slices, sugar and cinnamon. Saute until apples are glazed; set aside. Beat together eggs, flour, milk and salt. Pour into a heated 8-inch ovenproof skillet in which 1 T. butter has been melted. Bake for 10 minutes at 450°; reduce heat to 350° and bake 10 minutes longer. Remove from oven and cut into wedges. Pour apple filling into center of pancake. Drizzle heated strawberry preserves over top. Serve warm.

To serve flaming, combine 2 T. sugar and 1/2 t. cinnamon and sprinkle over pancake. Warm 3-4 T. cognac. Carefully ignite and pour over pancake. Serve immediately with sour cream.

## German Pancake Pie
Not as sweet as many pancakes                           Serves 6

4 eggs
1/3 c. sugar
2 c. milk
2 c. flour
1 t. salt
1 T. vanilla
2 T. butter
juice of 2 lemons
1/3 c. sugar
2 t. cinnamon

Combine eggs, sugar, milk, flour, salt and vanilla; blend with electric mixer. Pour into greased 10-inch glass pie dish. Bake at 375° for 40 minutes (center and sides will puff up, then drop). Let sit 3-5 minutes. Remove from pie pan onto large serving dish. Cut up butter and place on top; pour lemon juice over and sprinkle with mixture of cinnamon and sugar. Serve hot, in wedges.

## Cinnamon-Amaretto French Toast
Sprinkle with sliced toasted almonds                    Serves 2-3

6 slices stale French or
  Italian bread
2 eggs, beaten
1/4 t. salt
1/2 c. milk
cinnamon
butter, softened
powdered sugar
2-3 fresh lemon wedges
2-3 T. Amaretto liqueur

Dip bread slices in mixture of eggs, salt and milk. Put onto hot griddle. Sprinkle with cinnamon. Turn when brown on bottom; sprinkle other side with cinnamon. When second side is brown, place on plate, spread with butter, sprinkle with powdered sugar, and dribble lemon juice and Amaretto over all.

## Orange French Toast
Keep in your freezer for almost-instant breakfast                    Serves 6

2 eggs
1 c. orange juice
1 T. sugar
1/4 t. salt
8-10 slices of bread
6 T. butter or margarine

Orange Syrup:
1 c. light corn syrup
1 t. grated orange peel
1/4 c. orange juice

Beat eggs; add orange juice, sugar and salt. Dip bread into mixture, coating both sides. Place bread on baking sheets; freeze until firm, then wrap and return to freezer. When ready to serve, place bread in well-buttered shallow baking dish. Melt butter; drizzle over bread. Bake at 500° for 5 minutes; turn and bake until golden brown, 5-10 minutes more. In a saucepan, combine ingredients for syrup; simmer 5 minutes. Cool and refrigerate. Warm when ready to use.

## French Toast Fondue with Maple Butter
For variety, add strawberry butter to the menu                    Serves 4

Fondue:
1 loaf French bread
2 eggs, beaten
1/2 c. milk
1/4 t. salt
1 t. salt
peanut oil

Maple Butter:
1-1/2 c. powdered sugar
1/2 c. butter, softened
1/2 c. maple syrup
1 egg yolk
1 egg white, stiffly
  beaten

Cut bread into 2-inch cubes. In attractive mixing bowl, combine egg, milk, and 1/4 t. salt. Pour oil into fondue pot until half-full; heat to 375°. Add salt to oil. Set out bread and egg-mix and have each person dip own bread chunks, using fondue forks, in egg-mix. Allow excess to drip off; then cook in hot oil 2-3 minutes. Using dinner fork, dip "chunks" in maple butter.

For Maple Butter, beat powdered sugar with butter, maple syrup and egg yolk. Fold in beaten egg white. Chill.

## Stuffed French Toast

Strawberry preserves heated with Grand Marnier    Serves 6
are also a delicious topping

**Filling:**
1—8-oz. pkg. cream
  cheese, softened
1 t. vanilla
1/2 c. chopped walnuts

**French Toast:**
1 loaf French bread
4 eggs
1 c. whipping cream
1/2 t. vanilla
1/2 t. nutmeg

**Topping:**
1—12-oz. jar apricot
  preserves
1/2 c. orange juice

For filling, beat cream cheese and vanilla together until fluffy. Stir in nuts; set aside. Cut bread into 12 1-1/2-inch slices; cut a pocket in the top of each. Fill each with 1-1/2 T. of cheese mixture. Beat eggs, cream, vanilla and nutmeg together. Dip filled bread slices in egg mixture, being careful not to squeeze out the filling. Cook on lightly greased griddle until both sides are golden brown. Keep on cookie sheets in warm oven until ready to serve. Heat together preserves and juice. Drizzle over toast.

## Funnel Cakes

An old Pennsylvania Dutch specialty    Serves 4

2 eggs, beaten
1-1/2 c. milk
2 c. flour
1 t. baking powder
1/2 t. salt
1/2 t. cinnamon
oil for deep frying

In mixing bowl, combine eggs and milk. Sift in remaining ingredients and beat until smooth. Mixture should flow easily through a funnel; add more milk or flour if necessary. In a large skillet, heat 2 inches oil to 375°. Cover bottom opening of funnel with finger; pour a generous 1/2 c. batter into funnel. Release batter into hot oil in a spiral shape. Fry until bottom is golden, about 3 minutes. Turn with slotted spatula and fry 1 minute more. Drain on paper towels. Serve hot with butter and syrup.

## Fluffy Waffles

Chopped pecans, crisp bacon or blueberries
may be added to batter

Serves 5

2 egg yolks, well beaten
2 c. milk
2 c. cake flour
1/4 t. salt
3 t. sugar
4 t. baking powder
6 T. butter, melted,
   cooled
2 egg whites, stiffly
   beaten

Combine beaten egg yolks and milk; add flour sifted with salt, baking powder and sugar; add cooled butter. Beat until smooth; fold in egg whites. Bake on ungreased waffle iron.

## Pumpkin Nut Waffles

Wonderful with sausage and apple rings

Serves 6

2 c. flour
1 T. baking powder
3/4 t. pumpkin pie spice
1/4 t. salt
3 egg yolks
1-3/4 c. milk
1/2 c. vegetable oil
1/2 c. mashed cooked
   pumpkin
3 egg whites
1/2 c. chopped pecans

In a mixing bowl, thoroughly stir together flour, baking powder, pie spice and salt. Beat yolks; stir in milk, oil and pumpkin. Stir into dry ingredients. Beat egg whites to stiff peaks; fold into batter. Stir in nuts. Pour about 1 c. batter onto hot waffle iron; bake. Repeat with remaining batter. Serve hot waffles with butter and maple syrup.

## Whole Wheat Pecan Waffles

Serve with warm honey

Serves 6-8

1 c. whole wheat flour
1-1/4 c. all-purpose flour
2 T. sugar
1 T. baking powder
1/2 t. nutmeg
1 t. salt
1/2 c. chopped pecans
2 c. milk
1/2 c. vegetable oil
2 eggs, slightly beaten

In large bowl, combine dry ingredients. Add milk, oil and eggs. Mix until smooth; pour 1 c. batter evenly on preheated waffle iron. Close and bake about 5 minutes.

## Paté A Crepes
Very easy to make with a little practice                    Makes 24 crepes

1 c. cold water
1 c. cold milk
4 eggs
1/2 t. salt
2 c. flour, sifted
4 T. melted butter

Put water, milk, eggs and salt into blender container. Add flour, then butter. Cover and blend at high speed for 1 minute. If bits of flour adhere to sides of jar, dislodge with rubber scraper and blend for 2 to 3 seconds more. Cover and refrigerate at least 2 hours. To bake crepes, lightly butter a 7-inch skillet. Heat until a drop of water added to the pan sizzles (medium high heat). For each crepe, pour about 4 T. batter into the skillet and rotate it quickly to spread batter evenly. Cook about 1 minute, then turn crepe and brown other side about 30 seconds. Repeat until all batter is used, stacking crepes as they are finished. Crepes may be wrapped in foil and refrigerated 2 to 3 days, or frozen. Thaw in refrigerator before using.

## Buttermilk Crepes
These have a pleasant tanginess                    Makes 18 crepes

3/4 c. flour
1 c. buttermilk
1/2 c. milk
2 eggs
1 T. vegetable oil
1 t. sugar
1/4 t. salt

In mixer bowl, combine flour, buttermilk, milk, eggs, oil, sugar and salt; beat at low speed until blended. Heat a lightly greased 6-inch skillet; remove from heat; spoon in 2 T. batter. Lift and tilt skillet to spread batter. Return to heat, brown on one side only. Invert pan over paper toweling; remove crepe. Repeat, greasing skillet occasionally. Stack crepes with waxed paper between layers. Use immediately, refrigerate or freeze.

## Crepe Baskets
Each basket holds a perfect baked egg                    Serves 6

6 crepes
3 oz. cheddar cheese, grated
1—6-oz. can crab meat, flaked
6 eggs
salt
pepper
paprika

Grease six 10-oz. custard cups; place on cookie sheet. Place one crepe in each cup with bottom flat and sides ruffled. Put 1 T. cheese in each crepe; put 2 T. crab meat in each crepe; break one egg into each crepe; sprinkle each with paprika, salt and pepper. Bake at 350° for 15-20 minutes. Sprinkle another tablespoon cheese over egg and return to oven just until cheese melts.

## Avocado Crepes
Best filled with creamy seafood                    Makes 24 crepes

1 c. mashed avocado
8 eggs
1 c. flour
1/2 t. salt
1/18 t. cayenne pepper
3/4 c. milk
3/4 c. cold water

Mix all ingredients in blender container (batter will have consistency of heavy cream). Refrigerate at least 2 hours. Butter a 7-inch skillet; heat over medium heat until a drop of water sizzles on the pan. Pour in a scant 1/4 c. batter, rotating pan quickly to spread batter evenly. Cook until bottom is lightly browned, about 1 minute; turn and bake other side briefly. Continue with remaining batter, buttering for each crepe. Note: These are fragile to bake, so turn carefully with wide spatula or your fingers.

## Champion Chicken Crepes
A winner no matter when they're served                    Serves 8

**Filling:**
1 T. butter
1/4 c. minced onion
6 oz. Italian sausage
  (bulk), browned
2 c. diced cooked
  chicken
1—10-oz. pkg. frozen
  chopped spinach,
  defrosted and squeezed
  dry
3/4 c. Parmesan cheese,
  freshly grated
1/2 t. salt
1/4 t. pepper

**Sauce:**
6 T. butter
6 T. flour
3 c. milk, heated to
  steaming
1 c. Parmesan cheese,
  freshly grated
1 c. cheddar cheese,
  freshly grated
1/4 t. curry powder
3 drops hot pepper sauce

For Filling, saute onion in butter 4 minutes. Add sausage, chicken, spinach, Parmesan, salt and pepper, mix well. Place 1 large T. full of mixture in a stripe down center of each crepe. Roll up and place, seam side down, in a buttered 9 x 13-inch baking dish.

For Sauce, melt butter in large saucepan. Stir in flour and cook, stirring constantly, 2 minutes. Add milk and whisk over medium-high heat until thickened and bubbly. Add remaining ingredients and stir over low heat until cheese is melted and sauce is very smooth.

Assembly: Pour sauce over filled crepes and refrigerate, covered with plastic wrap. To serve, bake at 300° for 30 minutes or until heated through.

## Crab-Filled Crepes

Must be filled just before serving                    Serves 6

12 crepes
2 T. finely chopped
    onion
4 T. butter
4 T. flour
1-1/2 c. milk
3 T. sherry or white
    wine
1/2 c. chicken stock
salt and pepper
1 egg yolk
3 T. whipping cream
1/2 c. chopped
    mushrooms
1 T. butter
2 c. crabmeat
2 t. chopped chives
4 T. whipping cream
pinch of nutmeg

Saute onion in 4 T. butter. Stir in flour; add milk, sherry and chicken stock. Season to taste with salt and pepper. Cook, stirring, until thickened. Mix egg yolk with 3 T. cream. Stir into sauce; heat 2 minutes. Reserve 1/2 c. sauce.

Saute mushrooms in 1 T. butter; add crabmeat, mushrooms and chives to remaining sauce. Heat well. Fill crepes with crabmeat mixture; roll and tuck ends under. Place in a lightly greased 9 x 13-inch baking dish. Mix cream and nutmeg with reserved sauce; cover crepes with sauce and glaze them under the broiler. Serve immediately.

## Ham and Egg Crepes with Mushroom Sauce

May be assembled the night before baking                    Serves 6

2 T. butter
1-1/4 c. finely chopped
    ham
8 eggs
1/2 c. milk
1/4 c. water
1/2 t. pepper
12 crepes

Mushroom Sauce:
3 T. butter
8 oz. mushrooms, sliced
2 T. chopped onion
1 T. flour
1/8 c. milk
1 t. prepared mustard
1/2 t. salt
1/3 t. pepper
1/8 t. ground nutmeg
1 c. sour cream
2 T. chopped fresh
    parsley

Melt butter in large skillet; saute ham in butter about 5 minutes or until lightly browned. Combine eggs, milk, water and pepper; beat well. Add egg mixture to ham; cook, stirring occasionally, until eggs are firm but still moist. Spoon 1/4 c. egg mixture in center of each crepe; fold sides of crepe over filling. Place crepes, seam side down, in a lightly greased 13 x 9-inch baking dish, tucking ends under.

For Mushroom Sauce, melt butter in a large skillet; saute mushrooms and onion in butter 3-5 minutes or until onion is tender. Add flour, stirring until vegetables are coated. Cook 1 minute, stirring constantly. Gradually add milk; cook over medium heat, stirring constantly, until thickened and bubbly. Stir in mustard, salt, pepper and nutmeg; add sour cream and parsley. Cook, stirring constantly, until sauce is thoroughly heated. Pour mushroom sauce evenly over crepes. Cover and bake at 350° for 10-15 minutes or until thoroughly heated.

## Fiesta Crepes

Garnish with avocado slices                                    Serves 8

**Chicken Filling:**
3 T. butter
1 small onion, chopped
1/2 green pepper,
   chopped
3 fresh tomatoes,
   chopped (or 1—16-oz.
   can tomatoes, drained
   and chopped)
1/2 t. salt
1/4 t. chili powder
dash pepper
3 c. diced cooked
   chicken or turkey

**Cheese Sauce:**
2 T. butter
2 T. flour
1/2 t. salt
dash pepper
1/2 c. chicken broth
1/2 c milk
1/2 c. grated Swiss
   cheese
1/2 c. grated Parmesan
   cheese
16 crepes

For filling, melt butter in skillet. Add onion and green pepper; cook until tender. Add tomatoes and seasonings; simmer 15 minutes. Add chicken; cook 5 minutes longer. Set aside.

For cheese sauce, melt butter in saucepan; stir in flour and seasonings. Gradually stir in broth and milk. Cook over low heat, stirring constantly, until bubbly. Remove from heat. Add cheeses and stir until melted and smooth.

To assemble, put 1/4 c. of chicken filling in the center of each crepe; roll up. Place in 9 x 13-inch casserole dish with seam of crepe down. Spoon cheese sauce over crepes. Bake at 325° for 20 minutes or until heated through.

## Parisienne Chicken Crepes

Garnish with lots of parsley and orange slices                 Serves 8

8 crepes
2 T. butter
2 T. flour
1 c. chicken broth
1/4 t. salt
1 c. sliced mushrooms
1 egg yolk
1/4 c. whipping cream
2 c. cooked, diced
   chicken
1/4 c. grated cheddar
   cheese

Melt butter in saucepan. Blend in flour; add broth and salt. Stir and cook over moderate heat, about 2 minutes or until thickened. Stir in mushrooms; cook for 1 minute. Remove from heat. Mix egg yolk with cream. Stir small amount of hot mixture into egg yolk; stir egg mixture into saucepan. Cook over low heat for another minute. Stir in chicken. Fill crepes with chicken mixture; fold over; place in greased shallow baking dish. Sprinkle crepes with cheese. Cover and bake at 350° oven for 15 to 20 minutes.

## Panzerotte Crepes

May be prepared one day ahead                    Serves 10

20 crepes
2 eggs, beaten
1/2 c. grated Parmesan
2 c. cottage cheese
1-1/2 c. shredded Swiss
   cheese
1 lb. frozen chopped
   spinach, thawed and
   squeezed dry
1-1/2 c. soft bread
   crumbs
pepper
garlic powder

Sauce:
1/2 c. butter
1 c. whipping cream
1/2 c. grated Parmesan
   cheese
1/4 c. sherry

For filling, combine eggs, cheeses, spinach and bread crumbs; add pepper and garlic powder to taste. Spoon into crepes; roll up; place in greased 9 x 13-inch pan.

For sauce, melt butter; stir in cream, cheese and sherry. Pour sauce over crepes; bake at 350° for 30 minutes.

## Apple Betty Crepes

Top with ice cream for rave reviews                    Serves 10

Crepes:
1 c. flour
1-1/2 c. milk
1/2 c. sour cream
2 eggs
2 T. sugar
1/8 t. salt

Topping:
1/2 c. packed brown
   sugar
1/2 c. flour
1/4 t. cinnamon
1/8 t. nutmeg
1/8 t. salt
1/4 c. butter

Filling:
2 c. chopped apple
2 T. orange juice

Beat all ingredients for crepes until blended. Chill batter for 1 hour. In a heated skillet, bake a scant 1/4 c. batter for each crepe, turning once to brown.

For topping, combine brown sugar, flour, cinnamon, nutmeg and salt. Cut in butter until mixture is crumbly.

For filling, toss apples with orange juice. Add 1/2 c. topping mixture.

Assembly: Spoon about 1/4 c. of apple filling along center of each crepe. Fold the two opposite edges over the top of filling. Place crepes, seam side down, in greased 10 x 6-inch inch baking dish. Sprinkle with remaining topping. Bake 25 minutes at 375°. Serve warm.

@@4

## Florentine Crepe Cups
Sauteed mushrooms may be added      Serves 6

12 crepes
1-1/2 c. grated sharp
  cheese
3 T. flour
3 eggs, slightly beaten
2/3 c. mayonnaise
1—10-oz. pkg. frozen
  chopped spinach,
  thawed and squeezed
  dry
bacon and parsley for
  garnish

Fit crepes into wells of greased muffin pan. Toss cheese and flour; add eggs, mayonnaise and spinach; mix well. Fill crepes with egg mixture. Bake at 350° for 40 minutes. Garnish with bacon curls and parsley sprigs.

## Apple Rum Crepes
Serve with sausages for fall brunch      Serves 6

12 crepes
1/2 c. butter
3 lb. apples,
  pared and sliced
1 c. brown sugar
1 T. rum
1 t. cornstarch
1 t. water
whipped cream
cinnamon

Melt butter in a large skillet; add apples, brown sugar and rum. Cover and cook 5 minutes, stirring occasionally, until apples are beginning to soften. Mix cornstarch and water. Add to apple mixture and cook a few minutes until clear and slightly thickened. Cool slightly. Put 2 heaping tablespoons of apples in each crepe. Roll; top with whipped cream and sprinkle with cinnamon.

## Shrimp Piquante
Filling is also delicious in patty shells      Serves 6

12 crepes
1/4 c. butter
5 T. flour
1-1/2 c. milk
1/2 c. cream
1/2 c. green pepper, cut
  into strips
1/2 c. pimiento, cut into
  strips
2 c. cooked shrimp
2 egg yolks, beaten
1/2 c. mayonnaise
1/2 t. Worcestershire
  sauce

Melt butter in sauce pan. Blend in flour; add milk and cream slowly, stirring over medium heat until thickened and smooth. Add green pepper, pimiento and shrimp. When hot, add egg yolks. Cook one minute. Add mayonnaise and Worcestershire. Heat thoroughly and fill crepes. Serve immediately.

## Sausage-Filled Brunch Crepes

Inexpensive but elegant entree                                    Serves 8

16 crepes
2 lb. bulk pork sausage
1/4 c. chopped onion
1—3-oz. pkg. cream
   cheese, softened
1 c. shredded American
   cheese
1/4 t. celery salt
1/4 t. marjoram
1-1/2 c. sour cream,
   divided
1/2 c. butter, softened

Brown sausage and onion; drain well. Stir in cream cheese, American cheese, celery salt and marjoram. Remove from heat; stir in 1 c. sour cream. Place 2 T. sausage mixture down the center of each crepe; roll crepe and place seam down in greased 9 x 13-inch baking dish.

For sauce, combine butter and remaining 1/2 c. sour cream; spread over crepes; sprinkle with paprika. Bake at 350°, covered with foil, for 30 minutes.

## Crepes Maison

Sweet crepes which can also be filled with fresh fruit            Serves 12

7/8 c. flour
1/8 t. salt
1 T. sugar
3 eggs
1 t. vanilla
2 T. cognac
2 T. unsalted butter,
   melted
1-1/4 c. milk
4-5 t. melted butter, in
   small bowl

Filling:
4 T. butter
1-1/2 c. Cointreau
1 c. orange marmalade
   or blackberry
   preserves
6 T. grated orange rind

For crepes, sift flour, salt, and sugar 3 times; put in mixing bowl. Add eggs, one at a time, stirring constantly. Add vanilla, cognac and 2 T. melted butter; mix well. Add milk, a bit at a time, stirring constantly with a wooden spoon. Batter should have consistency of light cream. Pour batter into pitcher. Use an 8-inch crepe pan (preferably an iron skillet). Restir batter periodically to prevent lumping and lightly grease pan with melted butter for every other crepe. Heat pan until a drop of water on it will steam instantly. Pour about 1-1/2 T. of batter into pan, tilting pan to spread thinly over bottom. Cook until edges turn brown and crepe will slide easily in pan. Flip over with spatula (or use your fingers) and cook 30 seconds. Stack finished crepes on plate.

For filling, melt butter in large skillet; add Cointreau and heat over low flame. Add crepes, two at a time, and turn to coat. Spoon 2 T. marmalade in a strip on each crepe; roll each crepe over filling and push to side of pan. Repeat until all crepes are in pan and are slightly warmed. Sprinkle with orange rind.

## Strawberries 'n Cream Crepes

Good basic recipe for any dessert crepes                    Serves 8

1 qt. fresh strawberries,
   washed, hulled and
   sliced
1/2 c. sugar

Crepes:
1 c. flour
1 T. sugar
1/2 t. ground nutmeg
3 eggs, beaten
3 T. melted butter
1-1/2 c. milk
butter

Filling:
1—8-oz. pkg. cream
   cheese
1/2 c. powdered sugar
1/2 t. vanilla
reserved 1 c. strawberries

Reserve 1 c. sliced strawberries for filling. Sprinkle 1/2 c. sugar over remaining berries; stir occasionally until juicy. Refrigerate.

For crepes, mix flour, sugar, nutmeg and lemon peel. Blend eggs, melted butter and milk thoroughly. Add liquid all at once to flour mixture, beating until smooth. Melt small amount of butter in 6-inch skillet to coat pan. Pour 2 T. batter into pan and rotate quickly so batter covers bottom thinly. Cook over medium heat 1-2 minutes on each side until firm and very lightly browned.

For Filling: Beat cream cheese, sugar and vanilla with mixer until soft and creamy; blend in strawberries by hand.

To serve, spread 1 T. filling on each crepe; roll up. Place 3 filled crepes on dessert plate and top with ladle of sliced strawberries and juice. Serve immediately.

## Strawberry Crepes

In summer, these may be served chilled                  Serves 16

16 crepes
2 c. sour cream
3 T. sugar
2 T. orange liqueur
   (Cointreau or Grand
   Marnier)
2 c. sweetened sliced
   strawberries
2 T. butter
powdered sugar

Combine sour cream, sugar and orange liqueur. Spread crepes with equal amount of sour cream mixture and a few sliced berries; roll up. Place in shallow pan and put in refrigerator until serving time. Reheat in a skillet by adding 2 T. of butter to pan and place it over direct high flame. Heat thoroughly. (Or, place pan in oven and heat at 350° for about 20 minutes.) Ladle strawberries over the crepes and sprinkle with powdered sugar.

## Chocolate Crepes

Wonderful with cherry pie filling,                    Makes 16 crepes
whipped cream and grated chocolate

2 eggs
1 c. buttermilk
3/4 c. flour
2 T. sugar
2 T. unsweetened cocoa
2 T. butter, melted

In a blender container, mix all ingredients until creamy. Let stand 1 hour at room temperature. Using 1/4 c. batter for each, cook crepes in buttered skillet, turning once to brown both sides lightly. Fill as desired.

## Strawberry Butter

Especially tasty on hot French toast

1-1/2 c. fresh
    strawberries
1 c. butter, softened
1/2 c. powdered sugar

Puree strawberries in blender or food processor. With motor running, add butter gradually, then add sugar, to taste. Chill. Remove from refrigerator to soften about 1 hour before serving. Serve over pancakes, muffins, bagels, or any breakfast bread. Note: A 10-oz. package of frozen berries, with most of juice drained off, may be substituted for fresh berries.

sunday, may 9, 1984 sunny, windy, mild

tom heflin

# Egg Dishes

## Any-Kind-Of-Quiche
Be creative with your own combinations                                    Serves 8

**Crust:**
3 oz. cream cheese
1/2 c. butter
1 c. flour

**Filling:**
3 T. chopped shallot or
   onion
3 T. butter
5 eggs, beaten
1-1/2 c. half and half
   cream
1 t. salt
1/8 t. fresh ground
   pepper
1/8 t. nutmeg
choice of the following:

**Filling #1:**
3/4 c. cooked broccoli
1 c. chopped ham
1 c. grated Swiss cheese

**Filling #2:**
10 oz. pkg. frozen
   spinach, thawed and
   squeezed dry
1 c. crumbled cooked
   Italian sausage
1 c. mixed grated cheese-
   mozzarella and
   cheddar

**Filling #3:**
1-1/2 c. zucchini, thinly
   sliced, sauteed
1 c. sliced onion, sauteed
1/2 c. diced tomatoes
1 c. Monterey Jack
   cheese, grated

**Filling #4:**
1—6-oz. can crabmeat,
   flaked
2 c. mushrooms, sliced
   and sauteed
1 c. Swiss cheese, grated

For Crust, mix all ingredients in food processor or mixer until dough just forms a soft ball. Press into 10-inch quiche dish or pie plate. Flute edges. Chill while preparing filling.

For Filling, saute shallot or onion in butter for 3 minutes. Add, from your choice of fillings, any vegetables which require sauteing; cook until barely tender. Add other ingredients from your choice of fillings; spread this mixture evenly over unbaked crust. Beat together eggs, cream, salt, pepper and nutmeg; pour into crust. Bake at 375° for 40-50 minutes until set. Let stand 5 minutes before serving.

## Asparagus Quiche Supreme

Very attractive for a buffet                                    Serves 8

1 unbaked 10-inch pie
  shell with fluted crust
1—10-oz. pkg. frozen
  asparagus spears
3/4 c. milk
3/4 c. half and half
  cream
1/2 c. finely chopped
  green onion
1 t. salt
1/4 t. nutmeg
1/8 t. white pepper
5 eggs, beaten
1 c. shredded Swiss
  cheese, divided
1/4 c. Parmesan cheese,
  divided
1 c. ground baked ham

Bake pie shell at 400° for 8-10 minutes. Cook asparagus according to package instructions until tender. Combine milk, cream, onion, salt, nutmeg and pepper in saucepan. Bring to boil; simmer 1 minute. Mix small amount of hot mixture into eggs; then stir eggs into mixture. Sprinkle 3/4 cup Swiss and 2 T. Parmesan into pie shell. Sprinkle ham over cheese. Arrange asparagus spears in spoke fashion, trimming ends as necessary and putting pieces underneath. Pour egg mixture over. Sprinkle with remaining cheeses. Bake at 375° for 30-35 minutes or until knife inserted comes out clean.

## Crab Quiche

May be wrapped in foil and reheated                             Serves 6

1—6-oz. pkg. frozen
  crabmeat
3 T. chopped green
  onion
3/4 c. dry white wine or
  dry sherry
1 T. brandy
5 eggs
2-1/2 c. whipping cream
1/2 t. salt
1/8 t. pepper
1/4 t. nutmeg
paprika
8 oz. Swiss Gruyere
  cheese, grated
1—9-inch pastry shell,
  partially baked
  (5 minutes)

Clean crabmeat and put in small saucepan with onion; cover with wine and bring to boil. Simmer 2 minutes; remove from heat; add brandy; let cool. Drain off liquid. Combine eggs, cream and seasonings; blend. Stir in crabmeat, sprinkle cheese into pie shell. Pour crab mixture over. Sprinkle with paprika. Bake at 350° for 45-50 minutes.

## French Onion Pie

Serve with buttered broccoli or asparagus                    Serves 6

1 unbaked 9-inch pie
  shell
1—3-1/2-oz. can french
  fried onions, divided
4 eggs
2 c. milk
1 c. shredded cheddar
  cheese
1/2 t. salt
1/4 t. pepper
1 c. shredded cheddar
  cheese

Bake pie shell at 450° for 7-8 minutes. Remove from oven; reduce oven heat to 325°. Fill bottom of pastry with 1-1/2 cup onions. Beat eggs; add milk, 1 cup shredded cheese, salt and pepper. Pour over onions; sprinkle remaining cheese on top; follow with remaining onions. Bake at 325° for 55 minutes. Let stand 10 minutes before serving.

## Superb Spinach Pie

The colors are nice for a Christmas brunch                 Serves 6-8

1—3-oz. pkg. cream
  cheese, softened
1 c. shredded sharp
  cheddar cheese
5 eggs, lightly beaten
1/2 t. salt
1/4 c. chopped green
  onion
2 T. chopped parsley
1 unbaked 9-inch pastry
  shell
1—10-oz. pkg. frozen
  chopped spinach,
  cooked and drained
  well
1 tomato, thinly sliced
1/4 c. grated Parmesan
  cheese

Combine cream cheese, cheddar cheese, eggs, salt, onion, and parsley; beat lightly with a fork. Stir in spinach and pour into pastry shell. Arrange tomato slices on top and sprinkle with Parmesan cheese. Bake at 450° for 40-45 minutes or until set.

## Spinach Quiche

Would serve 40 as an hors d' oeuvre                           Serves 12

pastry for double crust
  pie
10 slices bacon, diced
2 medium onions,
  chopped
4 eggs, slightly beaten
2 c. milk
2 t. seasoned salt
2—10-oz. pkgs. frozen
  chopped spinach,
  cooked and drained
  well
1/2 c. mozzarella cheese
1/2 c. Monterey Jack
  cheese
1/2 c. Swiss cheese
1/4 c. grated Parmesan
  cheese

Roll pastry to fit 15 x 10-inch pan. Allow enough overlap to form rim. Carefully fit into pan; trim edges with sharp knife or flute with fork. Cook bacon in skillet until crisp. Remove bacon; drain on paper towel. Reserve 2 to 3 T. drippings in skillet; add onion and cook until lightly browned and tender; drain and set aside. Beat eggs, milk, and salt in mixing bowl until well blended. Stir in bacon, onion and spinach. Spoon into prepared pan, evenly distributing ingredients. Mix mozzarella, Monterey Jack and Swiss cheeses; spread over top. Sprinkle with Parmesan cheese before baking. Bake at 350° for 25 minutes or until filling is set. Cut into squares and serve warm.

## Spanakopita

Greek spinach pie                                            Serves 6-8

pastry for double crust
  9-inch pie
3 eggs
1 large onion, chopped
3 T. butter
1 c. cottage cheese
8 oz. feta cheese,
  crumbled
1—10-oz. pkg. frozen
  chopped spinach,
  thawed and squeezed
  dry
1/2 t. salt
1/4 t. pepper

Roll out pastry and line a 9-inch pie pan. Separate 1 egg and brush egg white on pie shell. Pour excess white into a large bowl. Add the yolk and remaining two eggs and set aside. In a skillet, saute onion in butter until tender. Meanwhile, beat the eggs; stir in cheeses, spinach, salt, pepper and onion. Turn into pie shell. Roll out remaining pastry and fit over pie. Crimp the edge; bake at 425° for 30 minutes or until crust is golden. Cool on rack for 10 minutes. Serve hot.

## Serbian Cheese Pie

Best if baked and served the same day                    Serves 6

1 lb. farmer's cheese or
    dry pot cheese, beaten
    well
2 eggs, beaten
1/2 c. sour cream
1 t. salt
1/8 t. white pepper
1/3 c. grated Parmesan
    cheese
6 T. melted butter
1/2 lb. frozen phyllo
    pastry, thawed

Add farmer's cheese to beatened eggs; blend well. Add sour cream, salt, pepper and Parmesan cheese. Brush the bottom and sides of a 9 x 9-inch baking pan with a little of the melted butter. Open packages of pastry sheets, remove one sheet and keep remainder covered with a damp towel to prevent drying out. Fit pastry sheet loosely into bottom of baking pan. Using pastry brush, butter first pastry sheet. Place another sheet atop, butter it and continue until there are 8 buttered layers in pan. Spoon on 1/3 of the cheese mixture. Add 2 more buttered pastry sheets, brushing top leaf with remaining butter. Bake at 350° for 35-40 minutes or until pie is golden brown and puffed. Cool slightly; cut in small squares and serve.

## Yogurt Quiche

Filled with delectable morsels                    Serves 6-8

1 unbaked 10-inch pastry
    shell
5 eggs, beaten
2/3 c. grated Swiss
    cheese
2/3 c. grated cheddar
    cheese
1 c. plain yogurt
1/2 lb. mushrooms,
    sliced
3 chopped onion
2 c. chopped green
    pepper
4 T. butter
2 c. diced cooked ham
1-1/2 c. chopped
    broccoli, cooked
    barely tender

Mix eggs, cheeses and yogurt. Saute mushrooms, onion and green pepper in butter; add to egg mixture. Stir in ham and broccoli. Pour into unbaked pie shell. Bake at 400° for 30-35 minutes. Let stand 10 minutes before serving.

## Savory Cheesecake

Puts an ordinary quiche to shame                    Serves 12

5 T. butter, melted
1-1/3 c. fine dry
   breadcrumbs, toasted
3—8-oz. pkg cream
   cheese, softened
1/4 c. whipping cream
1/2 t. salt
1/4 t. grated nutmeg
1/8 t. cayenne pepper
4 eggs
1 c. shredded Gruyere
   cheese
1—10-oz. pkg. frozen
   chopped spinach,
   thawed and squeezed
   dry
3 T. minced green onion
1 c. finely chopped ham
8 oz. mushrooms,
   chopped
3 T. butter
salt and pepper

Mix 5 T. butter with bread crumbs. Press mixture firmly onto bottom and sides of buttered 9-inch springform pan. Bake at 350° for 8 minutes. Cool. Reduce oven heat to 325°.

In blender, beat cream cheese, cream, salt, nutmeg and cayenne until smooth. Blend in eggs. Divide mixture between 2 bowls. Stir cheese into mixture in one bowl; add spinach, onion and ham to second bowl.

In a skillet, saute mushrooms in 3 T. butter for 8-10 minutes. Season with salt and pepper.

To assemble cheesecake, pour spinach mixture into crust; spoon mushrooms over. Carefully pour cheese mixture over top. Place pan on baking sheet; bake 1 hour 15 minutes. Turn off oven; let cheesecake cool in oven 1 hour with door slightly open. When cool, remove springform. Serve at room temperature.

## Cheese Pudding

Great for brunch or as a side dish with meat         Serves 6-8

16 slices day-old white
   bread
1 lb. sharp cheddar
   cheese, grated
6 eggs
3 c. milk
1 t. salt
1 t. dry mustard
1/4 t. paprika
1/2 t. Worcestershire
   sauce
1/4 lb. butter, melted

Remove crusts from bread; cut bread into 1/2-inch cubes. Divide cheese and bread each into 3 portions. Layer a buttered 2-quart casserole dish with 1/3 of the bread; 1/3 of the cheese; repeat twice. Beat eggs with milk and add all seasonings. Slowly pour this mixture over bread and cheese; pour melted butter over entire top. Cover casserole with plastic wrap and refrigerate overnight. Remove from refrigerator 45 minutes before baking. Place casserole in a pan of shallow water and bake uncovered at 350° for 1 hour and 15 minutes. Pudding should puff like a souffle and brown on top. Serve immediately.

## Any-Kind-Of-Strata
A recipe to challenge your own inventiveness                    Serves 8-10

12 slices bread, cubed
1 lb. cheddar cheese,
    shredded (or half Swiss
    cheese)
4 c. milk
8 eggs, beaten
1 t. dry mustard
2 t. minced onion
cayenne pepper, salt and
    pepper
3 T. butter

In buttered 9 x 13-inch pan, spread bread, then cheese. Beat milk, eggs, dry mustard, onion and seasonings. Pour over cheese. Dot with butter, refrigerate overnight. Bake one hour at 350°.

Variations:

Chicken Strata:
Add to the basic strata:
2 c. diced cooked
    chicken
1/4 c. finely chopped
    pimiento
1/2 c. finely chopped
    celery
1—10-oz. can cream of
    chicken soup
1/2 c. mayonnaise
reduce recipe to 4 eggs
    and 3 c. milk

Spinach or Broccoli Strata:
Add to basic strata:
2—10-oz. pkg. frozen
    chopped spinach, or
1—10-oz. pkg. chopped
    broccoli, cooked
8 oz. mushrooms, sliced
    and sauteed

Sausage Strata:
Add to basic strata:
1-1/2 lb. sausage, cooked
    and crumbled
8 oz. mushrooms, sauteed
    with 1 T. butter and
1/2 c. chopped green
    pepper

Ham Sauce:

1/4 c. mushrooms, sliced
1 t. minced onion
1 T. butter
1 c. medium white sauce
1/2 t. Worcestershire
    sauce
1/2-1 c. diced ham

Saute mushrooms and onion in butter. Add white sauce, Worcestershire and ham; heat well. Serve over strata.

## Bunch O'Brunch
Men love the hearty flavor                                    Serves 6-8

3 slices white bread,
  cubed
6 eggs, beaten
3/4 c. milk
1/2 t. salt
1/4 t. pepper
1/2 c. diced cooked ham
1/2 c. diced smoked
  sausage
1/2 c. cooked, crumbled
  bacon
1/2 c. diced Swiss cheese
1/2 c. diced cheddar
  cheese
1/2 c. sliced fresh
  mushrooms

Stir bread into beaten eggs. Add milk, salt and pepper. Stir in remaining ingredients, blending well. Pour mixture into a buttered 1-1/2-quart baking dish. Bake at 325° for 40 minutes or until set. Serve immediately.


## Crowd-Pleaser
Can be made an hour before baking                             Serves 12

1/4 c. butter
1/4 c. bacon grease
1/2 c. flour
4 c. milk
1/2 lb. dried beef
1/4 t. pepper
16 eggs
1 c. evaporated milk
1/4 c. butter
bread crumbs
paprika

Grease 9 x 13-inch baking dish. In skillet, melt butter and bacon grease. Add flour slowly; stir in milk; cook over low heat until thickened. Chop dried beef; add to flour mixture; add pepper. Beat eggs; add evaporated milk. Cook egg mixture in butter until soft, resembling scrambled eggs. Layer beef and egg mixtures in greased dish. Top with bread crumbs and paprika. Bake at 325° for 10 minutes, until thoroughly heated.

## Now-Famous Frittata
Was a big hit at a Junior League fundraiser                 Serves 8

3/4 c. chopped green
  pepper
1-1/2 c. sliced
  mushrooms
1-1/2 c. chopped zucchini
3/4 c. chopped onion
1 c. cubed ham
1 clove garlic, minced
3 T. vegetable oil
6 eggs, beaten
1/4 c. half and half cream
1—8-oz. pkg. cream
  cheese, diced
1-1/2 c. shredded
  cheddar cheese
2 c. cubed bread
1 t. salt
1/4 t. pepper

Saute green pepper, mushrooms, zucchini, onion, ham and garlic in oil until zucchini is crisp and tender; cool slightly. Beat eggs with cream. Add cream cheese, cheddar cheese, bread, salt, pepper and sauteed vegetables. Mix well. Pour into a well-greased 10-inch springform pan. Bake at 350° for 1 hour or until center is set. Cool 10 minutes before cutting.

## Cheese and Bacon Frittata
Good with hot curried fruit and muffins                 Serves 4

6 eggs
1 c. milk
1 minced green onion
2 T. butter, melted
1/2 t. salt
1/8 t. pepper
1/2 c. shredded cheddar
  cheese
8 strips bacon, cooked
  and crumbed

Grease 10-inch round pan or 9 x 9-inch baking pan. In medium bowl, beat eggs, milk, green onion, butter, salt and pepper until well blended; pour mixture into baking pan. Sprinkle cheese and bacon evenly over the top. Bake at 350° for 20 minutes or until set and golden brown.

## Salmon Souffle with Cucumber Sauce
Cold sauce is also nice with chilled salmon mold                    Serves 6

Souffle:
1—15-1/2-oz. can salmon,
  drained
1/2 c. milk
1/2 c. dry bread crumbs
3 eggs, separated
2 t. lemon juice
salt
pepper
lime or lemon wedges,
  optional

Cucumber Sauce:
1 c. sour cream
1/2 c. unpared, grated
  cucumber, undrained
1 t. minced parsley
1 t. lemon juice
1 T. grated onion
1/8 t. pepper

Remove bones and skin from salmon and flake. In 2-quart saucepan, cook breadcrumbs in milk a few minutes; remove from heat. Beat egg yolks and add to breadcrumbs with lemon juice, salmon and seasonings. Beat egg whites until fluffy; fold into salmon mixture. Grease a 1-quart baking dish and pour in mixture. Place in pan, half filled with water and bake at 350° for 35 minutes or until firm. (Bake souffle immediately after preparation.) Serve immediately with cucumber sauce.

For cucumber sauce; mix all ingredients and chill. At serving time, heat through over low flame; do not boil. Makes 1-1/2 cups. Pour into warm gravy boat and serve with souffle.

## Spinach Mushroom Souffle
Bits of ham or crisp bacon may be added                    Serves 6-8

1/4 c. butter
1/4 c. flour
1 c. milk
1/4 t. salt
1/8 t. pepper
1/4 t. dry mustard
3/4 c. cheddar cheese
1 t. Worcestershire
  sauce
2 T. sherry
3 egg yolks
2 t. minced onions
1/4 t. minced garlic
1—10-oz. pkg. chopped
  spinach, thawed and
  drained
1/2 c. canned sliced
  mushrooms, drained
3 egg whites
1/4 t. cream of tartar

Melt butter, add flour and stir until bubbly; remove from heat and stir in milk and seasonings. Cook over low heat until thick. Blend in cheddar cheese and Worcestershire sauce and sherry. Boil gently for 1 minute. Add egg yolks and stir well. Stir in onions, garlic, spinach and mushrooms. Beat egg whites with cream of tartar until stiff. Fold into spinach mixture. Pour into ungreased 2-quart casserole or souffle dish. Bake at 350° for 60 minutes or until puffed and golden and knife inserted into center is clean. Serve immediately.

## "Bauernfruhstuck"
German Farmers' Breakfast                                    Serves 6

1/4 c. butter
1-1/2 c. cubed uncooked
  potatoes (or frozen
  hash browns,
  defrosted)
1/4 c. finely chopped
  onion
1 c. cubed ham
1/4 c. chopped parsley
6 eggs
3/4 t. salt
1/8 t. pepper
2 T. half and half
  cream
1/2 c. shredded Monterey
  Jack cheese

Melt butter in 10-inch frying pan. Add potatoes and onion; cover and cook over medium-high heat, stirring occasionally to brown evenly, for about 20 minutes or until potatoes are tender and golden. Add ham and cook a few minutes longer until lightly browned. Sprinkle mixture with parsley. Reduce heat. Beat together eggs, salt, pepper, and cream until well blended. Pour egg mixture over potatoes and ham. Cover and cook until eggs are almost set, slipping spatula around edge of pan occasionally to allow egg mixture to run down, about 10 minutes. Sprinkle with cheese and cover until cheese melts. Cut in wedges to serve.

## Chicken Livers and Eggs
Serve with baked tomato halves, melon slices          Serves 6
and corn bread

4 oz. chicken livers
6 T. bread crumbs
6 slices Swiss cheese
3 T. butter
2 T. chopped onion
1 c. sliced fresh
  mushrooms
1/4 t. salt
1/8 t. pepper
1/2 t. thyme
6 eggs
3/4 c. whipping cream
2 T. grated Parmesan
  cheese

Wash and dry chicken livers; cut into small pieces. Butter 6 custard cups or ramekins. Sprinkle 1 T. bread crumbs in bottom of each. Cover with slices of Swiss cheese. In small skillet over medium heat, melt butter; saute chicken livers with onion, mushrooms, salt, pepper and thyme for 5 minutes, stirring occasionally. Divide mixture among custard cups, pushing up around sides and making an indentation in the center. Break an egg into each dish. Over each egg, spoon 2 T. cream; sprinkle with 1 t. grated Parmesan. Bake uncovered at 350° for 10-12 minutes, until eggs are set. Serve at once.

## Chiles Rellenos
Fast and easy in the microwave

Serves 4

5 eggs, beaten
2 c. shredded Monterey
   Jack cheese
1 c. cottage cheese, well
   drained
1/4 c. flour
2 T. diced green chiles
1 T. butter
1/2 t. baking powder

Combine all ingredients in mixing bowl and beat until well blended. Pour into 10-inch quiche dish. Cook uncovered in microwave on 70% power about 12 minutes, turning dish several times, until eggs are set. Or, cook in buttered skillet on top of stove, stirring occasionally, until set.

## Eggs-act-ly Perfect
Everyone can get into this act

Serves 4

8 bacon slices
1/4 c. minced onion
2 T. chopped green
   pepper
1/2 c. freshly cooked rice
1/2 c. cottage cheese
1 T. freshly grated
   Romano cheese
4 eggs, beaten
1/4 c. milk
1 T. chopped parsley
1/8 t. dillweed
1/8 t. pepper
1/4 t. salt
1/2 c. sour cream, at
   room temperature
1 T. Romano cheese

Chop 2 bacon slices into small pieces; fry pieces in large skillet over medium heat about 5 minutes. Add onion and green pepper; continue cooking until vegetables are tender, about 5-6 minutes. Drain all but 1 T. drippings from skillet. Add rice, cottage cheese, and 1 T. grated Romano cheese to skillet. Combine eggs, milk and seasonings in a medium bowl. Pour egg mixture into skillet and cook until just set, about 5-8 minutes. Meanwhile fry remaining bacon in another skillet over medium heat until golden but not crisp. Reduce heat to low. As each slice is removed from skillet, roll around prongs of fork to form curls. Fold sour cream into egg mixture and cook until warmed through. Transfer eggs to heated plate. Garnish with bacon curls and sprinkle with 1 T. Romano cheese. Serve hot. Note: Easy to make if one "chef" handles the bacon, one chops, and one cooks the eggs.

## Gold Rush Brunch
Makes a perfect one-dish supper, too                    Serves 8

1—10-oz. pkg. dry hash
  brown potatoes with
  onions
4 T. butter
1/4 c. flour
1/2 t. salt
1/8 t. pepper
2 c. milk
1 c. sour cream
2 T. parsley
8 slices Canadian bacon
8 eggs
salt and pepper

Prepare potatoes according to package directions and set aside. Melt butter in 3-quart saucepan. Blend in flour, salt and pepper. Add milk all at once; cook; stirring until thick and bubbly. Remove from heat. Add sour cream, parsley and hash browns. Put in 13 x 9-inch casserole; arrange bacon on top. Bake uncovered at 300° for 20 minutes. Place eggs in depressed areas made with a spoon; salt and pepper to taste. Bake for 15-25 minutes more until eggs are set.

## Good Morning Company
How to make overnight guests feel special                    Serves 6 to 8

12 slices Canadian bacon
12 slices Swiss cheese
12 eggs
1/2 c. half and half
  cream
1/4 c. Parmesan cheese

Line 9 x 13-inch glass baking dish with a layer of bacon, then a layer of Swiss cheese. Break eggs over all; drizzle cream over whites so yolks peek out. Bake at 450° for 10 minutes. Take out, sprinkle with Parmesan cheese; return to oven for 10 minutes, or until eggs are set. Cut in squares to serve.

## "Everyone Wants This Recipe" Casserole
Bake a coffecake along with this for a complete breakfast                    Serves 8

4 slices bacon
4 green onions, sliced
1 lb. mushrooms, sliced
1/2 t. salt
1/8 t. pepper
1/4 t. seasoned salt
2-1/2 c. shredded
  Monterey Jack cheese
8 eggs, well-beaten
1 c. milk

Cook bacon crisp; drain and crumble. Reserve bacon drippings and saute onions, then mushrooms. In large mixing bowl, combine bacon, onions, mushrooms, seasonings, cheese, eggs and milk. Pour into greased 2-quart casserole. Bake, uncovered, at 350° for 45-50 minutes.

## Scrambled Eggs and Mushrooms
Excellent for a buffet—the eggs stay creamy                    Serves 12

24 eggs
1 c. half and half
  cream
2 t. salt
1/4 t. pepper
4 T. butter
1 c. medium white sauce
parsley
1—8-oz. can sliced
  mushrooms, drained

Beat eggs with cream, salt, and pepper. Melt butter in a large frying pan or chafing dish and pour in egg mixture. Cook slowly, stirring occasionally, until almost set. Fold white sauce into eggs while they are still creamy. Keep mixture hot. Sprinkle with parsley and garnish top with mushrooms.

## Egg Croquettes with Mushroom Sauce
Must be refrigerated overnight before frying                    Serves 6

3 T. butter
3 T. flour
3/4 c. milk
1/2 t. salt
1/4 t. paprika
4 hard-cooked eggs,
  chopped
1 T. minced green onion
1 T. minced parsley
1/4 t. Worcestershire
  sauce
2 drops hot pepper sauce
1 c. cracker crumbs
1 egg, slightly beaten
oil for deep frying

Mushroom sauce:
2 T. butter
8 oz. mushrooms, sliced
2 T. flour
1 c. chicken broth
1/2 t. lemon juice
salt and pepper to taste
1/2 t. Worcestershire
  sauce

Melt butter in saucepan; stir in flour until blended. Blend in milk, salt and paprika. Stir continually over low heat until mixture is very thick, about 10 minutes. Remove from heat and add hard cooked eggs, onion, parsley and seasonings. Chill; when cold, shape into croquettes. Roll in cracker crumbs; dip in beaten egg and again in the crumbs. Refrigerate overnight. Deep fry in oil at 375° until golden brown, 2 to 5 minutes. Serve with mushroom sauce.

For mushroom sauce; melt butter in saucepan. Add mushrooms; cook about 5 minutes. Blend in flour and add chicken broth gradually. Cook until thickened, stirring constantly. Add seasonings and serve hot.

## Eggs Divan

May be baked in individual gratin dishes                    Serves 4-6

1 lb. broccoli spears
6 eggs, hard-cooked
1 c. minced ham
1/4 t. Worcestershire
    sauce
1/2 t. grated onion
1/2 t. salt
1/2 t. dry mustard
1 T. milk

Sauce:
2 T. flour
1-1/2 T. melted butter
1/2 t. dry mustard
1/2 t. salt
1 c. milk
1 c. grated sharp cheese
buttered bread crumbs

Cook broccoli until barely tender. Slice eggs lengthwise and remove yolks. Mash yolks and add ham, Worcestershire sauce, onion, salt, mustard, and milk. Mix well and fill egg whites. Place broccoli in a buttered 8 x 8-inch dish. Place eggs on top.

For sauce, blend flour, butter and seasonings in saucepan; add milk and cheese. Heat until thick and smooth, stirring constantly. Pour over eggs and top with bread crumbs. Bake at 350° for 25 minutes.

## Curried Eggs with Mushrooms

A new trick with Easter eggs                    Serves 4

1/2 lb. fresh mushrooms
4 T. butter
2 T. flour
1-1/2 c. milk
1 t. curry powder
1 T. ketchup
salt to taste
1/2 c. grated sharp
    cheese, divided
5 hard-cooked eggs,
    quartered
4 English muffins,
    toasted

Saute mushrooms in butter in covered skillet. Add flour and milk; cook and stir until thickened. Add curry, ketchup, salt and half of cheese. Stir until melted. Add quartered eggs. Pour into buttered casserole dish. Cover with remaining cheese. Bake at 350° for 30 minutes. Serve over English muffins.

## Deviled Eggs in Mushroom Sauce

Serve with or without a meat dish                                    Serves 6-8

**9 eggs**
**3 T. mayonnaise**
**2 t. grated onion**
**2 t. cider vinegar**
**2 t. Worcestershire sauce**
**3/4 t. mustard**
**3/4 t. paprika**
**1/4 t. salt**
**1/4 t. pepper**

**Sauce:**
**4 sliced green onions**
**8 oz. fresh mushrooms,**
  **sliced**
**1/4 c. margarine**
**1/4 c. flour**
**1 t. salt**
**1/4 t. pepper**
**2 c. milk**

Place eggs in deep saucepan; add enough cold water to cover. Bring water to boil. Reduce heat and cover; let simmer for 20 minutes; cool quickly with cold water; shell. Cut in half lengthwise. Force yolks through fine sieve. Mix yolks with mayonnaise, onion, vinegar and seasoning; blend well. Refill egg whites with yolk mixture.

For sauce, saute onion and mushrooms in margarine in a large skillet. Blend flour, salt and pepper; gradually add to onion and mushrooms. Add milk slowly; cook, stirring constantly until thickened. Spoon half of sauce into shallow 2-quart baking dish; place eggs in sauce. Spoon remaining sauce between eggs. Bake at 350° for 20 minutes, or until hot and bubbly. Serve over cooked rice.

## Egg Lasagna

Make ahead to delight weekend guests                              Serves 8

**1 lb. bacon, in 1-inch**
  **pieces**
**3/4 c. finely chopped**
  **onion**
**1/3 c. flour**
**1/2 t. salt**
**1/4 t. pepper**
**4 c. milk**
**12 lasagna noodles,**
  **cooked and drained**
**3—6-oz cans crabmeat,**
  **flaked**
**12 eggs, hard-boiled,**
  **sliced**
**8 oz. cheddar cheese**

Fry bacon until crisp; remove bacon from pan, reserving 1/3 cup drippings. Add onions to drippings and saute. Add flour, salt and pepper; stir over medium heat until smooth. Add milk; cook and stir until thickened. Grease a 13 x 9-inch pan. Layer in pan in order: 1/4 of sauce, noodles, bacon, crabmeat, remaining sauce, eggs and cheese. Bake at 350° for 30 minutes. Let stand 10 minutes before serving.

## Scalloped Bacon and Eggs
Best if assembled just before baking                    Serves 4

1/4 c. onion, chopped
2 T. butter
2 T. flour
1-1/2 c. milk
1 c. American cheese,
   shredded
6 eggs, hard-cooked,
   sliced
1-1/2 c. potato chips,
   crushed
10 slices bacon, fried
   crisp, crumbled

Saute onion in butter until tender. Blend in flour; add milk gradually. Cook, stirring constantly until thickened. Add cheese and stir until melted. Place half of egg slices in 10 x 6-inch baking dish. Cover with half of cheese sauce, half of potato chips and half of bacon; repeat layers. Bake at 350° for 15-20 minutes. Serve immediately.

## Eggs Oliver
Ripe olive-lovers rave about these                    Serves 6

4 T. butter
4 T. flour
2-1/4 c. half and half
   cream
1-1/3 t. yellow mustard
1/3 t. dillweed
1/2 t. salt
1/8 t. white pepper
6 eggs, hard-cooked and
   chopped
1 c. sliced ripe olives
1-1/2 c. ham strips
1 c. sliced mushrooms
1 T. butter
6 English muffins, split
   and toasted
12 tomato slices, broiled

Melt butter in saucepan; stir in flour and cook, stirring, 1 minute. Stir in cream; cook and stir over medium heat until thick; stir in mustard, dillweed, salt and pepper. Remove from heat; stir in eggs and olives. Saute ham and mushrooms in butter; add to sauce.

To serve, place one tomato slice atop each muffin half. Spoon some of sauce over.

## Stuffed Eggs Mornay
Sauce is also good on scrambled or poached eggs                    Serves 6-8

6 eggs, hard-cooked
1/2 c. finely chopped
  cooked mushrooms
5 green onions, chopped
2 T. butter, softened
1/2 t. tarragon
1/4 t. salt
3 T. Parmesan cheese
2 c. Sauce Mornay (or
  Microwave Sauce Mornay)

Sauce Mornay:
2 T. butter
2 T. flour
1 c. milk
1/4 c. whipping cream
salt, pepper and nutmeg
1 c. grated cheddar,
  Gruyere, or Swiss cheese

Microwave Sauce Mornay:
4 T. butter
4 T. flour
1/2 t. salt
2 c. milk
1 c. shredded Swiss,
  Gruyere, or Parmesan
  cheese
2 t. lemon juice
cayenne pepper

Halve eggs lengthwise. Press yolks through strainer, mix with mushrooms, onions, butter, salt and tarragon. Fill egg whites with mixture. Spread 1 cup sauce in flat baking dish. Lay eggs on top of sauce and spoon remaining sauce over. Sprinkle with cheese. Heat in 350° oven until sauce bubbles. Serve at once. Garnish with paprika or parsley if desire.

Sauce Mornay: Melt butter in saucepan over medium heat; add flour. Stir with wire whisk until blended. Add milk and cream, stirring rapidly with whisk. Bring to boil; cook until thickened and smooth. Add salt, pepper, and nutmeg. Remove from heat and stir in cheese.

In 1-quart glass measuring cup place butter, flour and salt. Microwave on high for 3-1/2 minutes, stirring twice. Gradually stir in milk. Microwave on high 2 to 5 minutes, stirring every minute until thick and bubbly. Add cheese, lemon juice and pepper to taste; stir until smooth.

## Deviled Muffin Puffs
Reminiscent of Eggs Benedict                                       Serves 4

4 English muffins
1—4-1/2-oz. can deviled
  ham
3/4 c. shredded
  American cheese
2 eggs, separated
1 t. prepared mustard
1/4 t. salt
1/8 t. pepper
2 drops hot pepper sauce
1/8 t. cream of tartar

Split and toast 4 English muffins. Spread with deviled ham. Sprinkle with cheese; place on baking sheet. Beat together egg yolks, mustard, salt, pepper, and hot pepper sauce until thick and lemon colored. Beat egg whites and cream of tartar until stiff peaks form; fold into yolk mixture. Spoon atop muffin halves. Bake at 350° for 12-15 minutes or until egg mixture is set.

## Eggs Pacific

Serve on toast points for an elegant supper                    Serves 6

12 hard-cooked eggs,
  peeled
1 lb. shrimp, cooked and
  peeled
3 T. butter
3 T. flour
1-2/3 c. half and half
  cream
2 t. prepared mustard
1 t. salt
1/8 t. white pepper
1 T. dry white wine
1 T. capers, drained
2 T. chopped parsley
1/4 t. thyme
1/2 c. shredded Swiss
  cheese

Slice eggs. Arrange half on bottom of buttered 13 x 9-inch baking dish. Arrange shrimp over eggs, and top with remaining eggs.

In a saucepan, melt butter and stir in flour. Cook 1 minute stirring constantly. Gradually stir in cream and cook until sauce thickens. Add mustard, salt, pepper, wine, capers, parsley and thyme. Pour sauce over eggs. Sprinkle with cheese.

Bake at 425° for 15 minutes, until sauce is bubbly. May be made ahead and refrigerated until baking time.

## Bagels a la Reine

Lettuce cups filled with fruit complete this menu           Serves 2

1 T. butter
1 T. flour
1/4 t. salt
1/4 t. pepper
1 c. milk
1/4 t. dry mustard
1/2 c. cheddar cheese
4 oz. mushrooms, sliced
2 T. butter
2 plain bagels, split and
  toasted
4 eggs, poached
2 oz. grated cheddar
  cheese

Melt butter over low heat; blend in flour, salt and pepper, stirring until mixture is smooth and bubbly. Add milk and bring to boil, stirring constantly. Add mustard and 1/2 cup cheese; blend until cheese is melted. Saute mushrooms in butter. Cover bagels with sauteed mushrooms, then with poached eggs. Pour sauce over top of eggs; sprinkle with grated cheddar cheese. Serve immediately.

## Swiss Eggs

If desired, line casserole first with ham slices                    Serves 4

1/4 lb. Gruyere cheese,
   thinly sliced
4 eggs
1/2 c. whipping cream
1 t. salt
1/2 t. pepper
grated cheese
toast or English muffins

Butter a shallow casserole; line with cheese slices. Break eggs neatly into the casserole, keeping them whole. Mix cream, salt and pepper; pour over eggs. Bake at 350° for 10 minutes. Sprinkle with grated cheese; brown the cheese topping under broiler for a few minutes. Serve over toast points or English muffins.

## Poached Eggs a la Bayard

Easy way to please one or a crowd                    Serves 1

1 tomato slice
1 egg
1-1/2 slices of bacon,
   cooked and crumbled
1/8 c. canned tomato
   sauce, heated
Parmesan cheese, grated

Grill tomato slice. Poach egg. Place poached egg on grilled tomato slice; sprinkle with bacon; drizzle sauce over, and sprinkle with Parmesan cheese.

## Eggs Sardou Florentine

One cup crabmeat may be sprinkled on eggs                    Serves 8

2—10-oz. pkg. frozen
   chopped spinach,
   cooked and well
   drained
8 artichoke bottoms
anchovy paste
8 eggs, poached
salt and pepper to taste
grated Parmesan cheese
2 c. Hollandaise sauce
paprika

Place spinach in buttered 1-1/2 quart casserole. Spread anchovy paste on artichokes and place on spinach. Poach eggs lightly and place on artichoke bottoms. Salt and pepper; sprinkle with Parmesan. Cover with Hollandaise; sprinkle with paprika. Bake at 350° for 20 minutes.

## Eggs St. Charles

Garnish with lemon curls, parsley and tomato wedges          Serves 6

**Hollandaise Sauce:**
**1/2 c. butter, cut into**
**    thirds**
**4 egg yolks**
**2 t. lemon juice**
**white pepper and salt**

**1/4 c. butter**
**12 trout fillets (6 trout)**
**12 eggs**

For Hollandaise Sauce, place egg yolks and one piece of butter into top of a double boiler. Over hot but not boiling water, stir rapidly and constantly. As mixture thickens and butter melts, add the second piece of butter, then the third. Do not allow the water to boil. When thickened, remove from heat; stir 2 minutes, add juice and seasoning to taste. Replace over hot water for 1-2 minutes, stirring constantly. Remove from heat. Should mixture curdle, immediately beat in 1-2 T. boiling water, beating constantly in order to rebind. Meanwhile, saute trout fillets in butter 10 minutes or until fish flakes easily. Set aside and keep warm. Poach the eggs in simmering water; when eggs are nearly done, place 2 trout fillets on each plate. Top each fillet with a poached egg; top with Hollandaise sauce. Serve additional sauce on the side.

## Maryland Eggs Benedict

You may never go back to the classic recipe          Serves 2

**2 English muffins**
**butter**
**1—6-oz. can crabmeat,**
**    flaked**
**2 T. butter**
**1/2 t. salt**
**4 eggs**
**1 c. Hollandaise sauce**

Split muffins and butter cut sides. Arrange on cookie sheet; broil until golden brown; keep warm. Saute crabmeat lightly in 2 T. butter. In medium skillet with cover, bring 1 inch of water to simmering. Add salt. Break one egg at a time into custard cup. Slip egg into water and simmer, covered, for 3 to 5 minutes. Spread crabmeat on muffins. With slotted utensil, place one egg on top of each muffin. Spoon on hollandaise sauce; broil until sauce is golden.

## Easy Eggs Benedict
Foolproof sauce is also nice on asparagus                    Serves 6

1—10-oz can cream of
   mushroom soup
3 egg yolks
2 T. lemon juice
3 drops hot pepper sauce
1/2 c. butter, melted
12 slices Canadian bacon
   or ham, heated
6 English muffins, split
   and toasted
12 eggs, poached

In blender, combine soup, egg yolks, lemon juice and hot pepper sauce. Cover; blend on high speed a few seconds. With blender still on high speed, remove cover. Very slowly pour butter in a steady stream into soup mixture. Blend 3 minutes more or until thick. Pour into sauce pan; heat; stir occasionally. Arrange bacon or ham on muffins; top with eggs. Pour sauce over all.

## Champignons Lyonnaise
Spear garlic clove on a toothpick for easy removal          Serves 3-6

1-1/2 lb. mushrooms,
   quartered
1/3 c. butter
3 whole cloves
1 clove garlic
1 bay leaf
1-1/2 c. tomato sauce
1/2 c. beef stock
salt and pepper to taste
1 T. butter
1 T. minced parsley
1 T. minced chives
1 T. minced onion
6 slices hot buttered
   toast
6 eggs, poached

Saute mushrooms for 5 minutes in 1/3 cup butter with cloves, garlic and bay leaf. Add tomato sauce, beef stock and salt and pepper to taste. Heat; turn into a 1-quart casserole dish. Cover and bake at 350° for 25 minutes. Remove cloves, garlic and bay leaf. Cream together 1 T. butter, parsley, chives and onion. Add gradually to casserole. Serve sauce on hot buttered toast, topping each serving with a poached egg.

# Artichoke Omelet

Serves 2

2 T. butter
1—7-oz. can artichoke
  hearts, drained and
  coarsely chopped
1—3-oz. can chopped
  mushrooms, drained
1/8 t. pepper
4 egg whites
2 T. water
1/4 t. salt
4 egg yolks
1 T. butter

Blender Hollandaise
  Sauce:
3 egg yolks
4 t. lemon juice
cayenne pepper
1/2 c. butter

In small saucepan, melt 2 T. butter. Add artichokes, mushrooms and pepper. Cook and stir until hot. Remove from heat and keep warm. Beat egg whites until frothy; add water and salt. Beat until stiff, but not dry. Beat yolks until very thick and lemon-colored. Fold yolks into whites. Heat 1 T. butter in a 10-inch oven-going skillet until a drop of water sizzles. Pour in egg mixture and spread with spatula, leaving higher at sides. Reduce heat; cook slowly 8-10 minutes until puffed and set; then bake at 325° for 10 minutes or until knife inserted in center comes out clean. Loosen sides of omelet with spatula. Place artichoke mixture on half of the omelet. Fold over and turn out onto warm platter. Serve with Blender Hollandaise Sauce.

For sauce, place egg yolks, lemon juice, and a dash of cayenne in blender container. Cover and quickly turn blender on and off. Heat 1/2 cup butter until melted and almost boiling. Turn blender on high speed; slowly pour in butter, blending until thick and fluffy. Serve immediately.

# Omelette Aux Fines Herbes
Wonderful with garden-fresh tomatoes

Serves 2

4 eggs
1/4 t. salt
1 T. cold water
2 T. minced fresh parsley
1 t. minced fresh
  tarragon leaves
1 t. minced fresh
  marjoram leaves
1/2 t. minced fresh
  thyme leaves
1 t. minced shallots
1 T. butter

Combine eggs, salt, and water in small bowl. Beat just until combined. Combine herbs and shallots; stir into eggs, mixing well. Slowly heat medium-size skillet. Add butter, heating until it sizzles briskly. Quickly turn egg mixture into skillet. Cook over medium heat. As omelet sets, loosen edge with spatula and tilt skillet. When omelet is dry on top and golden brown on bottom, fold it over. Tilt it onto plate and serve.

## Tasty Omelet
Marvelous over a campfire · Serves 3 to 4

**4 slices chopped bacon**
**2 c. shredded cooked**
 **potatoes**
**1/4 c. chopped onion**
**1/4 c. green pepper**
**4 eggs**
**1/4 c. milk**
**1/2 t. salt**
**1/4 t. pepper**
**1 c. shredded sharp**
 **cheddar cheese**

Cook bacon until crisp; remove and crumble. Leave drippings in skillet; add potatoes, onions and green peppers. Cook over low heat until underside is crisp and brown. Blend eggs, milk, salt and pepper; pour over potatoes. Top with cheese and bacon. Cover and cook over low heat about 10 minutes. Loosen omelet; invert on platter. Cut into wedges to serve.

## Omelette Mere Poulard
A good basic to which anything may be added · Serves 4

**8 eggs**
**2 T. whipping cream**
**salt and pepper**
**6 T. butter**

Separate eggs, placing whites in large bowl and yolks in medium bowl. With electric beater at high speed, beat egg whites until stiff peaks form. With same beater, beat egg yolks well; beat in cream, salt and pepper. Slowly heat 11-inch skillet. Add butter; heat until sizzling. Pour in egg yolk mixture. When it begins to set (5 to 10 minutes) fold in beaten egg whites. Cook over medium heat until omelet is puffy and almost set, 3 to 5 minutes. With spatula, quickly loosen omelet from skillet. Tilt skillet and fold omelet in half. Slip omelet onto plate and serve.

## Zucchini Omelet Casserole
Try this with fresh tomato sauce · Serves 6

**1 clove garlic, finely**
 **chopped**
**2 lb. small zucchini,**
 **sliced**
**1/4 c. butter**
**1/2 t. basil**
**2 t. salt**
**1/4 t. pepper**
**1/4 c. grated Parmesan**
 **cheese**
**4 eggs**

In a large frying pan, saute garlic and zucchini in butter 7 to 8 minutes. Add seasonings; continue to cook until zucchini is tender. About 30 minutes before serving, beat eggs and add zucchini mixture. Pour into a well-buttered 9-inch pie plate or casserole dish; and bake at 400° for 25 to 30 minutes or until center of casserole is set.

## Fresh Apple Omelet

Serve with ham slices and whole wheat muffins                    Serves 1-2

3 T. flour
1/4 t. baking powder
1/8 t. salt
2 egg whites
3 T. sugar
3 T. milk
2 egg yolks, well beaten
1 T. lemon juice
1 large red cooking
   apple, thinly sliced
1/4 c. sugar
1/4 t. cinnamon

Sift flour with baking powder and salt. In medium bowl with rotary beater, beat egg whites until foamy. Gradually beat in 3 T. sugar, beating until stiff peaks form. Into flour mixture in small bowl, beat milk and egg yolks until smooth. With rubber scraper, gently fold yolks into egg whites; add lemon juice. Slowly heat buttered 10-inch skillet. Pour batter into skillet, spreading evenly. Arrange apple slices in pattern over top. Sprinkle with 1/4 cup sugar mixed with cinnamon. Bake at 375° for 10 minutes, or until top is glazed. Serve warm.

## Sweet Peach Omelet

If canned peaches are used, omit sugar in filling                    Serves 2

4 eggs, separated
1/4 c. superfine
   granulated sugar
1/8 t. salt
1 t. water
2 T. clarified butter

Filling:
2-1/4 c. peaches, peeled
   and sliced
2 T. butter
1 t. brown sugar
1/4 t. ground cardamom

Preheat broiler to medium. Beat egg yolks with sugar. In separate bowl, add salt and cold water to whites and whip until stiff. Fold yolks into whites. Melt clarified butter and add to egg mixture. Pour into buttered 8-inch skillet and bang pan down on stove to settle. Cook over medium heat until set, then broil until puffed and golden. Meanwhile, toss sliced peaches in butter over moderate heat. Dust with brown sugar and cardamom to glaze. Place peaches in center of omelet. Fold out onto hot plate. Dust with superfine granulated sugar.

## SOUVENIRS

the basket was a gift from one of my art students.
the peacock feather from a dear friend who hung my
first one man show.
the money plant from an architect friend.
the milk weed pods came from one of my walks in the fields.
these souvenirs have sat on a table next to my easel
untouched for seven years.

wednesday february 1, 1984 sunny mild                    tom heflin

# Main Dishes

## Chicken-Bake Elegante
Serve sliced over toast points for brunch                    Serves 6-8

**6 whole chicken breasts,
  split, boned and skinned**
**1 T. paprika**
**1 T. garlic salt**
**1/4 c. melted butter,
  divided**
**1 T. lemon juice**
**8 oz. fresh mushrooms,
  sliced**
**2 T. flour**
**1 t. Worcestershire sauce**
**1/2 c. sliced, pitted black
  olives**
**3/4 c. sour cream**
**1/3 c. cream sherry**

Sprinkle chicken with paprika and garlic salt. Mix 1/8 cup melted butter with lemon juice; use to brush chicken. Place breasts in greased casserole dish; bake for 40 minutes at 325°. Meanwhile, in a frying pan, saute mushrooms in remaining butter for 5 minutes. Gradually blend in flour, Worcestershire sauce, olives and sour cream. Cook for 5 minutes, stirring constantly. Stir in sherry. Spread mixture over breasts evenly; return to oven and bake for 10 minutes longer.

## Chicken Breasts in Sour Cream
Marinade gives chicken a unique flavor                       Serves 6

**6 chicken breasts, split
  and boned**
**2 c. sour cream**
**1/4 c. lemon juice**
**2 t. salt**
**4 t. Worcestershire sauce**
**3 t. garlic salt**
**1/2 t. paprika**
**1/2 t. pepper**
**1 c. bread crumbs**
**1/2 c. margarine,
  melted**
**1/2 c. butter
  melted**

Wash chicken breasts and pat dry. In bowl, combine sour cream, lemon juice, and seasonings. Roll chicken breasts in sour cream mixture, place in bowl and top with any remaining sour cream. Cover; refrigerate overnight.

Remove chicken breasts, taking up as much of sour cream mixture as possible. Roll chicken in bread crumbs to coat well. Place in baking dish. Mix margarine and butter; pour half the melted butter and margarine over chicken and bake at 350° for 45 minutes. Pour remaining butter sauce over chicken and bake 5 minutes more.

## Citrus Chicken
Striking in a chafing dish                                    Serves 6

1/2 c. flour
1-1/2 t. salt
1/4 t. pepper
1 T. paprika
6 large chicken breasts
4 T. vegetable oil
1—4-1/2-oz. jar whole
　mushrooms, drained
1—16-oz. jar small white
　onions, drained
1—16-oz. jar baby
　carrots, drained
1 T. brown sugar
1/4 t. ginger
1—6-oz. can frozen
　orange juice
　concentrate, undiluted

Combine flour, salt, pepper and paprika; reserve 2 T. Use remaining mixture to flour chicken pieces. Brown chicken in oil in heavy skillet. Remove chicken to 5-quart dutch oven; put mushrooms, onions, and carrots on top of chicken.

In heavy skillet, make a sauce using 2 T. of the oil that was used to brown chicken, 2 T. reserved flour mixture, brown sugar, ginger and orange juice. Pour over the vegetables; cover and place in upper part of oven. Bake at 350° for 1-1/2 hours, stirring and basting occasionally.

## Marie's Chicken Cacciatore
Other chicken pieces may be substituted                      Serves 6

6 chicken breasts, boned,
　skinned and split
flour
salt and pepper
1/4 c. bacon drippings
1/4 lb. ham, in thin strips
1/2 c. chopped onion
1—2-oz. jar pimiento
1 clove garlic, minced
1-1/4 c. tomatoes, chopped
1 c. mushrooms, sliced
1 t. salt
1 c. water

Roll chicken breasts in flour seasoned with salt and pepper. In large skillet, brown chicken in hot bacon drippings until well browned. Add ham, onion, pimiento, garlic, tomatoes, mushrooms, salt and water. Cover and cook over low heat until chicken is tender, about 1-1/2 hours. Serve over pasta.

## Chicken Chardonnay

From Chef John Dargo and *Bellamy's*, home of          Serves 2
distinquished dining.

2—6-oz. chicken breasts,
  boned and skinned
2 T. butter
2 T. shallots, chopped
1 c. fresh mushrooms,
  sliced
1/4 c. Chardonnay (or
  other dry white wine)
1 T. lemon juice
flour
1 T. vegetable oil
1/4 c. heavy cream
chopped parsley

Pound chicken flat; set aside. In butter, saute shallots; add mushrooms and saute 2-3 minutes. Add wine and lemon juice; let simmer 6-7 minutes. Dredge chicken in flour and season if desired. Saute in oil in frying pan. Add cream to mushroom mixture and heat until reduced. On warm serving plates, place mushrooms over chicken breasts. Sprinkle with chopped parsley and serve immediately.

## Apricot Chicken

Easy enough for children to make          Serves 8

8 chicken breasts
salt and pepper
1 c. Russian salad
  dressing
1—8-oz. jar apricot jam
1 pkg. onion soup mix

Place chicken breasts in a greased 9 x 13-inch baking dish; add salt and pepper to taste. Mix salad dressing, jam and dry soup mix together; spread half of mixture over chicken. Cover and bake 35 minutes at 350°. Remove cover and spread remaining apricot mixture over chicken. Return to oven and continue to bake, uncovered, until chicken is tender, about 30 minutes more.

## Chicken with Artichokes

The cooking aroma is fantastic!          Serves 2

2 chicken breasts, boned,
  skinned, halved
1/4 c. flour
1/8 t. salt
1/8 t. pepper
2 T. butter
1 T. olive oil
1 T. chopped shallots
1—8-oz. can artichoke
  hearts, drained
1 T. lemon juice
1/2 c. Madeira wine
1 c. chicken broth
1 T. butter

Lightly flour chicken breasts; season with salt and pepper. Brown chicken in butter and oil; add shallots. When browned, add artichokes, lemon juice, Madeira and chicken broth; simmer 15-20 minutes. Remove breasts and artichokes to heated platter; keep warm. Cook sauce until thickened and reduced. Stir in 1 T. butter, pour over chicken and artichokes; serve immediately.

## Chicken Favorite
Garnish with purple grapes                                    Serves 12

**8 oz. dried beef**
**12 slices bacon**
**6 whole chicken**
  **breasts, split**
**2 c. sour cream**
**1—10-oz. can cream of**
  **mushroom soup**
**1/2 c. slivered almonds**
**hot rice or biscuits**

Grease a 9 x 13-inch baking dish and line with dried beef. Partially cook bacon; wrap the bacon around each piece of chicken and arrange in the dish over the chipped beef. Mix the sour cream and mushroom soup together and pour over chicken. Refrigerate overnight if desired. Top with almonds. Bake at 275° for 3 hours. Serve over hot rice or biscuits.

## Bratwurst-Stuffed Chicken Breast
Serve outdoors with your favorite hot bread                    Serves 6

**6 chicken breasts, boned**
  **and skinned**
**6 bratwurst, skin**
  **removed**
**1 egg, slightly beaten**
**2 T. water**
**1/2 c. flour**
**1/2 t. salt**
**1/4 t. pepper**
**1/2 c. butter**

Flatten chicken breasts; place one bratwurst on top of each chicken breast. Roll each chicken breast to enclose bratwurst; tie with string. Mix egg with water. Mix flour, salt and pepper in shallow dish. Dip each chicken breast in egg; dredge in flour mixture. Brown in butter. Place in glass baking dish; pour drippings over chicken breasts. Cover; bake at 350° for one hour.

## Chicken Breasts Hawaiian
Herbed rice pairs well with these                             Serves 8

**1/2 c. butter**
**1/2 c. flour**
**2-1/2 c. chicken broth**
**2 c. half and half cream**
**1 t. salt**
**1—4-inch strip lemon**
  **peel**
**8 chicken breasts, boned,**
  **skinned and split**
**16 small bay leaves**
**16 slices pineapple**
**powdered ginger**
**1/4 c. brandy**
**1/2 c. Macadamia nuts**

In large skillet, melt butter. Blend in flour; gradually add chicken broth and half and half.. Cook, stirring constantly until thickened. Add salt and lemon peel. Arrange chicken breasts in sauce, one bay leaf on top of each breast. Cover and simmer until tender, about 45 minutes.

In separate saucepan, heat pineapple. When serving, put heated pineapple slices on heated platter. Sprinkle each slice lightly with ginger. Remove bay leaves and place one chicken breast half on each pineapple slice. To the sauce add brandy and Macadamia nuts. Heat sauce quickly and pour over chicken.

## Pollo Marsala

From the *Old Rock River Deli*, offering                          Serves 4
imaginative light meals

2 chicken breasts, boned,
  skinned and halved
3 T. flour
salt and pepper
3 T. butter, divided
1 clove garlic, finely
  chopped
1/4 lb. fresh mushrooms,
  sliced
2 T. fresh lemon juice
1/2 c. dry white wine

Pound chicken lightly; cut into strips; dredge in flour seasoned with salt and pepper as desired. Melt 2 T. butter in large skillet. Saute garlic about 3 minutes. Add chicken and saute 8-10 minutes. Remove chicken to warm platter. In same skillet, melt 1 T. butter and saute mushrooms 3-4 minutes. Add lemon juice and white wine; stir in the chicken. Simmer several minutes until sauce thickens. Serve over spinach noodles or on bed of seasoned rice.

## Crab-Stuffed Chicken Breasts

May be prepared the night before serving                    Serves 8

4 chicken breasts, boned,
  skinned, halved
1/4 c. butter
1/2 c. thinly sliced green
  onion
1/4 c. thinly sliced
  mushrooms
6 T. flour
1/2 t. thyme
1 c. chicken broth
1 c. milk
1 c. dry white wine
salt and pepper
8 oz. crabmeat
1/3 c. chopped parsley
1/3 c. dry bread crumbs
1 c. shredded Swiss
  cheese

Pound chicken between 2 sheets of plastic wrap until 1/4-inch thick. Set aside. Melt butter in large skillet; saute onions and mushrooms; add flour and thyme. Blend in broth, milk and wine; cook and stir until thickened; add salt and pepper to taste. Remove 1/4 cup sauce. Make stuffing of 1/4 cup sauce, crabmeat, parsley, and dry bread crumbs. Spoon crab mixture evenly on 8 chicken breasts. Roll meat around filling and place seam side down in greased 8 x 12-inch baking dish. Pour remaining sauce over chicken breasts. Sprinkle with cheese. Cover and bake at 400° for 35 minutes; uncover and bake 10 minutes more.

## Chicken, Mushroom and Almond Casserole

Easily doubled                                                    Serves 3

1 T. butter
1-1/2 T. grated onion
2 oz. sliced fresh
  mushrooms
2 T. butter
2 T. flour
1 c. milk
1 c. chicken broth
1/2 t. salt
dash cayenne pepper
1-1/2 c. diced cooked
  chicken
1/3 c. slivered almonds,
  toasted
1/4 c. sliced stuffed
  olives
1/3 c. shredded sharp
  cheddar cheese
1 c. buttered bread
  crumbs

Melt 1 T. butter in small frying pan. Add onions and mushrooms; cook until tender; do not brown. Set aside. Melt the 2 T. butter in another pan. Stir in flour; gradually add milk and chicken broth. Cook and stir until sauce boils and thickens. Add seasonings. Layer half of chicken in a 1-qt. casserole. Top with half the almonds, olives, mushrooms and onions. Cover with half the sauce; repeat layers. Mix cheese and buttered crumbs. Sprinkle over top. Bake uncovered at 375° for 30 minutes.

## Chicken Hashed with Cream

Serve with a colorful salad                                       Serves 6

3 T. butter
3 T. grated onion
3 T. flour
1 c. chicken broth
2 c. half and half cream
1 t. curry powder
2 c. finely chopped
  cooked chicken
10 oz. chopped water
  chestnuts
salt
baking powder biscuits,
  split and buttered
  (or patty shells)

Melt butter in saucepan; add onion and cook over low heat 5 minutes. Stir in flour; slowly add broth, cream and curry powder. Whisk over low heat until thickened. Add chicken, water chestnuts and salt to taste. Cook and stir 5 minutes or until heated. Serve over biscuits or patty shells.

# Wild Rice, Chicken & Ham Casserole
Our favorite "do ahead" casserole                                    Serves 12

2—6-oz. pkg. long grain
   and wild rice
3—10-oz. cans cream of
   chicken soup
1-1/2 c. mayonnaise
3 t. lemon juice
2 t. curry powder
4 c. cooked chicken or
   turkey, cubed
1 lb. ham, cubed
8 oz. sliced fresh mushrooms
1/2 c. slivered almonds
2 T. chopped parsley

Cook rice as package directs. Combine soup, mayonnaise, lemon juice and curry powder in a bowl. Layer rice, chicken, ham and mushrooms in a 9 x 13-inch pan. Pour sauce over all. Top with slivered almonds. Bake at 350° for 45 minutes. Sprinkle with chopped parsley before serving.

# Crunchy Chicken Casserole
Parsley and pimiento may be added for color                          Serves 6-8

1/2 c. milk
2—10-oz. cans cream of
   mushroom soup
3 c. diced cooked chicken
1/4 c. minced onion
1/4 c. diced celery
1—5-oz. can sliced water
   chestnuts
1 c. chow mein noodles
3 c. almonds, sliced

Blend milk into soup. Mix gently with chicken, onion, celery, water chestnuts and 3/4 cup of noodles. Pour into greased 2-quart casserole dish. Top with remaining noodles and almonds. Bake at 325° for 40 to 45 minutes.

# Sour Cream Chicken Squares
Quiche-like dish with unusual flavor                                 Serves 6

2 c. biscuit mix
1/2 c. cold water
1 c. chopped cooked chicken
1—4-oz. can mushroom
   pieces, drained
1—2-oz. jar pimiento, drained
1/3 c. sliced green onion
1 c. shredded cheddar cheese
1 c. sour cream
1/3 c. mayonnaise
3 eggs
1 t. garlic salt
1/3 t. pepper

Grease 13 x 9-inch baking dish. Mix biscuit mix and water until soft dough forms; beat vigorously 20 strokes. Place dough on floured board, knead 5 times. Roll dough into 14 x 10-inch rectangle. Place dough in dish so edges are 1/2 inch up sides. Mix remaining ingredients; pour evenly over dough. Bake at 350° about 25 minutes, until edges are golden and knife inserted in center comes out clean.

## Hot Chicken Mousse with Mushroom Sauce
A food processor is essential for the mousse                    Serves 4-6

1-1/2 lb. chicken breasts,
   boned and skinned
2 c. whipping cream
2 egg whites
1—3-oz. pkg. chicken
   broth mix
1/4 t. cayenne pepper
1/4 t. salt
1/8 t. white pepper

Mushroom Sauce:
8 oz. mushrooms,
   chopped
1/2 c. chopped onion
6 T. butter
6 T flour
1 c. chicken broth
1 c. whipping cream
1/4 c. dry sherry
salt and pepper

In food processor, puree small amount of chicken with some of cream, gradually adding more until all is processed smooth. Add egg whites, broth mix and seasonings; process to blend well. Butter a 1-1/2-quart oven-proof mold; fill with chicken mixture. Cover and refrigerate. About 45 minutes before serving, place mold in shallow pan of hot water in a 350° oven. Bake for 30-35 minutes. Unmold onto hot platter.

For sauce, saute mushrooms and onion in butter. Mix in flour and broth; heat and stir while adding cream. Bring to boil. Remove from heat and add sherry; season to taste. Pour some of sauce over chicken mousse; pass remaining sauce.

## Savory Chicken Squares
Cranberry sauce or salad completes this entree                    Serves 8

4-5 lb. stewing hen,
   cooked, boned, and
   chopped (about 4 c.
   meat)
6 c. stale bread crumbs
1/2 c. chicken fat or
   margarine, melted
1/4 c. chicken broth
2 eggs, well beaten
3/4 t. salt
1-1/2 t. powdered sage
1/2 c. chopped celery
3 T. chopped onion
2 T. chicken fat

Gravy:
3 T. chicken fat
3 T. flour
2-1/2 c. chicken broth
salt and pepper

Spread chicken in 9 x 13-inch baking dish. Toss bread with the combined fat, broth, beaten eggs, salt, and sage. Saute celery and onion in 2 T. chicken fat. Combine with bread mixture and spread over chicken.

For gravy, melt fat in saucepan. Stir in flour; bring to boil. Add chicken broth, salt and pepper. Bring to boil, stirring constantly. Pour gravy over chicken. Bake at 350° for 50 minutes or until firm.

# Chicken Jambalaya

This easy one-dish meal is great outdoors                 Serves 6

3 medium onions,
    chopped
4 chopped celery stalks
2 cloves garlic, minced
2 green peppers, chopped
1/4 c. vegetable oil
1—3-oz. can tomato paste
1—29-oz. can stewed
    tomatoes
1 lb. smoked sausage,
    thinly sliced
4 c. cooked, cubed
    chicken
1/2 t. cayenne pepper
1 t. chili powder
1 T. chopped parsley
1 T. Worcestershire
    sauce
2 drops hot pepper sauce
2 t. salt
1/2 t. pepper
2-1/2 c. chicken broth
1 c. rice

In large skillet, saute onions, celery, garlic and peppers in oil. Add tomato paste, tomatoes, sausage, chicken and seasonings. Cook over low heat 30-35 minutes; add chicken broth and uncooked rice. Cook until tender, about 20 minutes.

# Chicken-Rice Casserole

All this needs is a crisp salad                 Serves 6

1 c. sliced celery
1 onion, chopped
1 c. mayonnaise
1 c. tomato-vegetable
    juice
1 whole chicken,
    cooked, deboned and
    cubed
1—6-oz. pkg. wild rice,
    cooked
3 T. butter
4—8-oz. cans whole
    mushrooms
1—8-oz. pkg. sliced almonds
salt and pepper
1 c. croutons, lightly
    crushed

Saute celery and onion in butter. Mix mayonnaise and juice in large bowl. Add chicken and all ingredients except croutons; mix well. Salt and pepper to taste. Place in 8 x 11-inch baking dish. Top with croutons. Bake at 375° for 30 minutes.

## Deluxe Chicken a la King
Serve on waffles, pastry shells or toast cups.                    Serves 6-8

1/4 c. chopped green
  pepper
1 c. sliced, fresh
  mushrooms
1 T. chopped onion
2 T. butter
3/4 t. salt
2 T. flour
2 c. half and half cream
2 c. cooked chicken,
  diced
2 T. dry sherry
1 T. lemon juice
3 egg yolks
1/2 t. paprika
1/4 c. butter, softened
2 T. chopped pimiento

In saucepan, cook green pepper, mushrooms and onion in 2 T. butter, until tender. Add salt and blend in flour. Stir in cream; cook and stir until thick and bubbly. Add chicken, sherry and lemon juice; heat. Meanwhile, in a small bowl, blend egg yolks, paprika and 1/4 cup butter; when chicken is bubbling, add yolk mixture all at once, stirring until blended. Remove from heat; stir in pimiento.

## Country-Baked Chicken
Makes lots of tasty gravy                    Serves 6-8

1/2 c. butter
6 lb. frying chicken,
  cut up
1/4 c. flour, seasoned
  with salt and pepper
1—13-oz. can evaporated
  milk
1—10-oz. can cream of
  mushroom soup
1 c. grated cheddar
  cheese
1 t. soy sauce
1/2 t. salt
1/4 t. pepper
1—10-oz. jar small
  onions, drained
8 oz. mushrooms, sliced
paprika

Melt butter in a 9 x 13-inch casserole dish. Coat chicken with seasoned flour. Arrange in a single layer in melted butter in casserole, skin side down. Bake uncovered at 400° for 30 minutes. Turn pieces and bake 20 minutes more until nicely browned. Pour off excess fat. Combine milk, soup, cheese, soy sauce, salt and pepper. Add onions and mushrooms to chicken; pour milk mixture over all; sprinkle with paprika. Cover with foil and continue baking 30 minutes more at 350°.

# Chicken Almond Ding

From *The China Place*, featuring authentic                    Serves 4
Cantonese cuisine in Rockton, Illinois

1/2 lb. raw chicken
   cut in 2/3-inch cubes
1 egg white
1 T. cornstarch
1 T. soy sauce
3 T. peanut oil, divided
several dashes garlic salt
dash ground ginger
5 T. diced celery
2 T. chopped onion
2 T. diced green pepper
1/4 c. chopped carrots
1/2 c. sliced fresh
   mushrooms
1/2 c. sliced water
   chestnuts
1/2 c. diced bamboo
   shoots

Sauce:
2 T. dry white wine
2 t. soy sauce
1/2 t. sugar
1/2 t. salt
1/4 t. sesame oil
1/4 t. white pepper

Marinate chicken in egg white, cornstarch, and 1 T. soy sauce for 30 minutes. Heat 1 T. oil in large fry pan or wok to 300° and stir-fry chicken pieces rapidly for about one minute or until chicken loses pink color. Remove from pan and drain on paper toweling.

In same pan, heat 2 T. oil until hot; sprinkle with garlic salt and dash of ginger. Immediately add remaining vegetables and stir-fry for 10 to 20 seconds. Return chicken to mixture. Add 2 T. dry white wine and the sauce ingredients. Cook until done, about 6 minutes. Add a little cornstarch mixed with water to thicken if necessary.

# Pineapple Chicken

Serve with fried rice or chow mein noodles                    Serves 2-3

1/4 c. peanut oil
3/4 c. raw chicken, in
   1-inch pieces
4 T. chicken stock
1/4 c. pineapple chunks
1/4 c. diced green pepper
1/4 c. chopped tomatoes
1/2 c. pineapple juice
2 T. cider vinegar
1/4 c. brown sugar
2 T. cornstarch
1/2 t. salt
2 eggs, hard-cooked and
   sliced

In hot oil, saute chicken 2 minutes. Add chicken stock; cover pan and steam gently 10 minutes. Pour off liquid from chicken; add pineapple, green pepper, and tomatoes. In separate saucepan, mix pineapple juice, vinegar, brown sugar, cornstarch and salt. Bring to a boil; lower heat and simmer 5 minutes, stirring often. Combine sauce with chicken and vegetables. Garnish with hard-cooked egg slices.

## Chicken Livers Madeira
Accompany with baked stuffed tomatoes                    Serves 4-6

1 lb. chicken livers
1/2 c. flour
1/2 t. salt
1/4 t. pepper
1 T. oil
3 T. butter
1/2 c. beef bouillon
1/3 c. Madeira wine
1 c. sauteed mushrooms
1 c. diced sauteed ham
2 T. minced parsley

Roll livers in flour seasoned with salt and pepper. Saute livers in oil and butter in a large frying pan until lightly browned, 3-4 minutes. Add bouillon, wine, mushroom and ham. Simmer 3-4 minutes. Set aside and reheat just before serving. Garnish with parsley.

## Cheese-Crumbed Cornish Hens
Wonderful hot or cold                    Serves 4

2 Rock Cornish hens,
   split
1/4 c. garlic-flavored sour
   cream dip
1 c. crushed cheese
   crackers (20 crackers)
1/4 t. dried thyme,
   crushed
1/8 t. pepper

Coat hens well with sour cream dip. Combine cracker crumbs, thyme and pepper. Roll hens in cracker crumb mixture. Place skin side up in shallow baking pan. Bake at 350° for 45-60 minutes or until done. Garnish with watercress and cherry tomatoes, if desired.

## Cornish Hens in Wine Sauce
Bake ahead and reheat to serve                    Serves 8

1/4 c. vegetable oil
1/2 c. white wine
1 clove garlic, minced
1/2 t. coarse pepper
1 small onion, grated
1 t. marjoram
1 T. cornstarch
4 Rock Cornish hens,
   thawed and halved
1/2 c. butter

In saucepan, mix oil, wine, garlic, pepper, onion, marjoram and cornstarch; cook until slightly thickened; set aside. Place hens in shallow pan; brush with butter. Bake uncovered 1 hour at 400°, turning and basting frequently with butter. Pour sauce over top; bake for 20 minutes longer.

## Cornish Hens Seville
Easy pressure-cooker method                                    Serves 4

**2 Rock Cornish hens,
   thawed and halved
soy sauce
flour
3 T. vegetable oil
3 T. vinegar
3/4 c. sherry
1/2 c. orange marmalade
1-1/2 t. salt
1/4 t. white pepper
mandarin orange
   segments
watercress**

Brush hens with soy sauce; sprinkle lightly with flour. Heat oil in pressure cooker. Brown hens on both sides, one at a time. Combine vinegar, sherry, marmalade, salt and white pepper; pour over hens in cooker. Close cover securely; place pressure regulator on vent pipe. Cook 10 minutes. Let pressure drop naturally. Or, microwave on high 25 minutes. Garnish with mandarin orange segments and watercress.

## Turkey-Artichoke Casserole
Superb way to finish the Thanksgiving bird                     Serves 6

**2—9-oz. pkg. frozen
   artichoke hearts
1-1/2 c. sliced fresh
   mushrooms
2 T. butter
2 c. cubed cooked turkey
1-1/2 c. turkey gravy
1 c. diced Swiss cheese
1/8 t. crushed, dried
   marjoram
1 T. dry sherry
1 T. butter
1/2 c. soft bread crumbs
1 T. minced parsley**

Cook artichokes in water until tender; drain. Saute mushrooms in 2 T. butter until tender. Place artichokes, mushrooms, and turkey in 2-quart baking dish. Heat together gravy, cheese and marjoram until cheese melts. Stir in sherry; pour over chicken. Melt remaining 1 T. butter, toss with crumbs. Sprinkle crumbs on top of casserole. Bake, uncovered, at 350° for 40 minutes. Garnish with parsley.

## Peking Duck
Perfect for a patio party                                      Serves 4

1—4-6 lb. Long Island
  duckling
salt
6 green onions
1 piece ginger root
2 T. dry sherry
4 T. Hoisin sauce
2 T. honey
2 T. soy sauce

Rinse duck; rub salt on skin and cavity; let stand for 30 minutes. Crush onions and ginger root together; add sherry, Hoisin sauce, honey and soy sauce. Let sauce stand for 10 minutes. Marinate duck in sauce, pouring over and inside; let stand for at least 1 hour. Grill over hot coals on covered grill for 1 hour, or bake at 375° for 30 minutes, then reduce heat to 250°, bake 1 hour; increase to 400° and bake 30 minutes (2 hours total baking time). Let rest 10 minutes before carving.

## Roast Duck
A Cantonese favorite from *The Royal Dragon*              Serves 2-4

1 duck, about 5 lbs.
2 c. boiling water
parsley for garnish

Marinade:
1/2 t. allspice
1 t. salt
3 t. sugar
2 t. Hoisin sauce
3 slices ginger (or 1/2 t.
  ground ginger)
1 green onion
1 clove aniseed, crushed

Coating for duck:
1 t. honey
2 c. water
3 T. vinegar

Clean duck; dry with a cloth. Combine marinade ingredients and place inside duck; skewer to close. Pour boiling water over duck. For coating mixture, bring all ingredients to a boil; pour over duck. Place duck in cool place and allow the skin to dry for six hours. Place duck on a rack and roast in hot oven at 450° for 30 minutes; turn over and continue roasting for another 25 minutes at 400°. Cut duck into serving pieces and garnish with parsley.

## Duckling in Orange Sauce

Duck may be boned before serving                    Serves 8

2 ducklings, quartered
salt and pepper
poultry seasoning
sauce
2 t. cornstarch

Sauce:
2 T. butter
2 shallots, chopped
1—6-oz. can frozen
   orange juice, undiluted
1/2 c. water
1/2 c. currant jelly
1/4 c. sweet vermouth
2 small pieces fresh
   ginger root

Season ducklings with salt, pepper and poultry seasoning. Bake at 350° for 3 hours, draining fat from roasting pan at least twice. Baste with sauce during last 15 minutes of roasting. Mix remaining sauce with cornstarch; cook over high heat until boiling; serve over ducklings.

For sauce, combine all ingredients in saucepan, simmer for 30 minutes.

## Christmas Blue Goose

Use the same method for duck or pheasant           Serves 8

2 slices bacon
1 Blue Goose, cut into
   pieces
1 c. water
salt and pepper
1/4 t. thyme
2 bay leaves
1/8 t. marjoram
1—10-oz. can cream of
   mushroom soup
1/2 c. dry red wine

Fry bacon in large frying pan; remove from pan. In bacon fat, brown goose on both sides. Add water, salt, pepper, thyme, bay leaves, and marjoram. (Water should be about 1/2 inch deep.) Cover; place in oven at 325° for one hour. Mix soup and wine; pour over goose. Continue baking 30-60 minutes until goose is tender.

## Keshy Yena

Serve with loaves of crusty bread                          Serves 10

2 lb. beef round steak,
   cut into thin stripes
1/4 c. flour
1/2 t. salt
1/4 t. pepper
1/2 c. margarine
2 T. flour
1/2 c. red wine
1/2 c. butter
2 green peppers, chopped
1/2 c. chopped onion
8 oz. mushrooms, sliced
2 medium tomatoes,
   chopped
1/4 t. cayenne pepper
1/2 t. salt
1/4 t. pepper
1 T. pickle relish
2 T. raisins
6 small stuffed olives,
   chopped
1—10-oz. can cream of
   mushroom soup
1/2 c. water
28 oz. Edam cheese, in
   1/4-inch slices

Dredge beef strips in mixture of 1/4 cup flour, 1/2 t. salt and 1/4 t. pepper. In large frying pan, melt margarine and brown beef strips. Stir in 2 T. flour and cook 1 minute. Add wine; cook 2 minutes. Remove meat and sauce and set aside. In same pan, melt butter; add green pepper, onion and mushrooms; saute until tender. Add tomatoes, cayenne salt and pepper; cook and stir until liquid evaporates. Remove pan from heat. Stir in relish, raisins and olives. Add beef mixture. Dilute mushroom soup with water; stir in.

Line a 3-quart casserole dish with cheese slices. Fill casserole with meat mixture. Place any remaining cheese slices on top. Bake at 350° for 30 minutes until cheese is melted and bubbly.

## Italian Roast Beef

Add crusty Italian rolls and a huge green salad              Serves 12

5 lb. sirloin tip roast or
   rump roast
4 T. butter
salt and pepper
2 large onions, chopped
1-1/2 c. chopped celery
5 garlic cloves, chopped
2 c. water
1/2 t. rosemary leaves
2 beef bouillon cubes

Brown meat in butter; add salt and pepper. Add onions, celery and garlic; stir until sauteed. Add water, rosemary leaves, and bouillon cubes; bring to boil. Cover and simmer 1-1/2 to 2 hours, until almost done. Remove meat; chill overnight. Strain juice and refrigerate. Next day slice meat thinly into serving casserole; bring juice to a boil in sauce pan. Pour juice over meat; warm in oven at 350°for 30 minutes.

## Surf 'n Turf Skewers
Let guests join in the cooking                    Serves 6

1/2 c. Japanese soy sauce
1/2 c. honey
1/4 c. cream sherry
1 t. grated orange rind
1/2 t. garlic powder
2-1/2 lb. beef sirloin, in
   1-1/2-inch cubes
20 large raw shrimp,
   peeled and deveined
1 T. cornstarch
8 oz. whole mushrooms
2 green peppers, in wide
   strips
6 green onions, optional

Mix soy sauce, honey, cream sherry, orange rind and garlic powder in a deep bowl. Add beef and shrimp; cover and marinate overnight in refrigerator. Drain well, reserving marinade. Mix marinade with cornstarch and cook, stirring constantly, until bubbly. Remove from heat. Thread skewers with beef, shrimp, pineapple, mushrooms and green pepper. Grill over hot charcoal, brushing often with marinade.

Note: For a festive touch at an outdoor party, have guests use green onion "brushes" to baste their entrees: Trim green onions so that 8 inches of green stem remains. Make 2 lengthwise cuts in the shape of an X through the white portion of each onion. Place in ice water until onion curls to form a brush.

## Tournedos of Beef
Served with asparagus at a Junior League fundraising brunch    Serves 4

4 eggplant slices, peeled
   (1/4-inch thick)
flour
4 T. butter
1/4 c. chopped shallots
2 T. butter
1/2 c. beef broth
2 T. white wine
2 T. Burgundy wine
8 mushroom caps
salt and pepper
4—4-oz. beef tenderloin
   filets
flour
4 oz. prosciutto ham,
   sliced

Dip eggplant slices lightly in flour. In a large skillet, cook eggplant in 4 T. butter until browned on both sides, about 5 minutes. Remove and keep warm. In the same skillet, cook shallots in 2 T. butter for 1-2 minutes. Stir in beef broth and wines. Add mushroom caps; cover and cook 4 minutes more. Salt and pepper filets. Dip filets in flour; pan fry in hot fat to desired doneness, about 2 to 2-1/2 minutes per side for rare.

To serve, layer eggplant, prosciutto, and beef filet on plate. Remove mushrooms from sauce; spoon about 1 T. shallot sauce over filets. Top each serving with 2 mushroom caps, skewered on a toothpick.

## Kushi-Yaki

Easy Japanese steak kabobs                                        Serves 2-3

1 lb. beefsteak, in 1-inch
  cubes
4 leeks, white part only,
  in 1-1/2-inch slices
2 T. flour
2 T. vegetable oil
1/2 c. soy sauce
4 T. sugar
2 T. mirin (rice wine)
1/2 lemon, cut in 8 slices
finely ground pepper

Thread beef alternately with leeks on bamboo skewers, then roll in flour. Heat oil in skillet and sear meat over medium heat until brown. Drain off oil. Add soy sauce, sugar and mirin. Cover; cook each side for 2-3 minutes. Remove and simmer liquid until reduced to half. Return skewers to skillet briefly to heighten color. Serve immediately with lemon and pepper. Variations: Substitute pork, chicken or liver for beef, and white onion for leek.

## California Casserole

Meat mixture can be frozen to serve with pasta                    Serves 8

8 oz. spinach noodles
3/4 c. chopped onion
3/4 c. chopped green
  pepper
1/4 c. shortening
1 lb. ground beef
1—1-lb. can cream style
  corn
1—8-oz. can tomato
  sauce
1—10-oz. can tomato
  soup
1 c. sliced ripe olives
1/2 t. chili powder
1/2 t. salt
1/8 t. dry mustard
1/8 t. pepper
1-1/2 c. cheddar
  cheese, grated

Cook spinach noodles according to pkg. directions. Line bottom of greased 9 x 13-inch pan with drained noodles. In large skillet, saute onion and green pepper in shortening; add beef and cook until browned; drain. Add to skillet the corn, tomato sauce, soup, olives, chili powder, salt, mustard and pepper. Heat 5 minutes. Pour over noodles; sprinkle with cheese. Bake at 350° for 45 minutes.

## Austrian Beef Strudel

Garnish platter with Spiced Peaches (page 119)                    Serves 5

2-1/2 c. chopped cooked
   beef roast
1 egg
1/2 t. chopped onion
1/2 t. parsley
1-1/2 T. shortening
1 T. butter
2 T. flour
1/2 c. beef broth
1/2 t. salt
paprika
5 sheets phyllo dough
1/2 c. melted butter

Mix meat and egg. Saute onion and parsley in shortening; add to meat. In same skillet, melt butter; blend in flour and beef broth. Add meat mixture, salt and paprika. Spread out 5 sheets of phyllo dough. Spread meat mixture over half of each sheet. Brush remaining half with butter. Roll, starting from filled end. Place rolled strudel seam-side down on greased baking sheet and brush top with butter. Bake at 300° for 30 minutes.

## Scaloppine al Limone

From *Maria's*, known for its delicious                    Serves 4
Italian specialties

1-1/2 lb. veal scallops,
   cut 3/8-inch thick
salt
freshly ground black
   pepper
flour
2 T. butter
3 T. olive oil
3/4 c. beef stock, fresh or
   canned, divided
6 paper-thin lemon slices
1 T. lemon juice
2 T. butter, softened

Pound the veal scallops with salt and pepper, until 1/4-inch thick; dip them in flour and shake off the excess. In a heavy 12-inch skillet, melt 2 T. butter with the olive oil over moderate heat. When foam subsides, add veal, 4 or 5 scallops at a time. Saute scallops for about 2 minutes on each side or until they are golden brown. With tongs, transfer the scallops to a plate. Pour off most of the fat from the skillet, leaving a thin film on the bottom. Add 1/2 c. beef stock and boil it briskly for 1 or 2 minutes, stirring constantly and scraping in any browned bits clinging to the bottom and sides of the pan. Return the veal to the skillet and arrange the lemon slices on top. Cover the skillet and simmer over low for 10-15 minutes, or until veal is tender when pierced with tip of knife. To serve, transfer the scallops to a heated platter and surround with the lemon slices. Add the remaining 1/4 c. beef stock to the juices in the skillet and boil briskly until the stock is reduced to a syrupy glaze. Add the lemon juice and cook, stirring, for 1 minute. Remove pan from heat, swirl in the 2 T. soft butter and pour the sauce over the veal scallops. Serve immediately.

## Scaloppini Veal Marsala

A special treat from Rockford's Italian community                    Serves 3

1 lb. veal scallops
1/3 c. grated Parmesan
   cheese
1/4 c. butter
1 clove garlic
5 large mushrooms,
   sliced
1/8 t. cayenne pepper
1 t. meat extract
1/4 c. beef stock
1/4 c. Marsala wine

Cut veal in 2-inch pieces; pound each piece thin. Roll in cheese until well coated. Place in skillet; saute in butter and garlic until golden brown; set aside. Saute mushrooms in butter for 5 minutes; set aside. Combine pepper, meat extract and stock; add to skillet. Stir until dissolved. Add veal and mushrooms; cook over high heat until well heated. Stir in wine and serve immediately.

## Devils on Horseback

From *Jungle Jim's* restaurant, specializing                    Serves 4
in seafood and New Orleans cuisine

2 lb. veal scallops, cut
   3/8-inch thick
onion salt
fresh black pepper
flour
vegetable oil
16 large shrimp, cooked
   and deveined
8 slices thick-cut bacon
1/3 c. chopped onion
1 c. sliced fresh
   mushrooms
2 green peppers, chopped
1/2 c. butter
1/2 c. Japanese soy sauce
1/4 t. onion salt
1/4 t. fresh black pepper
1/2 c. flour
3 c. chicken broth

Pound veal scallops to 1/4-inch thickness; season with onion salt and pepper. Dredge in flour and brown on both sides in several T. of oil. Set aside on platter in 250° oven. Cut bacon strips in half and wrap around the shrimp. Broil until bacon is crisp and set aside with veal. Saute together onion, mushroom and green peppers in butter. Add soy sauce, onion salt, and pepper. Simmer 10 minutes. Add flour to make a roux. Stir continuously to avoid lumps. Add chicken broth and simmer 15 minutes or until thickened. For each serving: On warm plate, place several veal scallops; put 4 shrimp on veal. Top with several T. of sauce. Serve immediately. Pass additional sauce.

## Veal Medallions
One of the wonderful specialties from *Giovanni's*                Serves 2

2/3 c. fine bread crumbs
1 T. chopped parsley
rind of 1/2 lemon, finely
   grated
1/2 c. blanched almonds
2 T. oil
8—1-oz. veal ribeye slices
1/4 c. flour
4 eggs, slightly beaten
1/2 c. lemon butter
   (recipe follows)

Prepare breadcrumb mixture by combining bread crumbs, chopped parsley, and lemon rind. Toast almonds in oven at 350° for several minutes until lightly browned. Set aside. Heat skillet with oil over a medium flame. Dust veal in flour, shake off excess. Dip into eggs, then drop into bread crumb mixture. Do not grind crumbs into veal. Remove from crumbs. Pan fry, turning periodically, to golden brown. Serve 4 slices veal per person; garnish with almonds and lemon butter.

## Lemon Butter
*Giovanni's* recommends this for fish, chicken or veal                Serves 16-20

1/2 c. white wine
1/4 c. beef gravy
1 lb. butter
juice of 1 lemon

Mix wine and gravy together in saucepan. Over moderate heat, reduce down to a pliable, workable syrup. Divide butter into 8 segments. Remove pan from heat. With a wire whisk, mix in chunks of butter, constantly moving butter around. (Caution: sauce may break down if gravy base or saucepan are exceedingly hot. The creamier the butter, the better the appearance will be.) Whisk in lemon juice. Serve over any fish, chicken, or veal. For fish, we suggest sprinkling ground dillweed on butter.

## Stuffed Breast of Veal with Noodles Mornay
Transforms inexpensive cut of veal into gourmet's delight          Serves 4

4-5 lb. breast of veal
1/4 c. butter
1/2 c. chopped onion
4 oz. fresh mushrooms,
  sliced
3/4 c. water
6 slices bread, crusts
  removed, cubed
1/2 c. seasoned croutons
1 T. grated Parmesan
  cheese
1/8 t. dried basil
2 T. vegetable oil
1 c. dry white wine
1 T. butter
2 T. flour
1 T. Parmesan cheese
1/2 c. chicken broth
1/2 c. white wine
1—7-oz. pkg. whole
  wheat spinach noodles
minced parsley
paprika

Using long sharp knife, carefully slit along (and close to) rib bones of veal breast to form "pocket." Prepare stuffing: Melt 1/4 c. butter in medium saucepan; saute onions and mushrooms until tender, 3-4 minutes. Stir in water, bread, croutons, Parmesan and basil. Cool a few minutes; stuff into veal pocket. Secure with several poultry skewers.

In large dutch oven, heat oil; carefully brown veal on all sides. Pour 1 c. white wine over veal. Cover; bake at 325° for 2-1/2 hours. Remove veal to large oven-proof platter. Return, uncovered, to oven. Add 1 T. butter to veal drippings; stir in flour and Parmesan. Slowly blend in chicken broth and wine. Stir constantly over medium heat until thickened. Keep warm.

Prepare noodles according to package directions; drain; arrange on serving platter with veal. Pour half the sauce over veal and noodles. Sprinkle with parsley and paprika. Serve immediately and pass remaining sauce.

## Enchiladas
These freeze beautifully                                   Serves 4-6

1 pkg. enchilada
  seasoning mix
1—10-oz. can tomato
  bisque soup
1—6-oz. can tomato paste
3 c. water
1-1/2 lb. ground beef
1/2 c. chopped black
  olives
3 c. shredded Monterey
  Jack cheese.
10 large flour tortillas

In medium saucepan, blend enchilada mix with soup and tomato paste. Slowly stir in water. Bring to boil; reduce heat and simmer 15 minutes. Meanwhile, in skillet, brown ground beef. Drain; stir in chopped olives and half of cheese. Pour 1/3 of the sauce mix into greased 9 x 13-inch pan.

To assemble enchiladas: dip each tortilla in sauce, then stack on a plate. Place 3 heaping T. of meat mix on the top tortilla; roll carefully and set in pan. Repeat with remaining tortillas. Pour remaining sauce over top and sprinkle with remaining cheese. Cover with foil. Bake at 375° for 30 minutes.

## Layered Tortilla Pie
Tastes wonderful reheated                                    Serves 4-6

1-1/2 lbs. ground beef
1 onion, chopped
1 clove garlic, minced
1—8-oz. can tomato
   sauce
1—2-1/4-oz. can sliced
   ripe olives, drained
1 T. chili powder
1t. salt
1/4 t. pepper
6 buttered tortillas
2 c. shredded cheddar
   cheese
1/2 c. water

Brown beef, onions and garlic in large skillet. Add tomato sauce, olives and seasonings; cook over medium heat 20 minutes, stirring frequently. In a round 2-quart casserole dish, alternate tortillas, 1-1/2 c. cheese and meat sauce. Sprinkle remaining cheese over top. Pour water near edge of casserole into bottom. Cover and bake at 400° for 30-40 minutes. Uncover and let stand 5 minutes before cutting to serve.

## Mexican Ribs
Chef Keenan of *Grampa's* recommends these              Serves 6

6 lb. country pork ribs
3 c. Spanish sauce (recipe
   follows)
1/2 t. crushed red pepper

In large flat baking pan, spread ribs. Pour sauce over and sprinkle with red pepper. Bake at 325° for one hour. Turn ribs, baste, and cook one hour more or until tender. Serve with Spanish rice and beans.

## Spanish Sauce
From *Grampa's*, specializing in                       Makes 8 cups
outstanding Mexican dishes.

1—27-oz. can whole
   tomatoes
1—27-oz. can tomato
   sauce
1 onion, chopped fine
2 green peppers, chopped
14 oz. chopped green
   chiles
2 t. cumin
2 t. oregano
2 t. pepper
1/4 c. chicken base
1/2 c. sherry
1/4 c. cornstarch
1/2 c. cold water
9 oz. green tomatoes
   (optional)

Crush tomatoes. Add all other ingredients except cornstarch and water to large cooking pot or Dutch oven. Cook over low heat for 30 minutes, stirring occasionally. Add cornstarch to cold water and whip smooth. Add to sauce. Stir. Turn off heat; let cool. Use as needed, reheated, for *Chimichanga* or *Mexican Ribs*.

## Beef Chimichanga
Another specialty of Chef Keenan and *Grampa's*                    Serves 12

4 lb. boneless chuck
   roast
salt and pepper
3 c. water
2 c. Spanish Sauce
   (recipe above)
2 c. pinto beans
4 c. water
1-1/2 t. salt
1/2 c. lard, melted
24 large flour tortillas
oil for deep frying
2 lb. cheddar cheese,
   shredded
2 c. Spanish Sauce,
   warmed
sour cream
shredded lettuce
guacamole (or avocado
   slices)

In a Dutch oven covered, simmer chuck roast, salt and pepper and 3 c. water for 4 hours. Drain. Shred beef. Mix beef with 2 c. Spanish Sauce.

In separate kettle, mix pinto beans, 4 c. water and 1-1/2 t. salt. Bring to boil; simmer, covered, over medium low heat for 3 hours. Drain. Mash beans with melted lard.

To assemble, place 1/2 c. meat mix and 1/3 c. bean mix in center of each tortilla. Fold 2 sides of tortilla into center, then roll. Fasten with toothpick. Deep fry each tortilla in hot oil at 375°. Drain on paper towels.

To serve, spoon warm Spanish Sauce over tortillas. Sprinkle liberally with cheese. Serve with sour cream, shredded lettuce and guacamole.

## Savory Pork Almond Din
Garnish with toasted almonds                              Serves 4-6

2 lb. pork shoulder
   steaks
2 T. shortening
1 c. sliced celery
1—4-oz. can button
   mushrooms
1—8-oz. can water
   chestnuts, drained
1/3 c. chopped pimiento
1 c. frozen french green
   beans
2 t. salt
1/4 t. pepper
1/2 t. garlic salt
1 c. water
1 beef bouillon cube
2 T. cornstarch

Cut steak into thin strips. In skillet, brown meat lightly in shortening. Cover and simmer for 30 minutes. Cook celery 5 minutes in small amount of water; drain. Add celery, mushrooms and their liquid, water chestnuts, pimiento, green beans, and seasonings; stir well. Add bouillon cube and 1/2 cup water and stir until dissolved. Mix cornstarch and remaining 1/2 cup water; add to meat and vegetables and cook, stirring constantly until thickened. Cover and cook slowly 5 minutes, stirring occasionally. Serve over cooked rice.

## Sweet and Sour Pork

From *The Royal Dragon*, serving Cantonese          Serves 2-4
and American specialties.

10 oz. pork loin, cut into
   1-inch cubes
1/4 t. salt
oil for deep frying

Pickled vegetables:
1 T. salt
4 T. sugar
1/2 c. vinegar
1 carrot, sliced
1 small cucumber, sliced
1 green pepper, sliced
4 oz. pineapple chunks

Batter for pork:
1 egg
1/2 c. cornstarch
1/2 c. flour
3 T. oil
1-1/2 c. water

Deep fry pork, which has been salted and dipped in batter, in hot oil until golden brown. Combine pickled vegetables with sweet and sour sauce ingredients and bring to boil. Stir until slightly thickened. Add fried pork; mix well. Serve immediately.

Note: For pickled vegetables, mix all ingredients. Cover and refrigerate overnight. For batter, mix all ingredients until smooth. For sweet and sour sauce, mix all ingredients in jar; cover and shake until blended.

Sweet and sour sauce:
1 c. water
5 T. apple cider
5 T. sugar
2 T. tomato sauce
1-1/2 T. cornstarch
1 T. vegetable oil

## Pork Tenderloin Diablo

Try this with orzo (rice-shaped pasta)          Serves 4

1 lb. pork tenderloin
1/4 c. flour
1 t. salt
1/4 t. pepper
1 T. vegetable oil
2—8-oz. cans tomato
   sauce
1 clove garlic, minced
1/4 t. oregano
1/4 t. basil
1/4 t. sugar
1—4-oz. can mushrooms,
   drained
12 crosswise slices green
   pepper
1/2 c. onion slices

Cut tenderloin crosswise in 2-inch pieces; flatten slightly with meat hammer. Mix together flour, salt and pepper. Roll meat in flour mixture; brown well in oil in heavy skillet. Blend together tomato sauce, garlic, oregano, basil and sugar. Pour sauce over meat; cover and cook slowly 30 minutes. Add mushrooms, green pepper and onion slices; cook 30 minutes more.

## Pork Tenderloin Patties

Same method may be used for sausage or beef patties          Serves 6

6 pork tenderloin patties
1 egg, slightly beaten
1 T. cold water
3/4 c. fine salted cracker
    crumbs
1/4 t. salt
1/8 t. pepper
5 T. butter
8 oz. mushrooms, sliced
1—10-oz. can cream of
    chicken soup
1 c. sour cream
1/4 c. dry sherry

Dip patties into mixture of egg and water; roll in crumbs seasoned with salt and pepper. Brown in 3 T. butter. Saute mushrooms in 2 T. butter. Put patties in shallow casserole; add mushrooms to soup, sour cream and sherry. Pour over patties; bake at 350° for 1 hour.

## Maple-Barbecued Baby Ribs

Wonderful with any egg casserole          Serves 4

2 c. ketchup
1-1/2 c. maple syrup
1/2 c. cider vinegar
1/2 c. orange juice
1 t. grated orange peel
2 T. Worcestershire
    sauce
2 t. salt
2 T. minced onion
3-4 lb. baby pork ribs
orange segments for
    garnish

In a 2-quart saucepan, mix ketchup, maple syrup, vinegar, orange juice, orange peel, Worcestershire, salt and onion. Bring to boil; simmer, uncovered, 15 minutes; let cool. While sauce simmers, cook ribs until tender in simmering water or in microwave. Marinate ribs in sauce for 2 hours at room temperature (or 1-2 days in refrigerator). To serve, bake ribs at 350° for 40 minutes, until browned and glazed. Garnish with orange segments.

## Reuben Casserole
Even better than the classic sandwich — Serves 8

1—27-oz. can sauerkraut,
  drained well
3 medium tomatoes,
  sliced
1/2 c. butter or
  margarine
1—8-oz. bottle thousand
  island dressing
1/2 lb. corned beef,
  thinly sliced
1/2 lb. Swiss cheese,
  grated
1—8-oz. can refrigerated
  biscuits
4 crisp rye crackers,
  crushed
1/4 t. caraway seed

Grease a 13 x 9-inch pan. Spread sauerkraut on bottom; add tomato slices; dot with butter. Pour over thousand island dressing; cover with corned beef; sprinkle cheese on top. Bake at 425° for 15 minutes. Separate rolls and place atop casserole; sprinkle crackers and caraway seeds on top. Bake at 425° for 15-20 minutes.

## Cider-Sauced Canadian Bacon
Perfect meat dish for brunch — Serves 12

3/4 c. light brown sugar
2 T. fine, dry bread
  crumbs
1 t. dry mustard
1 T. vinegar
1—3-lb. piece Canadian
  bacon
1 c. apple cider

Combine brown sugar, bread crumbs, mustard and vinegar and set aside. Bake the bacon uncovered at 350° for 1-1/2 hours, basting every 10 minutes with cider. Spread brown sugar mixture over the bacon and bake for 20 minutes more, or until the mixture has glazed the bacon. Slice 1/2-inch thick and serve on a preheated platter.

## Gingered Ham Steak
A quick entree from the chefs at *Mauh-Nah-Tee-See Country Club* — Serves 1

1—8-oz. ham steak
2 T. brown sugar
1 T. butter
2-3 T. ginger-flavored
  brandy
4 green pepper rings
1 T. raisins

Saute ham steak in butter until lightly browned on both sides. Mix brown sugar and butter over low heat. Add ginger brandy. Stir until mixed. Add green peppers and raisins. Saute 1 to 2 minutes, turning ham. Place ham steak on warm platter and top with ginger brandy sauce.

## Apricot Ham Slice

Too easy for something tasting this good                                Serves 4

1/2 c. apricot preserves
2 T. prepared mustard
1 T. water
2 t. lemon juice
1 t. Worcestershire sauce
1/2 t. cinnamon
1 center-cut ham slice, 1
   inch thick

In saucepan, combine first 6 ingredients. Heat until preserves melt. Slash fat edge of ham. Pour sauce over ham in shallow dish. Refrigerate overnight or let stand at room temperature for 2 hrs.; remove ham, reserving marinade. Grill over medium coals 5 minutes each side. Brush one side with marinade, turn. Grill brushed side 4-5 minutes. Repeat with other side. Heat remaining marinade on edge of grill. Serve with ham.

## Ham Rolls Continental

Easy to make ahead; bake or microwave                                Serves 3

6 slices ham, 1/4-inch
   thick
6 slices Swiss cheese
1—10-oz. pkg. frozen
   broccoli spears, cooked
   and drained
1 c. onion slices
2 T. margarine
2 T. flour
1/2 t. salt
1/4 t. basil
1/8 t. pepper
1 c. milk

Top each ham slice with cheese and broccoli. Roll and secure with toothpick. Place in 10 x 6-inch baking dish. Cook onion in margarine until tender; blend in flour and seasonings. Gradually add milk; stir over low heat until thickened. Pour over ham; cover baking dish with foil. Bake 25 minutes at 350°.

## Ham Rolls

An easy picnic or Sunday supper                                Serves 6

6 hard French rolls
   (individual size)
3/4 lb. ham, ground
1/4 lb. cheddar cheese,
   grated
1/2 lb. American cheese,
   grated
8 stuffed olives, sliced
6 green onions, sliced
2 celery stalks, chopped
1/2 c. olive oil
1/2 c. tomato paste

Scrape out and butter center of hard French rolls. Let stand so centers will dry. Mix together cheddar cheese, American cheese, olives, onions, celery, olive oil and tomato paste. Fill rolls with ham and cheese mixture. Cover with foil and bake 10 minutes at 400°. Uncover and bake 20 minutes more.

## Rum-Flavored Ham

This method also perks up flavor of canned ham                Serves 8-10

1—6-lb. fully cooked
  ham
1-1/2 t. whole cloves
1 c. brown sugar
3 oranges, unpeeled and
  sliced
1-1/2 c. rum

Wrap ham in heavy-duty foil; bake at 300° for 2-1/2 hours. Remove from foil. Remove rind from ham and score fat. Stud with cloves. Place brown sugar on top. Pour off fat from pan. Arrange orange slices in bottom of baking pan. Set ham on bed of oranges. Slowly pour rum over ham. Return ham to oven for one hour. Baste ham every 10 minutes with liquid in pan. Total baking time is 3-1/2 hours, or 35 minutes per pound.

## Glazed Sausage and Fruit Compote

Curry powder may be added for unique flavor                Serves 5

8 oz. brown and serve
  sausage links
1—16-oz. can sliced
  pears
1—16-oz. can sliced cling
  peaches
1—16-oz. can apricot
  halves
1—8-oz. can pineapple
  chunks
10 maraschino cherries
3 T. melted butter
1/3 c. brown sugar
1 t. lemon juice
1/4 t. ground ginger

Drain fruit well. Arrange fruit and sausage links in a single layer in shallow baking dish. Combine butter, sugar, lemon juice and ginger; mix well. Spoon butter-sugar mixture over fruit and sausages. Bake at 350° for 30 minutes. Serve warm.

## Sausage Cornbread Breakfast

For a variation, substitute apple bits for pineapple                Serves 6

1—10-link pkg. brown
  and serve sausage
  (regular or bacon
  flavor)
1—13-oz. can pineapple
  tidbits, drained
2 T. brown sugar
1—7-oz. pkg. cornbread
  mix

Arrange sausage, uncooked, in bottom of 8 x 8-inch casserole pan. Spoon drained pineapple tidbits over sausage; sprinkle with brown sugar. Prepare cornbread as package directs; spread over sausage and pineapple, covering well. Bake at 425° for 30 minutes; then let stand in casserole for 5 minutes. Turn out, sausage-side up, on a platter. Cut into serving pieces. Serve with maple syrup.

## Apple Sausage Ring
Serve with eggs and biscuits                                    Serves 8

2 eggs, slightly beaten
1/2 c. milk
1-1/2 c. cracker crumbs
1/4 c. minced onion
1 c. peeled, chopped
  apple
2 lb. bulk pork sausage

Combine all ingredients, mixing well. Press into a greased 6 1/2-cup ring mold. Unmold onto a 15 x 10-inch jellyroll pan. Chill 1 hour (or overnight, covered with plastic wrap). Bake at 350° for 1 hour. Unmold on serving platter.

## Artichoke Casserole
Unusual and popular buffet dish                                 Serves 12

olive oil
Italian bread crumbs
3 lb. Italian sausage,
  casing removed,
  crumbled
3—8-oz. cans sliced
  mushrooms, drained
3—15-oz. cans artichoke
  hearts, drained and
  quartered

In the bottom of a 9 x 13-inch pan, place enough olive oil to coat. Sprinkle with bread crumbs. Layer sausage, mushrooms and artichoke hearts. Top with bread crumbs. Bake for 1 hour at 325°, stirring every 10 minutes and adding more bread crumbs as needed to absorb liquid.

## Curry in a Hurry
Any leftover meat may be substituted                            Serves 4

3/4 c. sliced onions
1 c. diced celery
1 clove garlic (or garlic
  powder)
2 T. shortening, butter
  or margarine
1-1/2 c. cubed cooked
  lamb
1 t. curry powder
2 c. gravy (diluted with
  water if necessary)
salt to taste

Saute onions, celery and garlic in fat. Add meat, curry powder, gravy and salt. Cover; simmer 30 minutes. If necessary thicken with mixture of flour and water. Serve over hot rice.

## Shrimp Curry with Serundang
Accompany with sliced cantaloupe and honeydew melon.          Serves 6

2 T. butter
3/4 c. finely chopped
   apple
1/2 c. finely chopped
   onion
2 t. curry powder
1—10-oz. can cream of
   shrimp soup
1 c. sour cream
2 c. frozen cooked
   shrimp, thawed
steamed rice

Serundang:
4 oz. shredded coconut
4 T. butter
4 T. brown sugar
1 c. salted peanuts
1 t. coriander
1/2 t. cumin

Melt butter in saucepan; add apple, onion, and curry powder. Simmer slowly until apple and onion are tender. Stir in soup and bring to boil. Add sour cream and shrimp. Heat to boiling, but do not boil. Serve over steamed rice, with Serundang.

Serundang: Brown coconut lightly in butter; stir in brown sugar and peanuts; heat well. Stir in coriander and cumin. Let cool.

## Golden Shrimp Casserole
Easy but special variation of a favorite          Serves 6

5 slices buttered bread
2 c. cooked shrimp
2 c. grated sharp cheddar
   cheese
1—10-oz. can cream of
   celery soup
2/3 c. milk
3 eggs

Cut bread into 1/2-inch cubes. Place half of bread in 2-quart casserole dish. Put half of shrimp on top; add 1 cup cheese. Repeat layers. Mix soup and milk. Beat in eggs; pour over casserole. Place casserole in a pan filled with warm water to an inch of top. Bake at 375° for 1 hour.

## Shrimp Casino

From *The Mayflower*, one of Rockford's finest restaurants          Serves 1

4 large fresh shrimp,
     peeled and deveined
     (leave last joint on
     tail intact)
4 slices bacon
2 T. melted butter
2 T. white wine
hickory-smoked salt
pepper
paprika
nutmeg
grated Monterey Jack
     cheese
lemon wedge
parsley for garnish

Wash and drain shrimp; wrap each shrimp with a bacon slice and lay in small casserole dish. Add melted butter and white wine. Season to taste with hickory-smoked salt, pepper, paprika, and nutmeg. Broil until shrimp is cooked. Top with some grated Monterey Jack cheese and place under broiler until cheese is melted and lightly browned. Garnish with lemon wedge and parsley.

## Shrimp Creole

Serve in deep bowls with lots of French bread          Serves 10

1 c. margarine
1 green pepper, diced
2 large onions, diced
2 stalks celery, diced
2 cloves garlic, minced
1 c. chopped parsley
2—3-lb. cans whole
     tomatoes, drained
1—12-oz. can tomato
     puree
1 c. flour
5 c. seafood stock (or
     3 c. clam juice and
     2 c. water, heated)
3 T. Worcestershire
     sauce
3/4 c. dry white wine
1 T. Louisiana hot sauce
     (or to taste)
salt and pepper
3 lb. shrimp, peeled and
     deveined
steamed rice

Melt margarine in gallon pot. Saute pepper, onions, celery, garlic and parsley; add tomatoes and puree and stir. In separate pot, blend flour into simmering seafood stock. Add this mixture to the vegetables in the gallon pot. (The secret is to have both stock and vegetables hot to keep flour from lumping.) Add Worcestershire sauce, wine and hot sauce. Salt and pepper to taste. Cook for at least 30 minutes on medium heat. Add shrimp and simmer for 30 minutes more. Serve over steamed rice.

## Baked Seafood Royal

For dinner, serve with baked rice or pasta                    Serves 6

1 lb. cooked shrimp
1/2 lb. crabmeat
1/2 lb. cooked lobster
3 T. lemon juice
1/2 t. hot pepper sauce
1 t. salt
3 T. sherry
3/4 c. melted butter
1/2 lb. mushrooms, sliced
4 T. butter

Divide shrimp, crabmeat and lobster among six casseroles or use one single casserole. Mix lemon juice, hot pepper sauce, salt, sherry and butter; pour over seafood. Brown mushrooms in 4 T. butter and arrange on casserole. Bake at 450° for 15 minutes.

## Crunchy Crabmeat Casserole

May substitute chicken or turkey for crab                    Serves 4

1—5-oz. can water
  chestnuts
1—10-oz. can cream of
  mushroom soup
1-1/2 c. unseasoned
  bread stuffing mix
1/2 c. mayonnaise
2—7-oz. cans crabmeat

Drain and slice water chestnuts. Add soup, stuffing mix and mayonnaise; mix well. Add crab meat and mix lightly. Pour into greased 2-quart casserole dish and bake 40 minutes at 350°.

## Jiffy Crab Casserole

For a kid-pleaser, substitute tuna for crab                    Serves 4-6

1 c. butter
1—13-oz. can evaporated
  milk
4 oz. pimiento cheese
3—6-oz. cans crabmeat,
  drained
1 c. chow mein noodles
1 c. garlic croutons

Melt butter, milk and cheese together in large saucepan or microwave. Mix with crabmeat and noodles. Place mixture in buttered 1-1/2-quart casserole dish and top with croutons. Bake at 325° for 45 minutes or microwave until heated through.

## Crabmeat Rice Squares with Shrimp Sauce
Something different and easy to prepare ahead                                Serves 6-8

**Rice squares:**
1/4 c. minced onion
1/4 c. minced parsley
1 c. grated mozzarella
   cheese
1 t. salt
1 t. Worcestershire sauce
2—6-oz. cans crabmeat,
   drained
3 eggs
2 c. milk
3 c. cooked rice
1 c. frozen peas,
   defrosted

**Shrimp sauce:**
1—10-oz. can cream of
   shrimp soup
1/2 c. sour cream
1 t. lemon juice
1 lb. frozen cooked small
   shrimp, thawed

Combine all ingredients for rice squares. Pour into greased 9 x 11-inch baking dish; bake at 350° for 45 minutes.

Combine all ingredients for shrimp sauce in medium saucepan. Heat just to boiling, stirring often. Serve in sauceboat with rice squares.

## Brunch Lobster
This sauce is special for any seafood                                       Serves 6

4 Danish lobsters per
   person (or 2 small
   lobster tails per
   person)
4 egg yolks
1 t. sugar
2 drops hot pepper
   sauce
1/8 t. paprika
2 T. fresh lemon juice
2 T. cider vinegar
2 c. vegetable oil
1/2 t. curry powder
freshly ground salt and
   pepper
bibb lettuce

Boil lobster in salted water just until tender; do not overcook. Cool. Loosen meat, but leave in shell. Chill, covered, until serving time.

Combine egg yolks, sugar, hot pepper sauce and paprika in mixer bowl and beat until very thick. Add lemon juice and vinegar alternately with oil to yolk mixture, beating constantly. Stir in curry powder, salt and pepper to taste; cover and chill at least 8 hours.

To serve, line serving plates with bibb lettuce. Divide lobster among plates; top each lobster with some of sauce. Pass remaining sauce.

## Sea Shells
May also be baked in a casserole dish                     Serves 6

1 c. rich cracker crumbs
2 T. melted butter
1 small green pepper,
   chopped
1 small onion, chopped
3/4 c. chopped celery
1 c. crabmeat, drained
   well
1 c. shrimp, cooked
1/2 t. salt
1/8 t. pepper
1 t. Worcestershire sauce
1 c. mayonnaise

Mix cracker crumbs with butter in large bowl. Add all remaining ingredients; mix well. Divide mixture among 6 large seafood shells; place on baking pan. Bake at 350° for 30 minutes.

## Seafood Pie
Filling may be made ahead and refrigerated                Serves 6-8

5 T. butter
1/4 c. chopped onion
1/4 c. chopped celery
1/2 lb. shrimp or lobster
   meat, uncooked
1 lb. whitefish
1-1/2 lb. scallops
1/2 lb. oysters
2 c. chicken broth,
   boiling
1/4 c. dry sherry
pastry for 2-crust 10-inch
   pie

In skillet, melt butter; saute onion, celery and shrimp (or lobster) until tender. In a separate pan, cook whitefish, scallops and oysters in chicken broth for 5 minutes. Strain and reserve liquid. Chop seafood.

Stir flour into celery-onion mixture; add reserved liquid from cooking seafood. Heat and stir until thickened. Add sherry. Remove from heat. Add chopped seafood and blend well.

Line a 10-inch pie pan with crust. Pour in seafood mixture. Add top pie crust; cut vents for steam. Bake at 375° for 20-25 minutes, until crust is browned. Let rest 10 minutes before serving.

## Salmon En Papillote

From the beautiful *Mauh-Nah-Tee-See Country Club*                Serves 1

1 sheet foil or parchment
   paper, 24 inches long
1 T. butter, softened
2 T. chopped green
   onion
1—8-oz. salmon fillet
1 small tomato, peeled
   and cubed
3-4 large mushrooms,
   sliced
1 t. dill weed
2 T. butter, melted
salt and white pepper
1/8 c. white wine
1 t. fresh lemon juice

Fold foil or paper in half and cut in a heart shape, then unfold. Butter the center of half the heart. Sprinkle chopped green onions over butter. Place salmon fillet on top of green onions. Cover salmon fillet with tomatoes, sliced mushrooms, dill weed, butter and salt and pepper to taste. Sprinkle wine and lemon juice over all. Fold foil and seal edge by a series of continuous folds. Bake at 400° for 10 minutes.

## Baked Fish Parmesan

For a speedy meal, prepare ahead and microwave                Serves 4-6

2 lb. cod fillets, thawed
1/2 c. dry white wine
1 t. seasoned salt
1/2 c. mayonnaise
2 T. butter, softened
1/3 c. grated Parmesan
   cheese
1/2 c. slivered almonds,
   toasted
parsley
lemon slices for garnish

In an 11 x 7-inch baking dish, pour wine over fish fillets and sprinkle with seasoned salt. Cover with plastic wrap; refrigerate 2-3 hours. Just before serving, pour off wine. Spread top of fillets with mixture of mayonnaise, butter and Parmesan which have been blended well. Bake at 375° for 15-20 minutes or microwave until fish flakes easily. Place under broiler 2-3 minutes. Carefully remove to warm serving platter and serve immediately with toasted almonds and parsley sprinkled over. Garnish with lemon slices.

# Sole John Paul
From Chef John Dargo at *Bellamy's*, known for elegant dining                Serves 1

1/4 c. celery, cut in
   julienne
1/4 c. carrots, cut in
   julienne
1/4 c. onions, cut in
   julienne
2 T. butter
1 T. lemon juice
1/4 c. Chablis
1/4 c. heavy cream
3-4 oz. fillet of sole
court bouillon

Saute julienne vegetables in melted butter in skillet until tender, about 4-5 minutes. Add lemon juice and Chablis; simmer until liquid is reduced. Add cream and simmer. While sauce is simmering, poach the sole in court bouillon. Do not overcook. Remove sole to hot plate; pour sauce over sole and serve immediately.

# Oriental Tuna Bake
Inexpensive light luncheon or supper dish                Serves 6

2 T. butter
1/4 c. chopped green
   pepper
1 T. flour
1/2 t. salt
1/8 t. pepper
1/2 c. milk
1 egg, slightly beaten
1/4 c. sour cream
1/2 c. mayonnaise
1—16-oz. can chop suey
   vegetables, rinsed
   and drained
1—6-oz. can tuna,
   drained
2 T. butter
1 can chow mein noodles

Melt 2 T. butter in saucepan; add green pepper and cook 2 minutes. Blend in flour, salt and pepper. Gradually add milk; cook, stirring, until slightly thickened. Blend together egg, sour cream and mayonnaise; stir into sauce. Add vegetables and tuna. Turn into 1-quart baking dish; bake at 375° for 25 minutes. Melt 2 T. butter in skillet; add chow mein noodles and heat until lightly browned. Sprinkle over top of tuna. Bake 5 minutes more; serve immediately.

# Hangtown Fry
Serve with toast points and lemon wedges                Serves 4-6

8 large oysters
flour
6 T. butter
6 eggs
3 T. cream
1/4 c. freshly grated
   Parmesan cheese
1/4 c. chopped parsley
salt and pepper

Dip oysters in flour and lightly saute in butter. Blend the eggs, cream, cheese and parsley. Add salt and pepper to taste. Pour over oysters in pan and cook over low heat until eggs are set. Serve from the skillet or flip onto a hot platter.

## Bieracks
Baked German sandwiches                                    Makes 12

1/2 c. shortening
1/4 c. sugar
1 c. bran flakes
1 c. boiling water
1—.5-oz. cake yeast
1 egg, beaten
1 t. salt
3 c. flour, sifted
1 lb. ground beef
2 c. sauerkraut, squeezed
  dry
salt and pepper

Place shortening, sugar and bran flakes in bowl; pour water over mixture. Cool; add yeast. Add egg, salt and flour; knead into dough. Place in greased pan; set in warm place to rise 1 hour, covered. Fry ground beef until it turns gray; add sauerkraut, salt and pepper.

Roll half of dough out on floured board to 1/4-inch thickness. Cut into six 6-inch squares. Place a spoonful of meat mixture in center of each square. Fold corners to center; seal. Repeat with remaining dough and meat. Place bieracks on baking sheet and let rest in warm place until doubled in bulk. Bake at 400° for 25-30 minutes; serve hot. May be frozen and reheated.

## Stuffed French Bread
Much better made 2-3 days before serving.                  Serves 8

1 loaf French bread
1 can anchovy fillets in
  oil, undrained
8 oz. cream cheese,
  softened
1 T. capers
2 T. chili sauce
1/4 c. chopped onion
1 T. Worcestershire
  sauce
1/2 c. butter
1/2 c. watercress or
  green onion tops

Split bread lengthwise and pull out soft center in the top and bottom, forming a cavity. Beat together anchovies, cream cheese, capers, chili sauce, onion and Worcestershire; fill bottom cavity. Mix together butter and watercress or onion tops and fill top cavity. Put bread back together and wrap tightly in aluminum foil. Refrigerate. Slice bread thinly with sharp knife and serve.

## Crab Muffin Sandwich

Perfect soup and sandwich luncheon                    Serves 4

2—7-oz. cans king
  crab, drained
1—10-oz. can shrimp
  soup
1/4 c. minced celery
1/4 c. minced green
  pepper
2 T. minced onion
2 drops lemon juice
1/4 c. mayonnaise
salt and pepper
4 English muffins, split
  and toasted
8 tomato slices
grated Parmesan cheese

Flake crabmeat. Measure 1/3 c. undiluted soup and mix with crab, celery, green pepper, onion, lemon juice, mayonnaise, salt, and pepper. Put muffins on cookie sheet and top with tomato slices. Spread with crab mix; sprinkle with cheese. Bake 15 minutes at 425° until bubbly. (Remaining soup may be prepared and served with sandwiches.)

## Kasetoast Hawaii

Kids love making, and eating, these easy sandwiches           Serves 4

4 slices toasted bread
4 slices ham
4 slices pineapple
4 slices Gouda, brick or
  Swiss cheese

Butter toast lightly; put ham, pineapple, and cheese on top. Bake in preheated oven at 375° until cheese is melted. Serve hot.

## Breezy Cheezy Crabmeat Sandwiches

Garnish with black olive slices                    Serves 10

1 c. butter
1 lb. American cheese
2 T. lemon juice
2 T. Worcestershire
  sauce
1 t. garlic salt
2—6-oz. cans crabmeat,
  flaked
12 English muffins

Melt butter and cheese over low heat; add lemon juice, Worcestershire sauce, and garlic salt, mix well. Fold in crabmeat, mixing well. Chill several hours. Cut muffins in half or break apart. Spread each half with chilled crabmeat mixture. Place close together on ungreased baking sheet. Bake at 350° for 15 to 20 minutes. Serve immediately.

## Cheesey Sandwiches
Great for kids' brunch or late-night snack                    Serves 4

1/2 c. chopped onion
1/4 c. margarine
1/4 c. mayonnaise
2 c. grated cheddar
  cheese
2 drops hot pepper sauce
1/4 c. chopped pimiento
1/4 c. chopped parsley
12 slices white sandwich
  bread

Mix all ingredients together except bread. Cut crusts from 12 slices sandwich bread. Spread each slice with mixture and roll up. Hold with toothpick. Place in casserole dish; spread any remaining mixture over top. Bake uncovered at 350° for 10 minutes.

## Dijon Butter
From *Giovanni's*, specializing in fine continental dining     Serves 8-12

1 lb. butter
1/4 c. finely chopped
  onion
1 T. white wine
2 T. Dijon mustard
2 drops hot pepper sauce
1/8 t. garlic powder
1 T. Worcestershire
  sauce

Mix all ingredients together in blender container. Blender whip to three times the starting volume.

Suggested uses: On pan-fried chicken or Shrimp Dijon (4 shrimp per casserole dish with bread crumb coating. Pour dijon butter over. Heat over low flame just until melted.) Do not lose the creamy foam-like texture.

## Orange Marmalade Sauce
Excellent for chicken or duck...an easy treat from *Bellamy's*     Makes 3 cups

1-1/2 c. honey
2 c. orange marmalade
2 T. curry powder
2 T. garlic powder
2 T. brown mustard
2 T. onion powder
1/4 c. lemon juice
1 T. turmeric

In heavy saucepan, combine all ingredients and bring to a slow boil. Simmer 20 minutes.

### RED DELICIOUS

apples from emmerts orchard.
they're not all that pretty because i dont spray the
trees, but they sure do taste good, even though i do
have to eat around a few worm holes.

tuesday september 28 1983 sunny warm          Tom Heflin

# Vegetables
# & Side Dishes

## Apples and Bacon
Serve with omelets or scrambled eggs                Serves 6

**3 large, tart apples**
**6 slices bacon, cooked,**
   **drained**
**4 T. sugar (approximate)**

Peel and core apples and slice thickly. Cook bacon in skillet having a tight-fitting lid. Remove bacon, leaving 1/4 cup bacon grease in skillet. Add apple slices which have been sprinkled with a light dusting of sugar. Cover; cook over low heat until apples are tender. Remove cover and turn apples carefully without breaking slices. Brown lightly. Serve on hot platter surrounded with bacon.

## Apple-Yambake
Great accompaniment to poultry                Serves 6-8

**2 apples, peeled, cored,**
   **and sliced**
**1/3 c. chopped pecans**
**1/2 c. packed brown**
   **sugar**
**1/2 t. cinnamon**
**2—17-oz. cans drained,**
   **halved yams**
**1/4 c. butter**
**1 c. miniature**
   **marshmallows**

Toss apples and nuts with brown sugar and cinnamon. Alternate layers of apples and yams in greased 1-1/2 qt. casserole dish. Dot with butter.

Cover and bake at 350° for 35-40 minutes. Sprinkle marshmallows over top and broil 2-3 minutes or until lightly browned.

## Hot Fruit Salad
Good with any egg dish and muffins                Serves 14

**1—16-oz. can purple**
   **plums**
**1—16-oz. can pears,**
   **quartered**
**1—16-oz. can peaches,**
   **quartered**
**1—16-oz. can pineapple**
   **chunks**
**1/2 c. maraschino**
   **cherries**
**1/2 c. brown sugar**
**1/4 c. butter, melted**
**1—20-oz. can applesauce**
**2 bananas, sliced**
**1/2 c. chopped nuts**
**1/4 c. brown sugar**

Drain plums, pears, peaches, pineapple, and cherries. Dissolve 1/2 cup brown sugar in melted butter. Pour over drained fruit in large casserole dish. Add applesauce. Refrigerate several hours. Just before baking, add bananas. Bake at 350° for 45 minutes. Sprinkle with nuts and 1/4 cup brown sugar and bake 15 minutes more. Serve hot.

## Curried Pears
Garnish with maraschino cherries or chopped peanuts          Serves 6

3 large ripe winter pears,
    unpeeled, halved
    and cored
3 T. butter, softened
3 T. brown sugar
3 t. curry powder
1/4 t. salt

Place pear halves in shallow baking dish. Combine butter, sugar, curry, and salt. Divide mixture into 6 parts. Place 1 part in cavity of each pear half. Bake at 350° for 30 minutes.

## Sherried Fruit Compote
Serve warm or cooled in individual dishes          Serves 12

2 lb. mixed dried fruit
8 c. cold water
2 c. sugar
juice of 2 lemons
1 c. dry sherry
2 c. cold water
3 T. cornstarch

Soak fruit overnight in enough warm water to cover. Next morning, drain. Add 8 cups cold water to fruit; stir in sugar and lemon juice. Bring to boil; lower heat and simmer until tender, about 30 minutes. Add sherry. In small bowl, blend cornstarch with additional 2 cups water; add to fruit and cook until bubbly and clear, 15-20 minutes.

## Artichoke-Spinach Casserole
Unique and delicious!          Serves 6-8

1—8-oz. jar marinated
    artichoke hearts,
    drained
2—10-oz. pkg. frozen
    chopped spinach,
    thawed
1 t. salt
1/4 t. pepper
1—8-oz. pkg. cream
    cheese, softened
2 T. butter, melted
1/4 c. milk
1/2 c. grated Parmesan
    cheese

Place artichokes in buttered 1-quart casserole. Press liquid from spinach and season with salt and pepper. Arrange spinach over artichokes. Beat cream cheese with butter and milk using electric mixer until smooth. Spoon over spinach. Top with Parmesan. Bake, covered, at 350° for 30 minutes. Uncover and bake 10 minutes longer.

## Fresh Asparagus Casserole
Also works with green beans or zucchini                    Serves 4

| | |
|---|---|
| 1 lb. fresh asparagus | Steam or microwave asparagus until tender. |
| 1/4 t. salt | Drain. Place in bottom of greased casserole. |
| 1/4 c. seasoned Italian bread crumbs | Sprinkle with salt, bread crumbs and Parmesan cheese. Dot with butter. |
| 1/4 c. Parmesan cheese | |
| 2 T. butter | Bake at 350° for 15 minutes. Serve immediately. |

## Quick Sauteed Fresh Asparagus
Garnish with toasted sesame seed or lemon peel                    Serves 6

| | |
|---|---|
| 1 lb. fresh asparagus | Wash asparagus; trim bottom ends. Cut spears into thirds on bias. Set aside. Place wok or heavy frying pan with a tightly-fitting lid over high heat. Sprinkle sugar in middle of pan; when it melts and edges begin to brown, add butter and oil. Add asparagus, salt, pepper. Stir quickly; distribute asparagus around edges of the pan so middle is empty. Cover; cook 2 minutes. Lower heat to medium. Remove cover; stir. Distribute asparagus throughout pan. Cover again; remove from heat. Let stand 5 minutes before serving. |
| 1/4 t. sugar | |
| 2 T. butter | |
| 1 T. corn oil | |
| 1/2 t. salt | |
| 1/8 t. cayenne pepper | |

## Festive Broccoli Platter
Very impressive for special occasions                    Serves 6

| | |
|---|---|
| 2—10-oz. pkg. frozen broccoli spears | Cook broccoli in salted water until barely tender. Drain well. Beat egg whites, salt, and onion powder together until stiff peaks form. Gently fold in mayonnaise. Arrange cooked broccoli spears in a circle with stems pointing towards the center on an oven-proof platter. Drizzle melted butter over broccoli. |
| 2 egg whites | |
| 1/4 t. salt | |
| 1/4 t. onion powder | |
| 1/3 c. mayonnaise | |
| 1 T. melted butter | |
| grated Parmesan cheese | |

Spoon mayonnaise mixture in the center of the platter, covering the broccoli stems. Sprinkle mixture with Parmesan cheese. Bake in 350° oven for 10-12 minutes or until topping is golden.

## Broccoli Florets in Cream
Same technique is delicious with cauliflower                Serves 6

4 c. fresh broccoli florets
2 T. olive oil
1 t. minced garlic
1/2 t. salt
1/4 t. pepper
1 c. whipping cream
1/2 c. freshly grated
  Parmesan cheese

Blanch broccoli in boiling water for 3 minutes. Drain well. Heat olive oil in large skillet; add garlic, broccoli, salt and pepper; saute 2 minutes, stirring often. Pour cream over broccoli; boil slowly, basting often, until cream is nearly absorbed. Fold in Parmesan cheese. Serve hot.

## Broccoli-Corn Casserole
A good winter vegetable dish                Serves 6-8

1—10-oz. pkg. frozen
  chopped broccoli,
  thawed
1/2 c. melted butter
1-1/2 c. coarsely crushed
  chicken-flavored
  crackers
1—16-oz. can cream-
  style corn
1—7-oz. can whole
  kernel corn, drained
1/2 t. salt
1/4 t. pepper

Drain broccoli. Mix butter with cracker crumbs; reserve 1/2 cup. Mix remaining crumbs with broccoli, corn, and seasonings. Turn into a buttered, shallow 1-1/2 quart casserole. Top with reserved crumbs.

Bake at 350° for 30 minutes.

## Broccoli with Pecans
Adds a crunchy contrast to any meat dish                Serves 8-10

4—10-oz. pkg. chopped
  frozen broccoli, or one
  large bunch fresh
  broccoli
1—8-oz. can water
  chestnuts, drained and
  sliced
1 c. chopped pecans
1 envelope dry onion
  soup mix
1 egg, beaten
3/4 c. bread crumbs
1/2 c. butter, melted

Cook broccoli according to package directions. (If using fresh broccoli, clean, then quarter the flowerets. Remove stems and slice diagonally in 1/4-inch slices. Boil 6-8 minutes, until almost tender.)

Drain broccoli; place in large mixing bowl. Stir in water chestnuts, pecans, soup mix, and egg. Spoon evenly into greased 13 x 9-inch baking dish. Cover surface with bread crumbs. Pour melted butter over crumbs. Bake at 350° for 30-40 minutes. Let stand a few minutes before serving, then cut in squares.

## B and B Excellence
A nice change from the ordinary                                   Serves 4-6

1—10-oz. pkg. frozen
  chopped broccoli
1—10-oz. pkg. frozen
  baby lima beans
1 can water chestnuts,
  sliced
1—10-oz. can cream of
  mushroom soup
1/2 c. sour cream
1/2 c. crisp rice cereal,
  lightly crushed
1/4 c. melted butter

Cook broccoli and lima beans until almost done. Mix water chestnuts, soup and sour cream. Add soup mix to broccoli and beans. Pour into greased 1-1/2-quart baking dish. Top with rice cereal. Pour melted butter over top. Bake at 350° for 45 minutes.

## Spiced Red Cabbage
For best flavor, must be made ahead                               Serves 6-8

1 small head red cabbage
2/3 c. water
2 T. butter
3 whole cloves
1 t. salt
2 tart apples, peeled,
  cored and sliced
2 T. butter
2 T. sugar
2 T. fresh lemon juice

Discard outer leaves of cabbage. Halve, core, rinse and shred cabbage.

Combine water and 2 T. butter in large skillet over medium heat. Add cabbage, cloves and salt; stir well. Add apple slices and stir to blend. Cover tightly, reduce heat to low, and simmer until cabbage is tender, about 45 minutes. Add 2 T. butter, sugar, and lemon juice, and continue simmering, covered, for 5 minutes. Cool. Cover and refrigerate overnight.

Before serving, remove cloves and heat through. Serve hot.

## Herbed Carrots
Serve garnished with fresh parsley                                Serves 4

2 T. butter
2 T. water
1 t. sugar
4 c. carrots, quartered
salt and pepper
1 t. chopped parsley
1/4 t. dried tarragon,
  crushed

In a heavy saucepan, combine butter, water, and sugar. Add carrots. cover tightly and cook over low heat 15-20 minutes. Check occasionally to be sure all water has not evaporated. If so, add a little more water. Season to taste. Sprinkle with parsley and tarragon. Do not drain.

## Carrots in Madeira
Makes everyone a carrot-lover                    Serves 6

1/4 c. olive oil
1 medium onion, sliced
1-1/2 lb. carrots, in
   1/4-inch slices
2 large cloves garlic,
   mashed
salt and pepper
paprika
1/4 c. beef bouillon
3/4 c. Madeira wine
1 T. chopped parsley

Heat olive oil in heavy saucepan; add onions and cook gently 3-4 minutes, stirring. Add carrots; cook slowly, covered, about 10 minutes, tossing from time to time. Add garlic; season with salt, pepper, and paprika. Simmer for 10 minutes.

Bring bouillon and wine to a boil. Pour over carrots; when liquid returns to a boil, reduce heat and finish cooking carrots, very slowly, uncovered, for about 15 minutes. Place in serving dish and sprinkle with parsley.

## Marinated Carrots
Adapted from a New England favorite                    Serves 8

5 c. carrots, cut on bias
1 onion, chopped
1 small green pepper,
   chopped
1—10-oz. can tomato
   soup
1/2 c. vegetable oil
1/2 c. cider vinegar
1/2 c. sugar
1 t. dry mustard
1 t. Worcestershire
   sauce
1/4 t. cayenne pepper

Cook carrots in salted boiling water until crisp-tender, 5-6 minutes. Combine remaining ingredients in large bowl. Drain carrots; while carrots are still hot, stir them into the marinade mixture. Refrigerate 24-48 hours. Toss several times. Serve cold.

## Cauliflower-Broccoli Marinade
May also include pitted ripe olives and red peppers                    Serves 8

1 large head cauliflower,
   in flowerets
1 large bunch broccoli,
   cut into 1-inch pieces
3/4 c. mayonnaise
1/4 c. sugar
1/2 c. salad oil
1/2 c. cider vinegar
1/2 t. salt
1/8 t. cayenne pepper

Place vegetables in large bowl or casserole. In large jar, combine remaining ingredients and shake until well blended; pour over vegetables. Cover; refrigerate at least 6 hours. Toss several times before serving.

## Celery Supreme
Add bean sprouts and cashews for an entree with steamed rice      Serves 8

6 c. diced celery
1/2 c. water
1 t. salt
1 can sliced water
  chestnuts, drained
1—2-oz. jar pimiento,
  drained
1/2 green pepper, diced
1—10-oz. can cream of
  celery soup

Topping:
1/4 c. melted butter
1 c. coarse bread crumbs
1/2 c. sliced almonds

Simmer celery in water and salt for 10 minutes; drain. Combine celery, water chestnuts, pimiento, green pepper, and soup. Mix gently. Place in greased 9 x 9-inch casserole.

Combine butter, crumbs, and almonds. Spread over celery mixture.

Bake at 350° for 30 minutes.

## Perfect Corn-on-the-Cob
Best if it's just-picked Illinois corn!      Serves 4-8

8 ears sweet corn,
  husked
1/2 t. sugar
butter and salt

In Dutch oven, pour in water to depth of about 3/4 inch. Cover. Bring to boil. Sprinkle sugar into water. Add corn, cover, and return to boil. Time exactly 3 minutes from time water returns to boil. Remove corn and place on warm platter. Serve immediately with butter and salt to taste.

## Corn Puff
A perfect partner with grilled breakfast meats      Serves 6

1 T. butter, melted
3 eggs, well-beaten
1—17-oz. can whole
  kernel corn, drained
1—17-oz. can cream-
  style corn
2 T. flour
1 c. milk
1 t. sugar
1/2 t. salt
1/8 t. pepper

Preheat oven to 350°. Combine all ingredients. Pour into greased 1-1/2-quart casserole dish. Place casserole in oven in pan of water. Bake, uncovered, 1 hour and 20 minutes, or until knife inserted comes out clean.

## Stuffed Eggplant

Impressive on a buffet or carried to a "pot-luck"                    Serves 6

1 medium eggplant
1 c. raw mushrooms
4 T. butter
1/2 c. chopped onion
1 c. minced smoked ham
1/4 t. salt
1/8 t. pepper
buttered bread crumbs
grated American or
   cheddar cheese

Cut slice from top of eggplant. Scoop out meat to within 1/2 inch of outer skin. Chop mushrooms and pulp of eggplant coarsely; saute in butter with onion and ham, about 10 minutes. Add seasonings.

Fill eggplant shell and sprinkle top with buttered bread crumbs.

Bake at 400°for 15 minutes. Top with cheese and bake 15 minutes more. Slice in wedges to serve.

## Garden Casserole

Especially fast with a food processor                    Serves 8-10

1 T. melted butter
2 c. fresh green beans,
   in 1-inch pieces
3 carrots, in thin strips
1 green pepper, in 1-inch
   pieces
1 onion, thinly sliced
2 c. sliced celery
1-1/2 t. salt
1/2 t. pepper
1 T. sugar
2 T. cornstarch
1—16-oz. can whole
   tomatoes, undrained,
   chopped
3 T. butter, softened

Pour melted butter into 3-quart baking dish or casserole to coat the surface. Layer the green beans, carrots, green pepper, onion, and celery in dish. In a small bowl combine salt, pepper, cornstarch, and sugar; sprinkle over vegetables. Top with tomatoes and dot with butter.

Bake at 350° for 1 hour or until vegetables are tender.

## Green-Garden Casserole

May be assembled early and refrigerated until needed          Serves 6-8

1—10-oz. pkg. frozen
  chopped spinach,
  thawed
2 T. oil
1-1/2 c. chopped,
  unpared zucchini
1—10-oz. pkg. frozen cut
  green beans, thawed
  (or 1-1/2 c. fresh cut
  green beans)
1 onion, chopped
1/4 c. water
1/2 t. garlic salt
1 t. salt
1/8 t. pepper
1-1/2 t. basil
1/8 t. nutmeg
4 eggs, beaten
1/4 c. Parmesan cheese,
  grated
paprika

Drain spinach. In skillet, cook spinach in hot oil 2-3 minutes. Add zucchini, beans, onion, water, and seasonings. Cover and simmer 10-12 minutes. Remove from heat. Gradually stir some of the hot liquid into the beaten eggs, then return egg mixture to skillet; mix well. Turn into greased 10x6x2-inch baking dish or casserole. Place in larger shallow pan with 1 inch water. Bake, uncovered, at 350° for 25-30 minutes. Sprinkle with Parmesan and paprika. Return to oven for 2-3 minutes more. Cut into squares to serve.

## Green Bean Casserole

Cold casserole is enhanced with garden-fresh tomatoes          Serves 6

4 slices bacon, diced
1 large onion, sliced,
  separated into rings
2 lb. fresh green beans,
  in 2-inch lengths
1-1/2 t. salt
1/4 t. pepper
1 c. mayonnaise
2 t. fresh horseradish
1 T. lemon juice
2 eggs, hard-cooked,
  sliced thinly

Combine bacon, onions, beans, salt, and pepper in large saucepan. Cover with water. Bring to boil; simmer 1 hour, uncovered. Drain. Combine mayonnaise, horseradish, lemon juice, and sliced eggs. Mix with green bean mixture. Pour into serving dish. Serve hot, or chill several hours to serve cold.

## Mushrooms Magnifique
Perfect for midnight breakfast                                    Serves 6

4 T. butter
1 medium onion, finely
   diced
1 lb. mushrooms, sliced
1/4 t. salt
1/8 t. pepper
1 t. paprika
1 t. lemon juice
1-1/2 c. sour cream
6 slices grilled ham
   (1/4-inch thick) or
   Canadian bacon
6 slices buttered toast
fresh parsley, minced

Melt butter in large skillet; add onion and saute until tender. Add mushrooms and saute until tender, but not limp. Add salt, pepper, paprika, lemon juice, and sour cream. Heat through gently—do not allow mixture to bubble. To serve, place a slice of grilled ham or Canadian bacon on each slice of buttered toast or toast points. Spoon mushrooms over ham and sprinkle with minced fresh parsley.

## Mushroom Souffle
Light and unusual for a main or side dish                  Serves 8-10

1 lb. mushrooms, sliced
1/2 c. butter
10 slices white bread,
   buttered, in 1-inch
   cubes
1/2 c. onion, finely
   chopped
1/2 c. celery, finely
   chopped
1/2 c. green pepper,
   finely chopped
1/2 c. mayonnaise
4 eggs, well beaten
1-1/2 c. milk
3/4 t. salt
1/4 t. pepper
1—10-oz. can cream of
   mushroom soup
1 c. grated cheddar
   cheese

Saute mushrooms in butter. Reserve. Put half the bread cubes in a shallow 2-quart baking dish. Combine mushrooms and remaining ingredients, except soup and cheese. Spoon over bread, top with half of remaining bread cubes. Refrigerate overnight. Before baking, spread soup over all. Top with remaining bread cubes and bake at 300° for 40 minutes; sprinkle with grated cheddar and bake 20 minutes more.

## Mushrooms Farci
Garnish a meat and vegetable platter with these          Serves 12

40 mushrooms, large
1/2 c. grated fresh
  Parmesan cheese
1/2 c. dry breadcrumbs
1/4 c. grated onion
2 small cloves garlic,
  minced
2 T. chopped parsley
1/2 t. salt
1/4 t. pepper
1/2 t. oregano
1/2 c. butter, melted

Clean mushrooms; trim stems; carefully remove stems from caps. Chop stems and mix with cheese, breadcrumbs, onion, garlic, parsley, salt, pepper, and oregano. Fill mushroom caps with this mixture. Do not overstuff. Place caps in shallow baking dish. Spoon butter evenly over mushrooms. (May be refrigerated at this point until baking.) Bake at 350° for 25 minutes. Serve immediately.

## Swiss Cheese Mushrooms
Great "make-ahead" side dish—tastes similar to pizza topping     Serves 8-10

2 lb. fresh mushrooms,
  in 1/4-inch slices
4 T. butter
2 t. lemon juice
2/3 c. sour cream
1/2 t. salt
1/4 t. freshly ground
  pepper
2 T. flour
1/4 c. chopped parsley
1-1/2 c. shredded
  Swiss cheese

In large skillet, saute mushrooms in butter. Cover and cook until mushrooms are just tender; drain. Sprinkle mushrooms with lemon juice. In small bowl, mix together sour cream, salt, pepper, and flour. Stir in mushrooms and blend well. Place mixture in 9x12x2-inch casserole dish. Sprinkle with parsley and shredded cheese. Cover and refrigerate. When ready to serve, bake at 450° for 10 minutes (or longer at lower temperature) to heat thoroughly.

## Onions Au Gratin
Easy, tasty companion for beef          Serves 4-6

2-1/2 c. sliced onions,
  (about 10 medium-
  sized onions)
4 T. butter
2-1/2 c. grated cheddar
  cheese, divided
1/3 c. packaged biscuit
  mix
1/4 t. salt
1/8 t. pepper
3 T. melted butter

Saute onions in 4 T. butter until tender. Mix onions with 2 cups cheese, biscuit mix, salt, pepper, and melted butter. Pour into greased 1-1/2 quart casserole. Sprinkle remaining 1/2 cup cheese on top and bake at 350° for 30 minutes.

## Spinach and Cheese Casserole
Dresses up the taste of spinach                                    Serves 6-8

1 T. butter
8 oz. sliced fresh
  mushrooms
1/4 c. chopped onion
3 chopped scallions
  (including greens)
1/4 t. garlic powder
1/2 t. dried dill weed
salt and pepper
3—10-oz. pkg. frozen
  chopped spinach,
  cooked,
  well drained
1—3-oz. cream cheese,
  softened
1 egg, beaten
1/2 c. shredded sharp
  cheddar cheese

Saute mushrooms, scallions and onions in butter 5 minutes. Add garlic powder, dill weed, and salt and pepper to taste. Stir in spinach, cream cheese and egg; mix well. Place in a buttered round 1-1/2-quart casserole dish; sprinkle with cheese. Bake at 350° for 20 minutes, until cheese is melted and casserole is hot.

## Spinach Casserole
Easy to make the night before a brunch                              Serves 6-8

4—10-oz. pkg. frozen
  chopped spinach,
  thawed and squeezed
  dry
2 c. sour cream
1 pkg. dry onion soup
  mix
2 c. bread stuffing mix
1/4 c. melted butter

In a large bowl, mix together dry spinach, sour cream and soup mix. Cover; refrigerate 8 hours or overnight. When ready to bake, place mixture in greased baking dish or casserole. Top with stuffing mix which has been tossed with melted butter.

Bake at 350° for 35-40 minutes.

## Delectable Spinach
A real fooler with "gourmet" taste                                 Serves 8

3—10-oz. pkg. frozen
  chopped spinach
1 c. sour cream
1/2 pkg. dry blue cheese
  salad dressing mix
1/4 c. Parmesan cheese

Cook spinach according to package directions. Drain well in sieve, pressing with spoon to extract all liquid. Mix spinach with sour cream and salad dressing mix. Place in 1-1/2-quart casserole dish. Sprinkle with Parmesan. Bake at 350° for 30 minutes.

## Elegant Spinach
May be made with green beans or peas                    Serves 6-8

2—10-oz. pkg. frozen
  chopped spinach
1—5-oz. can water
  chestnuts
1/2 c. cheese sauce
12 slices bacon
1—3-1/2-oz. can French-
  fried onion rings

Cheese sauce:
2 T. butter
2 T. flour
1/4 t. salt
1/8 t. pepper
1/4 t. dry mustard
1 c. milk
1/2 c. grated sharp
  American cheese

Cook and drain spinach. While spinach is cooking, make cheese sauce (below). Thinly slice water chestnuts. In mixing bowl, combine spinach, chestnuts, and 1/2 cup cheese sauce. Spread in greased 10 x 6-inch baking dish.

Fry bacon until crisp; drain on paper towel; crumble over spinach mixture. Spread remaining cheese sauce over all.

Bake, uncovered, at 350° for 15 minutes. Top with onion rings and bake an additional 5-10 minutes.

For cheese sauce:
Melt butter over low heat in heavy saucepan. Blend in flour and seasonings, stirring until smooth and bubbly. Stir in milk; bring to boil and boil 1 minute. Cook until thickened, stirring constantly; cook 3 minutes more. Blend in cheese, stirring until melted and mixture is smooth.

## Pumpkin Squash Bake
A natural with turkey                    Serves 8

1 c. canned pumpkin
1—10-oz. pkg. frozen
  winter squash, thawed
1-1/2 c. applesauce
1/4 c. brown sugar
1/2 c. heavy cream
2 eggs, beaten
1/2 t. salt
1/8 t. nutmeg
1/2 t. pumpkin pie spice
4 T. melted butter

Topping:
1/2 c. soft bread crumbs
1/2 c. ground almonds
2 T. melted butter

In a large bowl, mix together pumpkin, squash, applesauce, brown sugar, cream, eggs, salt, nutmeg, pumpkin pie spice, and 4 T. melted butter. Put into a shallow, buttered 2-quart casserole dish.

Mix together bread crumbs, ground almonds and 2 T. butter. Sprinkle over casserole.

Bake uncovered at 350° for 45 minutes. Serve hot.

## Saucy Squash Boats
A special treat with pork roast or chops                    Serves 4

2 medium acorn
  squash
4 slices bacon
2 c. applesauce, smooth
  or chunky
cinnamon

Cut each squash in half crosswise, trimming stem points to make level. Remove seeds. Place each half, cut-side down, on lightly greased baking sheet; bake at 350° for 35 minutes. Turn squash right-side up and place a piece of bacon in each, curving it around inside of squash. Continue baking at 350° for 25 minutes. Remove from oven and set bacon aside.

Spoon 1/2 cup applesauce into each cavity and sprinkle with cinnamon. If bacon needs crisping, set on baking sheet; otherwise, set it atop applesauce. Bake 10 minutes more at 350°. Crumble bacon over squash and serve immediately.

## Squash Casserole
Super side dish for chicken or turkey                    Serves 8

3—10-oz. pkg. frozen
  squash, thawed
1/4 c. melted butter
1 t. chicken bouillon
  granules
3 green onions, sliced
2 medium carrots, grated
1 c. sour cream
1—10-oz. can cream of
  chicken soup
1/4 c. butter
2 c. herb-seasoned
  bread stuffing mix,
  crumbled

In greased 3-quart casserole dish, combine squash, 1/4 cup melted butter, bouillon granules, green onion, carrots, sour cream, and soup. Stir to blend completely. In medium saucepan, melt remaining 1/4 cup butter; add stuffing crumbs and toss well to mix. Sprinkle crumbs over top of casserole. Bake at 350° for 40-45 minutes.

# Pennsylvania Dutch Fried Tomatoes
Delicious side dish for ham loaf                                    Serves 6

**4 large green tomatoes**
**1/2 c. flour**
**salt and pepper**
**2 T. butter**
**1/2 c. brown sugar**
**1 c. whipping cream**

Slice tomatoes lengthwise, in medium-thick slices, to maintain firmness. Coat in flour and season lightly with salt and pepper. Melt butter in large skillet; add tomatoes and fry quickly on both sides. Sprinkle with brown sugar. Continue frying until tomatoes are soft and easily pierced with a fork. Remove to warm plate.

Pour cream into skillet; turn heat to high and stir constantly until thick, smooth, and bubbling. If necessary, stir in an additional 1 T. flour to thicken. Season to taste.

Pour sauce over tomatoes and serve at once with fresh snipped parsley.

# Stuffed Tomatoes Florentine
To serve a dozen, simply stuff tomato halves                       Serves 6

**6 medium tomatoes,**
**  very ripe**
**1—8-oz. pkg. cream**
**  cheese, softened**
**2/3 c. sour cream**
**2 T. chopped onion**
**2 T. fresh dill**
**  (or 1 t. dillweed)**
**1 clove garlic, crushed**
**3 c. cooked spinach,**
**  drained, squeezed and**
**  chopped**
**salt and pepper**

Cut top slice off tomatoes. Scoop out pulp; set aside tomatoes. Put pulp in strainer; let drain for 1 hour.

In large bowl, combine cream cheese, sour cream, onion, dill, and garlic. Mash with fork until mixture is smooth. Add cooked spinach, salt and pepper. Mix until all ingredients are well blended. Chill 1 hour.

Stir drained pulp into chilled mixture. Stuff tomato shells with mixture. Bake at 350° for 20 minutes or until heated through.

## Herbed Tomato Casserole
Excellent with pork dishes                                    Serves 6-8

2 T. butter
6 green onions, sliced
  (use entire onion)
2 T. brown sugar
2—28-oz. cans tomatoes,
  undrained
1/2 t. salt
1/8 t. pepper
1/4 c. butter
2 T. brown sugar
2 c. herb-seasoned bread
  stuffing mix

In large saucepan, saute onions in 2 T. butter for 3 minutes. Stir in brown sugar until dissolved. Add tomatoes, breaking them up slightly with fork. Add salt and pepper. Pour into large, greased casserole or souffle dish. In same pan, melt remaining 1/4 cup butter; blend in 2 T. brown sugar and stir until dissolved. Add stuffing and toss with butter-sugar mix. Pour stuffing mix over tomatoes. Bake at 350° for 40 minutes.

## Sweet Potatoes with Mincemeat
Great with turkey, chicken, or ham                            Serves 6

6 large sweet potatoes
1/2 c. water reserved
  from cooking potatoes
1/2 c. brown sugar
1/2 c. butter, softened
1—16-oz. can
  mincemeat

Boil sweet potatoes in water to cover until fork pierces potatoes easily, about 30 minutes. Drain, reserving 1/2 c. cooking water. Cool and skin potatoes. Cut into halves or quarters. Remove center of each. Mix reserved water with brown sugar, butter and mincemeat. Fill center of sweet potatoes with mincemeat mixture.

Warm at 300° for 15-20 minutes before serving.

## Brandied-Candied Yams
Lovely at Thanksgiving, baked in hollowed-out oranges          Serves 8

1—2-1/2-lb. can sweet
  potatoes, drained
  (or 2-1/2 lb. yams,
  cooked in jackets until
  soft, cooled, skinned)
6 T. butter, melted
1 t. vanilla
1/2 t. salt
1/2 c. brown sugar
1/2 c. orange juice,
  made double strength
  from concentrate
3 T. brandy
2 eggs, slightly beaten

Topping:
1/2 c. brown sugar
2 T. flour
2 T. cold butter
1/4 t. cardamom or
  cinnamon
1/4 c. chopped pecans

Mash sweet potatoes in large mixing bowl. Add melted butter, vanilla, salt, brown sugar, orange juice, and brandy. Mix in eggs at medium speed until smooth. Turn into 11 x 7- inch shallow baking dish (or individual dishes). For Topping, cut butter into brown sugar, flour, and spices. When crumb-like, stir in pecans and sprinkle evenly over sweet potatoes.

Bake uncovered at 350° at least 30 minutes until potatoes are heated through and topping is golden brown.

## Cheesey-Zucchini Casserole
Serve with maple-barbequed pork and fruit          Serves 8

2 lb. medium zucchini,
  thinly sliced
1—4-oz. can
  mushrooms, drained,
  sliced
1 T. butter, melted
2 eggs, separated
1 c. sour cream
2 T. flour
1/2 t. salt
1-1/2 c. shredded,
  cheddar cheese
6 slices bacon, cooked,
  crumbled
1/4 c. dry bread crumbs
1 T. melted butter

Combine zucchini, mushrooms, and 1 T. butter in skillet. Cook over medium heat until zucchini is tender, stirring occasionally. Beat egg yolks; add sour cream, flour, and salt. Stir until blended. Beat egg whites until stiff. Fold into sour cream mixture.

Layer half squash mixture, half sour cream mixture, half cheese, and half bacon in 12 x 8- inch baking dish. Repeat layers. Sprinkle with bread crumbs; drizzle 1 T. melted butter over. Bake at 350° for 25 minutes.

## Zucchini Canoes

Results are worth the extra preparation time                    Serves 6

3 slices bacon
6 medium zucchini
1 egg, slightly beaten
1/4 c. whipping cream
1 c. shredded Swiss
  cheese
1/8 t. nutmeg
salt and pepper
2 T. dry bread crumbs

In skillet, cook bacon until crisp. Drain on paper towels; crumble and set aside (reserve fat in skillet). Cut thin slice lengthwise from each zucchini; with teaspoon, hollow out each zucchini in canoe shape, reserving pulp. Blanch "canoes" in boiling water for 2 minutes; drain and set aside.

Chop reserved zucchini pulp; saute in bacon drippings until crisp-tender; combine with bacon, egg, cream, cheese, and nutmeg. Add salt and pepper to tast. Sprinkle 1 t. bread crumbs into each canoe. Fill with zucchini mixture. Place in shallow baking dish. Pour 1 inch hot water into dish.

Bake at 350° for 30 minutes, or until knife inserted in zucchini mixture comes out clean.

## Zucchini in Dill Cream

Great for accompanying seafood entrees                    Serves 6-8

7 c. unpared zucchini
  strips, in 3-inch
  lengths
1/4 c. chopped onion
1/2 c. water
1 t. salt
1 t. instant chicken
  bouillon granules
1/2 t. dillweed
2 T. butter, melted
2 t. sugar
1 t. lemon juice
2 T. flour
1/2 c. sour cream

In large saucepan, simmer zucchini, onion, water, salt, bouillon, and dillweed 5 minutes. Do not drain. Add butter, sugar, and lemon juice. Blend flour into sour cream. Stir half of the hot squash liquid into sour cream. Blend, then return all to pan. Cook over low heat just until bubbly.

Pour into heated serving bowl and serve immediately.

# Zucchini-Rice Casserole
Good way to use leftover rice                                    Serves 6

2 lb. small zucchini
1/4 c. butter
1/4 c. vegetable oil
1-1/2 c. cooked rice
1/2 c. freshly grated
   Parmesan cheese
1/2 c. grated sharp
   cheddar cheese
salt and pepper
2 eggs, slightly beaten
3/4 c. dry bread crumbs
4 T. melted butter

Cut ends from zucchini and steam until tender. Reserve 2 zucchini for garnish, then dice remaining zucchini. Combine butter and oil in Dutch oven; heat until butter is melted. Add rice and diced zucchini; saute until golden, stirring often. Stir in cheese until melted; add seasonings. Cool slightly; stir in eggs quickly. Pour into a greased shallow baking dish. Sprinkle generously with bread crumbs. Slice reserved zucchini and arrange slices on end around sides of the dish. Drizzle melted butter over top. Broil 6 inches from heat until lightly browned and bubbly.

# Sauce for Vegetables
Leftover sauce is great on sandwiches                          Makes 1 cup

1 c. sour cream
   (at room temperature)
1 T. prepared yellow
   mustard
1 T. fresh lime juice
2 T. chopped parsley
dash cayenne pepper
1/4 t. salt

In small bowl, blend all ingredients. Spoon over hot vegetables. Serve at once.

# Serundang (for Curry)
Good with any curry recipe                                       Serves 8

1/2 c. shredded coconut
4 T. butter
4 T. brown sugar
1 t. ground coriander
1/2 t. cumin
1 c. salted peanuts

In medium saucepan, brown coconut lightly in butter. Add sugar. Stir well. Add seasonings and peanuts. Heat through. Cool. Serve with fruit and curry.

Leftover mixture will keep one week in tightly closed container. Do not refrigerate.

## Sensational Au Gratin Potatoes

Any cream soup may be substituted to vary the flavor          Serves 8

1—2-lb. pkg. frozen
   country-style hash
   brown potatoes,
   thawed
1/2 c. melted butter
1 c. sour cream
2 T. minced green onion
1/4 t. garlic powder
1—10-oz. can cheddar
   cheese soup
1 c. shredded cheddar
   cheese
parsley for garnish

Combine all ingredients except shredded cheddar cheese in large mixing bowl. Stir to mix. Pour into greased 13 x 9-inch baking dish. Sprinkle with shredded cheddar cheese. Cover tightly with foil; bake at 350° for 1 hour. Garnish with parsley before serving.

## Cruzan Potatoes

Smoked meats may be added for a one-dish meal          Serves 8-10

1/2 c. butter
1 c. chopped onion
1 c. chopped green
   pepper
1 c. celery
1 c. raisins
1—6-oz. can tomato
   paste
2 T. crushed thyme
2 drops hot pepper sauce
6 eggs, beaten
6 c. prepared mashed
   potatoes

In large skillet, saute onions, peppers, and celery in butter for about 10 minutes. Stir in raisins. Blend in tomato paste, thyme and hot pepper sauce. In a separate bowl, mix eggs with potatoes. Combine both mixtures and pour into an 8 x 10-inch baking dish.

Bake at 350° for 25-30 minutes, or until firm.

## Potatoes Baked in Cream

May also be baked in foil on the grill          Serves 12

5 lb. potatoes, peeled
1/2 c. melted butter
1 T. salt
2 c. half and half cream
4 oz. sharp cheddar
   cheese, grated

Several hours before serving, boil potatoes in salted water until tender. Drain well and refrigerate until chilled. Peel and grate cooked potatoes; place in buttered 9 x 13-inch baking dish. Add melted butter, salt, and half and half. Top with grated cheddar cheese. Bake uncovered at 350° for 25-30 minutes.

## Breakfast Potato Casserole
Increase baking time 10 minutes if casserole is cold                    Serves 6

2 lb. potatoes,
   unpeeled
6 oz. Canadian bacon,
   sliced
1/3 c. chopped green
   onion
1 c. shredded sharp
   cheddar cheese
5 eggs, beaten
1 c. milk
3/4 t. salt
1/2 t. marjoram
1/8 t. pepper
snipped parsley
   for garnish

Cook potatoes in water until tender, about 40 minutes. Peel and slice 1/4-inch thick. Cut bacon slices in half. In buttered 11 x 7-inch baking dish, alternate slices of potato and bacon. Sprinkle onion, then cheese over top. Combine eggs, milk, and seasonings; pour over all. Casserole may be refrigerated overnight at this point.

Bake at 375° for 35 minutes or until knife inserted near center comes out clean. Garnish with parsley.

## Hash Brown Casserole
Easy to make ahead and bake just before serving                    Serves 12

1—2-lb. bag frozen hash
   brown potatoes,
   thawed
1/2 c. margarine, melted
1 c. chopped onions
1 c. shredded cheddar
   cheese
1—10-oz. can cream of
   chicken soup
1 t. salt
1 t. garlic salt
2 c. sour cream

Topping:
1/4 c. margarine, melted
2 c. crushed corn flakes

Mix all casserole ingredients together. Put into greased 9 x 13-inch pan. Mix topping ingredients. Sprinkle on casserole. Bake at 350° for 1-1/2 hours, uncovered.

## Baked Potatoes Romano
Sour cream, chives or paprika may be beaten in          Serves 12

10 medium potatoes,
   peeled and
   quartered
1/3 c. butter
2/3 c. milk
3 egg yolks
1—8-oz. pkg. cream
   cheese, softened
1/2 c. grated Romano or
   Parmesan cheese

Cook potatoes in water until tender. Drain well. Place in large mixing bowl with butter, milk, and egg yolks. Beat until well blended and no lumps remain. Beat in cream cheese. Pour into well-greased, large casserole dish having high sides. Sprinkle with cheese.

To serve, bake at 350° for 25-30 minutes. If preparing ahead, cover and refrigerate. When ready to serve, bake at 350° for 45 minutes.

## Potatoes Savoyarde
Serve with beef, poultry or eggs          Serves 8

8 large potatoes
4 T. butter
salt and pepper
2 c. beef broth (or more)
1 c. grated Gruyere
   cheese
fresh snipped parsley

Peel and slice potatoes thinly. Generously butter a 9 x 13-inch baking pan. Place a layer of potatoes in pan; season with salt and pepper to taste. Continue adding layers, seasoning each. Dot the top layer with butter. Pour in enough beef broth to cover potatoes.

Bake at 350° for 45 minutes until potatoes are tender. If too much liquid remains, pour off most of it. Sprinkle with grated Gruyere and return to oven until the cheese browns nicely and potatoes are thoroughly cooked, about 15 minutes more.

Garnish with snipped fresh parsley.

## Stuffed Baked Potatoes
May be assembled ahead and reheated just before serving          Serves 4

**2 large Idaho baking
  potatoes
4 strips bacon, quartered
1/4 c. chopped shallots
2 T. grated Parmesan
  cheese
1/2 c. sour cream
1/2 t. salt
1/2 t. white pepper
1 T. melted butter
paprika**

Scrub potatoes well and bake for one hour at 400° (or microwave until tender). Fry bacon pieces until crisp. Drain off all but 3 T. bacon fat. Add shallots to fat and saute slowly. Remove skillet from heat.

Cut potatoes in half lengthwise and scoop insides into skillet without breaking potato skins. Add cheese, sour cream, salt and pepper to potato, shallot and bacon mixture, mashing to blend thoroughly. Return skillet to low heat and heat through. Stuff mixture into potato skins, drizzle with melted butter, and sprinkle with paprika. Bake 15-20 minutes at 350°.

## Garlic-Cheese Grits
Serve as a side dish with eggs or meat          Serves 6-8

**1-1/2 c. quick-cooking
  grits, cooked
2 eggs, beaten
1 c. garlic-flavored
  cheese spread
1/2 c. butter
paprika**

Grease 3-qt. casserole dish. Add eggs, 3/4 cup cheese and butter to grits. Mix well. Pour into prepared dish. Top with remaining 1/4 cup cheese. Sprinkle with paprika.

Bake 1 hour at 350°.

## Baked Rice
After cooking, pack into buttered mold and unmold immediately    Serves 6

**1/4 c. butter
1/4 c. chopped green
  onion
2-1/2 c. chicken broth
1 c. rice
1 c. golden raisins
1/4 c. minced parsley
1/2 c. sunflower seeds**

Melt butter in medium skillet over medium heat. Add onion and saute until slightly softened. Transfer to 2-quart baking dish. Stir in chicken broth, rice, raisins and parsley. Cover tightly and bake at 350° until broth has been absorbed, about 45 minutes.

Using fork, mix in sunflower seeds. Serve immediately.

## Hot Mexican Rice Ring
Colorful and spicy                                                   Serves 8

2 c. cooked rice
1 c. shredded Monterey
　　Jack cheese
1—4-oz. can green chile
　　peppers, drained
　　and chopped
1 t. salt
1 t. pepper
2 c. sour cream
1/4 c. chopped pimiento,
　　drained
2 T. chopped green
　　pepper

Mix all ingredients together and spoon into a small, buttered ring mold. Bake at 350° for 30 minutes. Remove from oven and let stand 5 minutes before unmolding onto serving dish.

## Old-Fashioned Rice Pudding
Makes a custard layer, delicately flavored                       Serves 10

1/2 t. vanilla
7 eggs, slightly beaten
1/2 c. sugar
1/2 t. salt
1/2 c. golden raisins
1 c. cooked rice
4 c. milk, scalded
nutmeg

Mix together vanilla, eggs, sugar, salt, raisins, rice, and milk. Pour into deep, greased casserole. Sprinkle nutmeg on top. Bake uncovered at 450° for 5 minutes, then bake at 325° for 20 minutes. Turn off oven and allow pudding to sit in oven at least 30 minutes, until knife comes out clean. Serve warm or chilled.

## Rice with Black Olives
Easy side dish with seafood or poultry                         Serves 4-6

1—6-oz. pkg. long grain
　　and wild rice,
　　uncooked
1 medium tomato,
　　chopped
3/4 c. water
1/2 c. butter, melted
1 medium onion,
　　chopped
1—5-oz. can pitted black
　　olives, sliced
1/2 lb. American cheese,
　　cubed

Mix all ingredients except cheese in 8 x 8-inch casserole dish. Sprinkle cheese on top. Cover; bake at 350° for 1 hour 15 minutes.

# Risotta alla Milanese (Braised Rice with Saffron)

Compliments of Jake Cason and *Maria's*,
a Rockford favorite for Italian cuisine                     Serves 6-8

**7 c. chicken stock, fresh
or canned
4 T. butter
1/2 c. finely chopped
onions
2 c. plain white raw rice,
preferably imported
Italian rice
1/2 c. dry white wine
1/8 t. powdered saffron
or saffron threads
crushed to a powder
4 T. butter, softened
1/2 c. freshly grated
imported Parmesan
cheese**

Bring the chicken stock to a simmer in a 3-quart saucepan and keep it barely simmering over low heat.

In a heavy 3-quart flameproof casserole, melt 4 T. butter over moderate heat. Cook onions in butter, stirring frequently, for 7-8 minutes. Do not let them brown.

Stir the rice into the onions and cook for 1 minute, or until the grains glisten with butter and are somewhat opaque. Pour in the wine and boil until it is almost completely absorbed. Then add 2 cups of the simmering stock and cook, stirring occasionally, uncovered, until almost all of the liquid is absorbed. Add 2 more cups of stock and cook, stirring occasionally.

Meanwhile, stir the saffron into 2 cups of stock and let it steep for a few minutes. Then pour it over the rice. Cook until the stock is completely absorbed. By now, the rice should be tender. If it is still firm, add the remaining stock, 1/2 cup at a time, and continue cooking and stirring until the rice is soft.

Stir in 4 T. butter and the grated cheese with a fork, taking care not to mash the rice. Serve at once while rice is creamy and piping hot.

## Stroganoff Wild Rice
Easily doubled or tripled for a crowd                                Serves 6

1 T. melted butter
1/2 c. sliced onion
4 oz. fresh mushrooms,
  cleaned, sliced
2-1/2 c. water
1 T. ketchup
1/2 t. Kitchen Bouquet
1—6-oz. pkg. long grain
  and wild rice
2/3 c. sour cream

In large saucepan, saute onion and mushrooms in butter until tender, about 3 minutes. Add water, ketchup, and Kitchen Bouquet. Stir in both packets from rice package. Bring to boil, then cover and simmer 25 minutes. Just before serving, stir in sour cream.

## Shanghai-Style Fried Rice
Only a salad is needed to complete a light Chinese meal        Serves 6-8

4 T. vegetable oil
3 eggs, slightly beaten
3-4 c. cooked long-grain
  rice
1/2 c. frozen peas
2 scallions, chopped

Options:
1/2 c. chopped Chinese
  ham, or 1/2 c. chopped
  cooked shrimp, or
  1/2 c. shredded
  leftover roast pork

Heat empty wok. Heat 2 T. oil in hot wok; add eggs. Saute, stirring lightly, only until all liquid is gone (do not overcook) and remove immediately onto wooden board. Slice into thin strips. Add 2 T. remaining oil to wok; heat. Add cooked rice and stir-fry 2 minutes. Add peas, scallions, and meat to rice in wok; stir-fry 2 minutes. Stir in eggs and stir fry briefly. Serve on warm platter.

## Sweet Koogle
A wonderful alternative to rice or potatoes                   Serves 12-16

1—8-oz. pkg. wide
  noodles, cooked
1/2 c. butter, softened
1—8-oz. pkg. cream
  cheese, softened
1/8 t. salt
6 T. sugar
4 eggs, beaten
1-3/4 c. milk

Drain noodles well. Set aside. Beat butter and cream cheese; add salt, sugar, and eggs. Add milk and blend well. Stir in drained noodles. (Mixture will be very runny.) Pour into a greased 9 x 13-inch baking dish and bake for 45 minutes at 350°.

Serve hot or chilled. May be wrapped well and frozen.

CHRISTMAS '83
getting presents wrapped for christmas once again, but this
year there are gifts for our first grandchild.

tom heflin    thursday december 22, 1988 sunny, cold 1:30

# Desserts

## Deep Dark Secret
Best served with a large spoon                    Serves 10-12

12 oz. chopped dates
1 c. chopped pecans
4 eggs, separated
1 c. sugar
2 t. vanilla
1/2 c. flour
1 t. baking powder
1/4 t. salt

Topping:
3-4 bananas, peeled and
     sliced
2 oranges, peeled and
     sliced
1—16-oz. can crushed
     pineapple, undrained
1 c. whipping cream,
     whipped
maraschino cherries

Mix dates and pecans; set aside. Beat egg yolks with sugar until light; add vanilla. Stir in sifted dry ingredients. Beat egg whites just until stiff; fold into yolk mixture with dates and pecans. Spread in a greased and floured 9 x 13-inch pan. Bake at 350° for 30-40 minutes. Cool.

To assemble, break up half the cake and arrange it flat on a large platter. Top with bananas and oranges. Break up the remaining half of the cake and mound it on top of fruit. Pour crushed pineapple and juice over the whole cake. Frost with whipped cream. Decorate with cherries. Refrigerate at least 2 hours, or overnight.

## Chocolate Eclairs
Nice served on paper doilies                        Serves 10

2—3-oz. pkg. regular
     chocolate pudding mix
3 c. milk
3 T. Grand Marnier
1 c. water
1/2 c. butter
1 c. flour
4 eggs
1 c. whipping cream,
     whipped
1/3 c. chocolate chips
1/4 c. evaporated milk
1 c. powdered sugar
1 t. light corn syrup
1/2 t. vanilla

Prepare pudding according to package directions using 3 cups milk. Remove from heat; stir in Grand Marnier. Cover and refrigerate. Heat water and butter in a 3-quart saucepan to boiling. Stir in flour and cook until mixture forms a ball and leaves sides of the pan. Remove from heat. Beat in eggs one at a time until smooth. Shape dough into finger shapes, by dropping heaping tablespoons, 3 to 4 inches long, onto greased cooking sheet. Bake 35-40 minutes at 400° Cool.

Fold whipped cream into chilled chocolate pudding mixture. Cut off tops of eclairs and save. Spoon out any soft dough and discard. Fill eclairs with pudding mixture; replace tops. Heat chocolate chips and evaporated milk over low heat until melted. Remove from heat. Stir in sugar, corn syrup and vanilla until smooth. Use chocolate mixture to frost eclairs. Refrigerate until serving.

## Chocolate Icebox Pudding

May also be layered in parfait glasses                    Serves 12

18 ladyfingers or one
   spongecake
4—1-oz. squares
   unsweetened chocolate
1/4 c. hot water
3/4 c. sugar
pinch of salt
4 egg yolks
1 t. vanilla
4 egg whites, stiffly
   beaten
1 c. whipping cream,
   whipped
3 T. powdered sugar

Line bottom and sides of 9-inch springform pan with ladyfingers or spongecake. In double boiler, melt chocolate. To the chocolate add water, sugar and salt. Stir until sugar is dissolved and mixture blends. Remove top of double boiler from the heat and egg yolks one at a time, beating after each one. Place over boiling water again and cook 2 minutes or until thick, stirring constantly. Remove from heat; add vanilla and fold in egg whites. Pour immediately into lined springform pan and chill overnight. Before serving cover with whipped cream, sweetened with powdered sugar.

## Chocolate Fondue

Easy, fast and fun                                          Serves 6

4—1-oz. squares
   unsweetened chocolate
1/2 c. butter
2-1/4 c. powdered sugar
2/3 c. evaporated milk
2 T. dark rum

Dippers:
Chunks of bananas,
   apples, pineapple,
   peaches, strawberries,
   mandarin oranges and
   pound cake

In top of double boiler, mix chocolate, butter, powdered sugar and evaporated milk. Cook over simmering water 30 minutes, stirring often. Pour into mixer or blender and beat until smooth. Stir in rum. Serve warm with an assortment of dippers. Spear fruit or cake on fork and twirl in chocolate.

## Barb's Chocolate Mousse

Peppermint flavoring may replace bourbon                    Serves 6-8

1 c. chocolate chips
2 egg yolks
3 T. bourbon
1-1/4 c. milk or cream,
   warmed

Mix all ingredients in blender container, blending until smooth. Pour into individual serving dishes. Chill 3 hours.

## Triple Chocolate Sin
Don't count the calories—just the compliments                     Serves 10

**Crust:**
1-1/4 c. graham cracker
  crumbs
3 T. sugar
3 T. unsweetened cocoa
1/3 c. butter or
  margarine, melted

**Cheese Layer:**
12 oz. cream cheese,
  softened
3/4 c. sugar
2 eggs
1 T. vanilla
1 T. creme de cocoa
1 c. sour cream
1 oz. unsweetened
  chocolate, finely
  grated

**Chocolate Layer:**
1-1/2 t. instant coffee
2 T. boiling water
4—1-oz. squares
  semisweet chocolate
4 eggs, separated
1/3 c. sugar
1/2 t. vanilla
2 T. dark rum, divided
1 c. whipping cream
shaved chocolate for
  garnish

For crust: In a 9-inch pie pan, combine crumbs, sugar and cocoa; add butter or margarine and stir until well coated. Press mixture into bottom and sides of pan. Bake at 350° for 8 minutes; cool slightly.

For cheese layer: In large mixer bowl, beat cream cheese and sugar until light and fluffy; add eggs, one at a time, and continue beating until well mixed. Stir in vanilla and liqueur. Pour mixture into baked pie crust. Bake for 30 minutes at 350°. Cool exactly 10 minutes; evenly spread sour cream over baked cheese layer. Sprinkle on grated unsweetened chocolate. Refrigerate.

For chocolate layer: Meanwhile, in top of double boiler, dissolve coffee in boiling water. Add chocolate and melt over hot (not boiling) water, stirring until smooth. In small bowl, beat egg yolks until thick and lemon colored; gradually add sugar and continue beating until a light yellow. Stir in chocolate mixture, vanilla and 1 T. rum until well mixed. In another small bowl, beat egg whites until stiff peaks form. Stir 1/4 of egg whites into chocolate mixture. Gently fold chocolate mixture into remaining egg whites. Refrigerate mixture until cheese layer is chilled. Evenly spread chocolate mixture over cheese layer; chill.

To serve, whip cream until stiff peaks form; add remaining T. rum. Spread cream over chocolate layer. Sprinkle with shaved chocolate.

## Chocolate Sundae Crunch

Children will enjoy helping with this                          Serves 6-8

1 c. flour
1/4 c. brown sugar
1/2 c. butter
1/2 c. chopped pecans
1—3-oz. pkg. instant
  vanilla pudding
2 c. milk
1 pint vanilla ice cream
1/4 t. almond extract

Topping:
1/2 c. chocolate chips
1/2 c. miniature
  marshmallows
3 T. whole or evaporated
  milk

Combine flour and brown sugar; cut in butter until crumbly; add nuts. Pat into a 9-inch square pan. Bake at 350° for 25 minutes or until golden. Cool completely. Crumble mixture and save 1/2 cup for the topping. Lightly press remaining crumbs into same pan. Combine pudding mix with milk; beat at low speed until blended. Add ice cream and almond extract; blend until smooth. Pour over crumb base. Sprinkle remaining crumb mixture over the pudding mixture. Melt chocolate chips, marshmallows and milk in saucepan or microwave until smooth. Drizzle over the top of crumbs. Chill at least 2 hours.

## Eggnog Dessert

Attractive in a ring mold                                      Serves 8

2 T. unflavored gelatin
1/2 c. cold water
1 qt. eggnog, divided
2 T. rum
2 c. whipping cream,
  whipped

Sauce:
1—12-oz. box frozen
  raspberries, thawed,
  undrained
1/2 c. currant jelly
1 T. cornstarch

Soften gelatin in water. Heat 1 cup of the eggnog. Pour gelatin over and stir to dissolve. Add remaining eggnog and rum. Fold cream into eggnog mixture. Pour into mold; chill until set.

For sauce, mix all ingredients in saucepan. Heat until bubbly and thickened. Strain to remove seeds; chill. Spoon over dessert just before serving.

## Light Cream Dessert
Serve with favorite sauce                                    Serves 6

3/4 c. fine sugar
1/2 c. cold water
1 T. unflavored gelatin
1 c. whipping cream
1-1/2 c. sour cream
1 t. vanilla

Combine sugar, water and gelatin. Let stand 4 to 5 minutes. Place over medium heat until it comes to a boil. Remove from heat; gradually blend in unwhipped cream. Combine sour cream and vanilla in a separate bowl. Gradually add warm mixture to sour cream mixture. Whisk until smooth. Pour into custard cups or ramekins. Refrigerate at least 4 hours.

## Four Seasons Fruit
Arrange fruit in circles or spokes                           Serves 8

**Shell:**
1/4 c. soft butter
2 T. sugar
3 T. almond paste
1/2 t. grated lemon peel
1 egg white
3/4 c. sifted flour

**Pastry Cream:**
1—3-oz. pkg. vanilla
   pudding mix
1-1/2 c. milk
1 t. vanilla
4 ladyfingers, split
2 t. Kirsch

**Apricot Glaze:**
1/2 c. apricot preserves
2 T. water
13 banana slices,
   cut diagonally
1/3 c. fresh raspberries
1/3 c. seedless green
   grapes
8 fresh strawberries,
   halved
1/4 c. fresh blueberries

For shell, grease and flour an 8 x 1-1/2-inch round layer cake pan. In a small bowl at medium speed, cream butter, sugar, almond paste and lemon peel until well combined. Add the egg white and beat at high speed until smooth. Gradually beat in flour. With fingers, press evenly onto bottom and sides of pan. Bake shell at 300° for 50 minutes or until golden brown.

For pastry cream, combine pudding mix with milk in a small saucepan and cook as package directs. Remove from heat and put in a bowl to cool; add vanilla. Place a sheet of waxed paper on surface of pudding. Refrigerate until cooled. Spread half of the pastry cream over the bottom of the shell. Arrange split ladyfingers on top of cream. Sprinkle with Kirsch; cover with remainder of the cream.

Apricot glaze: In a small saucepan, heat apricot preserves with water. Stir until melted; strain and cool. Arrange fruit decoratively over cream; brush surface with glaze. Refrigerate until serving.

## Fruit Pizza
Beautifully easy

Serves 12

**Crust:**
**1 roll sugar cookie dough**

**Icing:**
**8 oz. cream cheese**
**1/2 c. sugar**
**1 t. vanilla**

**Fruit:**
**mandarin oranges**
**bananas, sliced**
**pineapple tidbits**
**seedless grapes**
**strawberries, sliced**
**walnuts, chopped**
**blueberries**

**Glaze:**
**1/2 c. apricot preserves**
**1 T. hot water**

For crust, slice cookie dough into 1/8-inch thick slices. Overlap the cookie slices on a cookie sheet or pizza pan and press into a 10-inch circle. Bake at 375° for 12 minutes; cool completely.

For icing, mix all ingredients well and spread on cooled crust.

For fruit, cover icing with mandarin oranges and bananas. Top with pineapple, grapes, strawberries and blueberries. Sprinkle with walnuts.

For glaze, mix well and spoon over fruit. Cover with plastic wrap and refrigerate until chilled.

## Fruit Blintzes
Serve warm or chilled

Makes 14-16

**2 eggs**
**1 c. milk**
**2 T. butter, melted and**
 **cooled**
**1/2 t. salt**
**1/8 t. nutmeg**
**1/2 c. flour**
**1 can fruit pie filling,**
 **any flavor**

Beat eggs, milk, butter and seasonings. Gradually add flour, beating until smooth. Refrigerate, covered at least 2 hours. Heat a 6-inch skillet and grease lightly. Put 2 T. butter in hot pan and rotate to cover whole pan evenly. Cook until lightly browned on bottom side. Turn out on waxed paper. Fill with 1 T. pie filling and roll up, tucking in ends. Repeat with remaining batter.

## Jim's Favorite Dessert
Different idea for a special birthday cake          Serves 12

8 eggs whites, at room
   temperature
1-1/2 t. vanilla
1 t. vinegar
2 c. sugar

**Filling:**
1 c. crushed pineapple,
   drained
3/4 c. maraschino
   cherries, drained well
   and quartered
2 c. whipping cream,
   whipped, divided

Beat egg whites with vanilla and vinegar until soft peaks form. Beat in sugar, one T. at a time. Beat until very stiff. Pour into two buttered 9-inch round cake pans; smooth tops; bake at 300° for 1-1/4 hours. Remove from oven and let cool in pans. Meringues will fall and crack. When cool, carefully remove from pans. Trim edges to form even layers.

For filling, mix pineapple and cherries into half of whipped cream. Spread on one meringue layer. Top with second layer; cover top with remaining plain whipped cream. Transfer to serving plate and chill 8 hours or overnight.

## Lemon Angel Fluff
Garnish with twisted lemon slices          Serves 12-15

1 large angel food cake
6 T. butter, softened
1-1/2 c. powdered sugar
4 eggs, separated
3 T. lemon juice
2 c. whipping cream,
   whipped, divided
1/2 of 7-oz. pkg. coconut

Slice cake into 1/2-inch slices. Set aside. Beat together butter and powdered sugar. Beat in egg yolks one at a time. Add lemon juice. In a separate bowl, beat egg whites until stiff; then fold into lemon mixture. Fold in half of whipped cream.

Line the bottom of a 9 x 13-inch pan with cake; cover with half the lemon mixture. Repeat, to make 3 layers of cake and 2 layers of filling. Spread remaining half of whipped cream over top layer of cake. Sprinkle with coconut. Cover and refrigerate several hours or overnight.

# Peach Melba Trifle
Vary this with seasonal fruits

Serves 8

**Custard:**
1 c. sugar
1 t. salt
1/2 c. cornstarch
4 c. milk
4 eggs, beaten
4 t. vanilla
3 T. butter

**Layers:**
1 small angel food cake
1/4 c. Triple Sec liqueur
1 pt. fresh raspberries
4 peaches, peeled, sliced
  and dipped in ascorbic
  acid color-keeper

**Topping:**
1 c. whipping cream
3 T. sugar

In saucepan, mix together sugar, salt and cornstarch. Stir in milk. Cook over low heat, stirring constantly, until mixture boils. Boil 1 minute. Remove from heat. Stir 1/2 cup of milk mixture into eggs; blend eggs into hot mixture in saucepan. Cook and stir over low heat just until mixture comes to the boiling point. Cool slightly; stir in vanilla and butter. Cool well before using.

To assemble dessert, cut cake into 1-inch cubes and sprinkle with Triple Sec. Reserve a few raspberries for garnish. In a large, clear glass bowl, layer 1/3 each of cake, custard, raspberries and peach slices. Repeat layers twice more, ending with fruit. Chill 4 hours or overnight. To serve, whip cream and sweeten with sugar. Top dessert with cream and reserved raspberries.

# Rhubarb Dessert
A tempting tart

Serves 12

**Crust:**
2 c. flour
2 t. sugar
1 c. butter or margarine

**Filling:**
1-1/2 c. sugar
2 T. flour
1—20-oz. pkg. frozen
  rhubarb (or 4-6 c.
  fresh), cut up
1/2 c. milk
juice of 1 orange
3 egg yolks, beaten

**Meringue:**
3 egg whites, stiffly
  beaten
6 T. sugar

For crust, mix flour, sugar and butter until crumbly; pat into a 9 x 13-inch pan. Bake 15 to 20 minutes at 375° or until golden brown.

For filling, put sugar and flour in a heavy 3-quart saucepan. Add rhubarb, milk and orange juice; cook until rhubarb is tender and mixture is fairly thick. Remove from heat and add egg yolks; return to heat. Cool. Pour filling on top of crust. Beat sugar into egg whites; spread over filling. Bake at 350° for 12 to 15 minutes or until meringue is golden brown. Cool.

## Strawberry/Raspberry Cream Puffs
Puffs may also be filled with chocolate mousse          Serves 6

1 c. water
6 T. butter (do not
  substitute)
1 c. flour
1/2 t. salt
3/4 c. eggs (4-5 large
  eggs)
1 qt. strawberries,
  washed, hulled and
  sliced
1 c. whipping cream,
  whipped

Raspberry Cassis Sauce:
1-1/2 c. frozen raspberries,
  thawed, undrained
1/4 c. Creme de Cassis
1 T. sugar

Heat the water and butter in a saucepan until water boils. Add flour and salt all at once and stir quickly with a wooden spoon until batter is stiff, leaves the side of the pan and forms a ball. Remove from heat. Add the eggs gradually but quickly, stirring vigorously until combined. Using a regular-size ice cream scoop, place 6-7 scoops of batter onto a lightly greased baking sheet, placing far apart to allow puffs to expand. Immediately place in preheated 400° oven and bake 35 minutes. Remove from oven and cool.

Sauce: Place all ingredients in a blender; process 1 minute. Strain through a sieve to remove seeds and pulp; chill.

To serve, cut the puffs in half horizontally and place the bottoms in each of 6 dessert bowls. Fill with the strawberries and whipped cream. Place the tops over the whipped cream and ladle the sauce over. Serve immediately.

## Strawberry Meringue
Exceptionally attractive dessert          Serves 10-12

6 egg whites, at room
  temperature
1 t. cream of tartar
1-1/2 c. sugar
1 c. whipping cream,
  whipped
1 banana, sliced
1 qt. large strawberries,
  hulled
1/2 gal. ice cream, any
  flavor

Beat egg whites with cream of tartar until stiff. Very gradually add sugar. Pour meringue into buttered 10-inch springform pan; set in a pan of hot water and bake 1 hour at 325°. Remove from oven and allow to cool a few minutes. Invert onto a serving platter. Cool. When ready to serve, fill center with ice cream. Cover completely with whipped cream. Arrange banana slices in center and surround with strawberries.

## Strawberry Bavarian

Serve with Old Fashioned Icebox Cookies (page 311)                    Serves 6

1 qt. strawberries, sliced
3/4 c. sugar
1 T. unflavored gelatin
1/2 c. cold water
2 T. lemon juice
1 c. whipping cream,
   whipped

Mix strawberries with sugar. Let stand until sugar dissolves. Sprinkle gelatin over cold water. Let stand 5 minutes, then heat gently until gelatin dissolves completely. Add gelatin and lemon juice to sliced berries. Fold in whipped cream. Pour into a 1-quart mold or serving dish. Chill until set. Unmold to serve.

## Zuppa Inglese

Fresh berries may be layered with filling                    Serves 8-10

Cake:
6 eggs, separated
1 c. sugar
1-1/2 t. vanilla
1 c. sifted flour
1/2 c. clarified butter,
   cooled but still liquid*
1 c. rum

Filling:
3 T. flour
3/8 c. sugar
1/8 t. salt
1 c. half and half cream
4 egg yolks, beaten
1/2 t. vanilla
1/2 t. almond extract

Topping:
1 c. whipping cream
2 T. powdered sugar
1/2 t. almond or rum
   extract

For cake; stir egg yolks and whites separately until slightly mixed; combine. Beat until light and fluffy, adding sugar gradually. Place bowl on a rack in a saucepan having a 2-inch depth of water. Do not allow bowl to touch water. Place pan over low heat for 7 minutes, until the egg mixture is just lukewarm, stirring constantly. When mixture becomes lukewarm and bright yellow, remove from heat, add vanilla, and beat at high speed with an electric mixer for 10 to 15 minutes, until it triples in volume and draws from beaters in ribbon fashion. Sprinkle flour, a little at a time, on top of the whipped mixture; fold in. Fold in butter. Pour into a 4-1/2 x 9-inch loaf pan; bake at 350° for 25-30 minutes. When cool, divide into 3 layers. Sprinkle layers with rum.

For filling; mix flour, sugar and salt in a heavy saucepan; gradually blend in cream. Cook over medium heat, stirring constantly until the mixture thickens. Add egg yolks slowly, stirring constantly. Continue to cook until slightly thicker; do not boil. Add the vanilla and almond extracts; blend well. Cool; fill cake. Top with whipped cream sweetened with sugar and flavored with almond or rum extract.

*To clarify butter: melt slowly over low heat; carefully pour off clear liquid; discard whey remaining in bottom of pan.

## Summer Trifle

Don't count on leftovers—there won't be any!                Serves 6-8

1/4 c. dark rum
1/4 c. water
2 T. sugar
1 c. whipping cream,
    whipped
2 T. powdered sugar
1 t. vanilla
12 ladyfingers, split
1 c. cubed fresh
    pineapple
3/4 c. fresh blueberries
4 T. black raspberry
    preserves (seedless),
    melted

In a saucepan, boil rum, water and sugar 5 minutes. Let the syrup cool. Flavor whipped cream with powdered sugar and vanilla; chill. To assemble, sprinkle ladyfingers with cooled syrup. In an 8-inch souffle dish or glass bowl, spread one-third of the whipped cream. Top with 1/2 cup pineapple and 1/4 cup blueberries. Spread with 2 T. melted preserves. Top with half the ladyfingers. Repeat layers. Decorate top with remaining whipped cream; garnish with remaining blueberries. Chill several hours or overnight, covered with plastic wrap.

## Amaretto Souffle

Perfect finale to an Italian meal                Serves 8

6 macaroon cookies
1 envelope unflavored
    gelatin
3 T. water
4 egg yolks
1/2 c. Amaretto liqueur
1 t. almond flavoring
1 c. whipping cream,
    whipped
6 egg whites
5 T. sugar
whipped cream,
    optional
slivered almonds,
    optional

Finely crumble macaroon cookies onto a baking sheet. Place on top shelf of 200° oven for 10-20 minutes, until dry and browned (watch carefully). Soften gelatin in water; dissolve over low heat. Set aside. Beat egg yolks until thick and light in color; add Amaretto and almond flavoring. Stir gelatin into egg yolk mixture. Let stand for 20 minutes or until mixture begins to thicken. Fold whipped cream into egg yolk mixture. Beat egg whites until peaks form. Add the sugar gradually and beat until stiff. Fold whites into egg yolk mixture; fold in dried macaroons. Pour mixture into a 1-quart souffle dish that has had a 3-inch foil collar wrapped around it, secured with tape. Refrigerate at least 4 hours. Remove foil and decorate with additional whipped cream and/or slivered almonds.

## Caramel Praline Souffle
Light and delicious                                    Serves 6

**Souffle:**
**1 envelope unflavored**
   **gelatin**
**1/2 c. cold water**
**28 soft caramels**
**2 T. sugar**
**1 c. hot water**
**5 eggs, separated**
**1/4 t. salt**
**1 c. whipping cream,**
   **whipped**

**Topping:**
**2 T. sugar**
**1/4 c. chopped pecans**

Soften gelatin in 1/2 cup of the water. Melt caramels and sugar with 1 cup hot water in a covered double boiler over low heat. Stir until smooth. Beat egg yolks; stir a small amount of the hot mixture into egg yolks. Return yolk mixture to the pan and stir constantly over low heat 3-5 minutes. Stir in gelatin. Cool; refrigerate until mixture begins to gel. Beat egg whites with salt until stiff. Fold egg whites and whipped cream into the caramel mixture. Pour into a 1-3/4-quart souffle dish; freeze. Let soften at room temperature for about 2 hours before serving.

For topping, melt 2 T. sugar in a pan over low heat, stirring until clear and caramel colored. Stir in chopped pecans. Spoon topping onto a greased baking sheet. Immediately separate nuts with 2 forks. Cool mixture; break into small pieces. To serve, sprinkle topping over souffle.

## Maple Bourbon Souffle
A sophisticated make-ahead dessert                    Serves 8

**5 T. sugar**
**2 eggs, plus 2 yolks**
**2 T. bourbon**
**3 T. pure maple syrup**
**2-1/2 c. whipping cream,**
   **whipped**
**1 c. chopped macadamia**
   **nuts**

**Sauce:**
**4 egg yolks**
**1/2 c. sugar**
**2 c. milk, heated to**
   **boiling**
**3 T. bourbon**
**2 T. pure maple syrup**

In top of double boiler, mix sugar, eggs, yolks and bourbon; heat over simmering water until mixture is very warm. Pour into mixer bowl and beat until very cool and fluffy. Beat in syrup; fold in whipped cream. Butter a 6-cup souffle dish and fit with foil collar. Pour mixture into dish and freeze.

For sauce, beat yolks with sugar in a medium saucepan. Stir in hot milk. Cook over low heat, stirring constantly, until mixture thickens enough to coat a spoon; do not boil. Remove from heat; stir in bourbon and maple syrup. Cool; refrigerate 1-2 days. To serve, remove collar from souffle. Press nuts into top and sides. Serve immediately, with sauce on the side.

## Luscious Peach Souffle
May be garnished with almonds                    Serves 12

3 c. peach halves
2 envelope unflavored
  gelatin
1/2 c. sugar
4 eggs, separated
1 c. milk
1 t. almond extract
1/4 c. sugar
1 c. whipping cream,
  whipped
3 c. peach slices

In a blender or food processer, puree 3 cups peach halves. In medium saucepan, mix gelatin with 1/2 cup sugar; blend in egg yolks beaten with milk. Let stand 1 minute. Stir over low heat until gelatin is completely dissolved; about 5 minutes. Stir in pureed peaches and almond extract. Pour into a large bowl and chill, stirring occasionally, until mixture mounds slightly when dropped from a spoon. In a large bowl, beat egg whites until soft peaks form. Gradually add 1/4 cup sugar and beat until stiff. Fold egg whites, whipped cream and remaining peaches into gelatin mixture. Turn into a 1-1/2-quart souffle dish with a 3-inch collar attached; chill until firm.

## Amaretto Chocolate Ice Cream Torte
May be frozen up to 2 weeks                       Serves 8

1/2 c. butter
1 c. flour
1/2 c. sugar
1/2 c. chopped, toasted
  almonds
1/4 c. Amaretto liqueur
1 c. whipping cream,
  whipped
1 qt. chocolate ice
  cream, softened

Melt butter in a large skillet; stir in flour, sugar and almonds. Cook over medium heat, stirring constantly, until mixture is golden and crumbly, 6 to 8 minutes. Reserve 3/4 cup crumb mixture; pat remaining mixture into a buttered 9-inch springform pan. Freeze at least 3 hours. Gently but quickly fold Amaretto and whipped cream into the ice cream. Spoon the mixture into the crumb-lined pan. Freeze until partially set; about 1 hour; sprinkle with reserved crumb mixture. Return to freezer and freeze until firm; at least 2 hours.

## Frozen Chocolate Cookie Chips
Easy way to serve a crowd                          Serves 18

1 c. butter
2 c. powdered sugar
4—1-oz. squares
   unsweetened
   chocolate, melted
4 eggs, beaten
1/2 t. peppermint extract
2 t. vanilla
1 c. vanilla wafer crumbs
1 c. whipping cream,
   whipped
maraschino cherries

Beat together butter and powdered sugar until light. Add melted chocolate and beaten eggs. Beat in peppermint and vanilla extracts. Sprinkle 1 T. wafer crumbs into each of 18 paper-lined cupcake tins. Spoon chocolate mixture onto crumbs; freeze. Top with whipped cream and maraschino cherries.


## Chocolate-Peanut Ice Cream Delight
Kids will be delighted to make this                Serves 16

42 cream-filled chocolate
   sandwich cookies
1/4 c. butter, melted
2 qt. French vanilla ice
   cream, softened
1 large jar fudge topping
1 c. crushed peanuts or
   chopped pecans
1—12-oz. container
   whipped topping

Crush cookies in blender or food processor. Mix butter with the cookie crumbs. Reserve 1/2 cup of this mixture. Press the remainder into bottom of a 9 x 13-inch pan. Bake at 300° for 5 minutes. Cool. Spread softened ice cream over this layer. Freeze until firm. Spread fudge topping over the ice cream and sprinkle with chopped nuts. Put back into the freezer to harden. Spread with whipped topping and sprinkle with reserved crumb mixture. Freeze until serving time.


## Brandied Orange Bombe
Sprinkle with coconut or nuts before serving       Serves 8-10

1/2 c. golden raisins
1/2 c. brandy
1 qt. orange sherbert
1-1/2 qt. vanilla ice
   cream, slightly
   softened

Soak the raisins in brandy overnight in a covered jar. Chill a 2-quart mold in the freezer. Spread the inside of the mold evenly with the orange sherbert and freeze. Drain the raisins and stir them into the softened ice cream. Fill the mold with the ice cream-raisin mixture. Cover the mold with foil or plastic wrap. Freeze for at least 6 hours. Unmold onto serving platter.

## Grasshopper Flower Pots

For a faster "garden", substitute ice cream for grasshopper mixture    Serves 9

1—7-oz. jar marshmallow
   creme
1/4 c. milk
10 drops green food
   coloring
1/2 t. peppermint extract
1 envelope whipped
   topping mix
1/2 c. cold milk
1/2 t. vanilla
1 c. whipping cream,
   whipped
30 chocolate wafer
   cookies
9 styrofoam cups
4 plastic drinking straws
9—3-inch clay pots
9 fresh flowers

In a large bowl, mix marshmallow creme with milk, food coloring, and peppermint extract. Set aside. Prepare topping mix with milk and vanilla according to package directions; fold into whipped cream. Fold cream into marshmallow mixture; spoon mixture into styrofoam cups. Crush chocolate cookies until they look like "dirt". Spoon a thick layer of "dirt" into each cup. Insert a 2-inch length of straw in the center of each cup. Freeze for at least 4 hours. To serve, remove from freezer five minutes before serving. Place styrofoam cup in a flower pot and insert a fresh flower stem in the straw.

## Frozen Grand Marnier Souffle

May be served with Grand Marnier-flavored whipped cream    Serves 8

1 c. sugar
1/3 c. fresh orange juice
6 egg yolks
1/4 c. Grand Marnier
   liqueur
2 c. whipping cream
1 angel food cake, cut
   into 1-inch cubes

In saucepan, mix sugar and orange juice. Bring to a boil over moderate heat and cook until syrup registers 220° on a candy thermometer. In mixer bowl, beat egg yolks until thick. Pour syrup in a thin stream into yolks, beating constantly until mixture is thick. Cool to room temperature. Beat in Grand Marnier. In separate bowl, whip cream until soft peaks form. Fold into Grand Marnier mixture. Fit a 4-cup souffle dish with a foil collar which extends 2 inches above rim of dish. Alternate layers of Grand Marnier mixture and cake cubes in dish until all of custard is used. Place in freezer and freeze at least 6 hours.

## Frozen Orange Souffles
Top with a swirl of whipped cream                    Serves 6

6 large navel oranges
3 egg yolks
3/4 c. sifted powdered
   sugar
1/4 c. orange juice
3/4 t. orange liqueur
2 t. grated orange peel
1 c. whipping cream,
   whipped

Cut top quarter off each orange. Remove fruit, leaving basket-like shell. Dry inside of shell with paper towel. Beat egg yolks and sugar until smooth; approximately 1 minute. Stir in orange juice, liqueur and orange peel. Fold in whipped cream. Pour about 3/4 cup of the souffle mixture into each orange shell. Freeze until firm, 4 to 6 hours.

## Peach Praline Sundae
In season, top fresh peach halves with ice cream balls          Serves 1

vanilla ice cream
fresh or frozen peaches,
   sliced and slightly
   sweetened
toasted pecan halves
praline liqueur

Top a scoop of ice cream with some peaches, a few pecan halves and 1 or 2 T. praline liqueur.

## Peppermint Freeze
Chopped candy canes can replace nuts              Serves 16-20

Crust:
30 chocolate wafer
   cookies, crushed
1/3 c. butter, melted

Peppermint Layer:
1/2 gal. peppermint ice
   cream, slightly
   softened

Chocolate Layer
3/4 c. butter
3—1-oz. unsweetened
   chocolate
4 eggs, separated
2 c. powdered sugar
1-1/2 t. vanilla
1/2 c. nuts, chopped

For crust, mix crushed cookies with butter; press into bottom of 9 x 13-inch pan. Spread evenly with ice cream; freeze.

For chocolate layer, melt butter and chocolate together. Cool well. Beat 4 egg yolks until thick. Gradually beat in chocolate mixture and sugar. Stir in vanilla. Beat egg whites until soft peaks form. Fold whites into chocolate mixture. Pour chocolate mixture over ice cream layer; sprinkle with nuts. Freeze. To serve, cut into 16-20 squares.

## Strawberry Champagne Sorbet
Other fruits may be substituted                    Serves 8

1 c. whipping cream
1/2 c. sugar
1-1/2 c. champagne
1—10-oz. pkg. frozen
  strawberries, thawed
2 egg whites
1/4 c. sugar
1/4 t. cream of tartar
red food color (optional)

In saucepan, combine cream and 1/2 cup sugar; cook and stir over medium heat until sugar has dissolved. Cool. Stir in champagne and undrained berries. Pour into an 8 x 8-inch pan; cover; freeze firm, about 4 hours. Beat egg whites and cream of tartar to soft peaks; slowly add 1/4 cup sugar and beat to stiff peaks. Break up frozen berry mixture and turn into chilled mixing bowl; beat smooth. Fold in egg whites. Tint with food color as desired. Cover, return to freezer and freeze firm. Serve in chilled sherbet glasses with fresh strawberries.

## Frozen Strawberry Dessert
Filling may also be poured into a baked pie shell        Serves 16-20

Crumb Crust:
1/2 c. butter
1/4 c. brown sugar
1 c. flour
1/2 c. chopped pecans

Mix crust ingredients lightly and sprinkle on-to a jelly roll pan. Bake about 15 minutes at 400°, stirring frequently, taking care not to let them burn. Press half of the crumbs in bottom of a 9 x 13-inch pan; reserve the rest for topping.

Filling:
1—10-oz. pkg. frozen
  strawberries, thawed
2 egg whites
1 c. sugar
1 t. vanilla
1 T. lemon juice
1 c. whipping cream

For filling, combine strawberries, egg whites, sugar, vanilla and lemon juice in mixing bowl. Beat at high speed for 20 minutes. Fold whipped cream into strawberry mixture. Pour into the crumb-lined pan and top with reserved crumbs. Freeze overnight. Cut into squares to serve.

## Cantaloupe with Strawberry Sauce
Cooling and colorful                               Serves 2

1/2 c. fresh strawberries
2 T. sugar
1-1/2 T. lemon juice
1 small cantaloupe,
  halved and seeded
2 mint sprigs

Mash strawberries or whirl in a blender. Add sugar and lemon juice; cover and process a few moments longer. Pour the sauce into the two cantaloupe halves. Cover and chill in re-frigerator 1 hour. Garnish with mint sprigs.

## White Chocolate Ice Cream
An exquisite taste                                    Makes 2 quarts

3/4 c. sugar
1 c. water
6 egg yolks
1 T. vanilla
10 oz. white chocolate
   (imported preferred),
   melted
2 c. whipping cream
bittersweet chocolate
   curls

Mix sugar and water in medium saucepan. Bring to boil; stirring only to dissolve sugar. Boil 5 minutes; remove from heat. In mixing bowl, beat egg yolks with vanilla about 7 minutes, until fluffy. Slowly pour syrup into yolks, beating constantly. Beat 7-10 minutes, until mixture is cooled. Gradually beat in chocolate until mixture is cool and smooth. Chill 1 hour. Lightly whip cream; fold into white chocolate mixture. Cover and freeze until firm, at least 5 hours. To serve, garnish with bittersweet chocolate curls.

## Banana Copacabana
From *Figg's Cafe*, which specializes in flaming desserts          Serves 1

1 banana, sliced
2 T. butter
2 T. raisins
1 t. cinnamon
1/2 c. banana ice cream
   topping
2 T. orange curacao
"151" rum
1 T. nuts, chopped
2 scoops chocolate ice
   cream

Brown sliced banana in butter. Add raisins and cinnamon along with banana topping and orange curacao; simmer. For the "show", add the "151" rum and ignite. When flame is out, pour over ice cream. Sprinkle with chopped nuts before serving. Be very careful when using "151" rum. Do not stand near the flame. The flaming is a nice touch, but is also dangerous if not used correctly.

## Microwave Bananas Foster
A sensational, and easy, finale                              Serves 6

1/2 c. butter or
   margarine
1 c. brown sugar
6 bananas
1/2 t. cinnamon
2 qt. vanilla ice cream
2 oz. banana liqueur,
   optional
2 oz. light rum, optional

Melt butter in microwave on high. Add brown sugar; cook on high 30 seconds. Peel bananas and cut lengthwise, then in half. Toss bananas with cinnamon lightly. Add to butter and brown sugar mixture. Put banana, brown sugar and butter mixture in microwave for 1-1/2 minutes on high or until bubbly. Let stand 2 minutes while filling desert dishes with ice cream. Stir liqueurs into banana mixture, if desired. Distribute evenly among the 6 desserts.

# Desserts

## Pineapple Tipsy
From *Figg's Cafe*, known for their fabulous flaming finales        Serves 1

3 pineapple slices
2 T. butter
lemon zest (peel finely
  minced)
1/2 c. apricot-pineapple
  sauce
1 T. orange curacao
1 T. apricot brandy
1 T. "151" rum
2 scoops ice cream (your
  favorite)

Brown pineapple slices in butter. Add lemon zest. Add pineapple sauce, curacao, and brandy; let simmer. For the "show" add the "151" rum and ignite. When flame is out, pour over ice cream. Be careful when using "151" rum. Do not stand near flame. The flaming is a nice touch, but is also dangerous if not used correctly.

## Lemon Mousse
May also be served in tart shells        Serves 6-8

1 c. whipping cream,
  whipping
1 envelope unflavored
  gelatin
2 T. cold water
1/3 c. lemon juice
4 eggs
1 c. sugar
whipping cream for
  garnish

Cover whipped cream and refrigerate. Soften gelatin in water in small saucepan. Heat slowly until gelatin is dissolved; cool. Add lemon juice. Beat eggs with sugar until thick and lemon colored. Beat in gelatin mixture. Fold in 1 cup of whipped cream and pour into individual dishes for serving. Refrigerate until set. Garnish with remaining whipped cream to serve.

## Peaches and Raspberries with Almonds
Almond liqueur may be added        Serves 2

4 peach halves, fresh or
  canned
1—10-oz. pkg. frozen
  raspberries, thawed
1/2 c. whipping cream,
  whipping
3 T. sugar
3 T. slivered almonds
1/8 t. almond extract

Place 2 peach halves in each dessert dish. Fill hollows with slivered almonds; spoon sweetened raspberries over the peaches. Mix whipped cream with sugar and almond extract. Top desserts with cream. Sprinkle with more almonds and serve immediately.

## Green Grape Dessert

Elegant served in stemmed goblets                    Serves 4

1 lb. seedless green
  grapes
1/4 c. honey
1/4 c. brandy
1 T. lemon juice
1/2 c. sour cream
1/2 c. brown sugar

Wash grapes; remove from stems. Blend honey, brandy and lemon juice with wire wisk. Pour mixture over grapes. Cover and refrigerate overnight. Spoon into serving dishes; top with sour cream, and sprinkle with brown sugar.

## Angel Pie

Really a "heavenly" dessert                          Serves 8

**Crust:**
5 egg whites
1/4 t. cream of tartar
1-1/4 c. sugar

**Filling:**
5 egg yolks
1/2 c. sugar
rind of 1 lemon, grated
3 T. fresh lemon juice
2 c. whipping cream,
  whipped

For crust, beat egg whites until frothy. Add cream of tartar and gradually add sugar, beating well until all sugar is dissolved. Carefully spread meringue in a well-buttered 10-inch pie plate. Bake for 20 minutes at 275°; turn oven to 300° and bake for 35 minutes. Remove from oven and cool.

For filling, beat 5 egg yolks well and add 1/2 cup sugar, lemon rind and lemon juice. Cook in the top of a double boiler over simmering water until thick; cool well. Carefully fold cream into lemon mixture; gently place in cooled meringue shell. Cover with plastic wrap and refrigerate for 24 hours.

## Cheese Apple Crisp

Just as good reheated                               Serves 6-8

2 T. flour
1/2 c. sugar
6-8 tart apples, peeled,
  cored and sliced
1 T. lemon juice
1/2 c. flour
1/2 c. sugar
1/4 t. salt
1/4 t. cinnamon or nutmeg
1/4 c. butter, softened
1-1/2 c. finely shredded
  cheddar cheese

Combine 2 T. flour and 1/2 cup sugar. Stir sugar mixture into apples to distribute evenly. Arrange apples in a 10-inch pie plate; sprinkle with lemon juice. Combine 1/2 cup flour, 1/2 cup sugar, salt and cinnamon. Cut in butter; stir in cheese. Spread on top of apples. Bake at 350° for 50 minutes. Serve warm.

# Schokoladencreme Nut Pie

A sweet chocolate pie                                    Serves 8

**Crust:**
3 c. flaked coconut
3/4 c. chopped pecans
1/4 c. butter, melted

**Filling:**
3/4 c. butter, softened
1 c. plus 2 T. superfine
  sugar
1-1/2—1-oz. squares
  unsweetened
  chocolate, melted
1-1/2 t. vanilla
3 eggs

**Topping:**
1 c. whipping cream,
  whipped
pecans for decoration

For crust; combine coconut, pecans and butter in a 9-inch pie plate and mix thoroughly. Press onto bottom and sides of pan. Bake at 325° for 15 to 20 minutes or until golden brown around the edges. (Bottom of crust will still be white). Place on rack to cool completely.

For filling, beat butter until creamy; add sugar a little at a time; continue beating; add melted chocolate and vanilla. Add 2 eggs and beat 3 minutes. Add remaining egg and beat 3 minutes more. Pour mixture into the cool pie shell and refrigerate. Before serving, top with whipped cream and pecans.

# Whipped Kahlua Pie

Men love this pie                                        Serves 8

**Crust:**
1/2 pkg. chocolate
  wafers, crushed
6 T. butter, melted
1/2 c. finely chopped
  pecans
1 T. sugar

**Filling:**
1 qt. coffee ice cream
2 c. whipping cream
1 t. vanilla
2/3 c. Kahlua
4 Heath candy bars,
  crushed

For crust, mix wafer crumbs with melted butter, pecans, and sugar. Pat into a 10-inch greased pie pan. Bake at 350° for 10 minutes. Cool.

For filling, soften ice cream slightly. Whip cream, adding vanilla and Kahlua. Gently fold crushed candy bars into whipped cream mixture. Gently blend in ice cream. Pour into crust and freeze.

## Lemon Pie
Beautiful variation of a classic                                          Serves 6

**Filling:**
1-1/3 c. sugar
1/2 c. cornstarch
1/4 t. salt
1-3/4 c. water
4 egg yolks
2 T. butter
1/2 c. lemon juice
1—9-inch baked pie crust

**Meringues:**
4 egg whites
1/4 t. cream of tartar
1/2 c. sugar

Thoroughly mix sugar, cornstarch and salt in a medium saucepan. Slowly add water, stirring constantly. Cook over medium heat, stirring constantly until it thickens and is bubbly. Let bubble one minute more, still stirring. Remove from heat. Beat egg yolks slightly. Slowly blend in 1/2 cup of hot mixture. Stir back into remaining mixture. Cook over low heat for 2 minutes, stirring gently. Remove from heat; stir in butter and lemon juice. Pour into cooled crust. Cover with plastic wrap; chill 3 hours.

For meringue, beat egg whites, slowly adding cream of tartar and sugar, until stiff peaks form. Lightly flour a baking sheet. On it form 7—2-inch diameter mounds of meringue by forcing meringue mixture through a pastry tube. Bake at 425° for 3 to 5 minutes. When pie is cool, set six meringues around top of pie and one in the center. Cut into 6 wedges.

## Fresh Peach Pie
Pass additional whipped cream when serving                                Serves 6

**Crust:**
1-1/2 c. graham cracker
   crumbs
1/3 c. powdered sugar
1/3 c. melted butter

**Filling:**
2 c. fresh peaches, peeled
   and chopped
3/4 c. sugar
2 T. lemon juice
1/8 t. salt
1 envelope unflavored
   gelatin
1/4 c. cold water
1/2 c. boiling water
1 c. whipping cream
1/8 t. vanilla
1 t. sugar

For crust, mix graham cracker crumbs with sugar and butter and press into a 9-inch pie plate; set aside.

For filling, combine chopped peaches with 3/4 c. sugar, lemon juice and salt. Soak gelatin in cold water for 5 minutes; then dissolve gelatin in the boiling water. When dissolved, stir into the peach mixture. Refrigerate until it starts to gel. Whip cream until stiff; add vanilla and 1 t. sugar. Fold the whipped cream into the peach mixture and pour into pie crust. Refrigerate for at least 2 hours.

## Sour Cream Peach Pie
Serve chilled or at room temperature                    Serves 6-8

1 unbaked 9-inch pie
   shell
6-8 fresh peaches, peeled
   and sliced
1 c. sour cream
3/4 c. sugar
4 T. flour
sugar and cinnamon

Fill unbaked pie shell with sliced peaches. Mix sour cream, sugar and flour; pour over peaches in the shell. Sprinkle with cinnamon and sugar. Bake at 450° for 10 minutes; lower heat to 350° and bake 45 minutes more. Cool well.

## Jay's Cheese Pie
Top with fruit sauce if you wish                    Serves 8-10

1-1/3 c. graham cracker
   crumbs
1/4 c. melted butter
3—3-oz. pkg. cream
   cheese, softened
1/2 c. sugar
2 eggs, at room
   temperature
1/2 t. vanilla

Topping:
5 T. sugar
2 c. sour cream
1/2 t. vanilla
1/8 t. cinnamon

Mix graham cracker crumbs and butter together; press into the bottom and sides of a 9-inch pie pan. Bake at 350° for 5 minutes; cool. Beat cheese well; gradually beat in sugar. Add eggs and vanilla; beat well. Pour into prepared pie shell. Bake at 325° for 20 minutes or until firm. Remove from oven and cool 10 minutes.

For topping, mix sugar, sour cream, vanilla, and cinnamon. Spread on pie. Return to the oven and bake at 325° for 5 minutes. Cool; chill.

## New York-Style Cheesecake
A rich, heavy cake                    Serves 8

4—8-oz. pkg. cream
   cheese, softened
4 eggs
1-3/4 c. sugar
1 t. vanilla
rind and juice of 1
   medium size lemon
butter
1/4 c. graham cracker
   crumbs

Beat cream cheese until smooth. Add eggs, sugar, vanilla, rind and juice of lemon. Coat an 8-inch round springform pan with hard butter, and dust with graham cracker crumbs. Pour in batter gently. Put springform pan into a larger pan, pour boiling water into outer pan to a depth of 1-1/2 inches. Bake 1-1/2 hours at 325°. Keep oven door closed; cool in oven for 30 minutes. Remove and cool. Chill well before serving.

## Almond Cheesecake

One of America's favorite flavors                                    Serves 10

1 c. less 2 T. sugar
1/4 c. butter
2—8-oz. pkg. cream
   cheese, softened
1/4 c. flour
2 T. honey
5 eggs, separated
1/2 c. half and half
   cream
1/4 t. almond extract
1 t. vanilla
1/2 c. finely chopped
   almonds

Topping:
1/4 c. brown sugar
1 t. cinnamon
1/4 c. finely chopped
   almonds

Cream together sugar and butter. Beat in cream cheese until fluffy. Blend in flour, honey, and egg yolks, beating well. Add cream and extracts. Beat egg whites until stiff; fold into cream cheese mixture. Fold in chopped almonds. Pour into a well-buttered 9-inch springform pan. Mix topping ingredients; sprinkle over batter; set on the lowest oven rack and bake at 325° for 1 hour. Turn off heat and cool in oven for 1 hour. Remove and cool.

## Praline Cheesecake

Maple flavoring may be substituted for vanilla                       Serves 16

Crust:
1-1/2 c. finely crushed
   vanilla wafers
1/4 c. melted butter
1/2 c. finely chopped
   pecans

Filling:
3—8-oz. pkg. cream
   cheese, softened
1-1/4 c. brown sugar
3 eggs
3 T. flour
1-1/4 t. vanilla
1/2 c. chopped pecans

Glaze:
3-4 T. maple syrup
16 pecan halves

Combine crust ingredients and press onto bottom and up sides of a 9-inch springform pan. Bake at 350° for 10 minutes. Blend all filling ingredients. Pour into crust. Bake at 350° for 50-60 minutes. Cool; chill in refrigerator for several hours. Spoon 3-4 T. maple syrup over the top to glaze. Garnish with 16 pecan halves around the edge of the top. Refrigerate 1-2 hours. Serve cold.

# Baba Au Rhum
Individual babas may be baked in muffin tins for 15 minutes          Serves 24

2 pkg. active dry yeast
1/2 c. warm water (110°)
4 c. flour
6 eggs, beaten
2/3 c. melted butter
1/4 c. sugar
1 t. salt
2/3 c. currants

Rum sauce:
1-1/2 c. sugar
2 c. water
4 thin slices lemon
4 thin slices orange
1 c. white rum

Apricot glaze:
1/3 c. apricot jam
1 T. lemon juice

Sprinkle yeast onto warm water; let stand 5 minutes. Measure flour into a large bowl. Stir yeast and combine with flour; beat in eggs. Beat thoroughly; let stand covered 30 minutes. Gradually add butter, a fourth at a time, working in with a spoon. Stir in sugar, salt and currants. Knead smooth with wooden spoon in bowl. Turn dough into greased 10-inch tube pan. Let rise in warm place until tripled in bulk (almost to top of pan). Bake at 375° for 45 minutes. Remove from pan and place on rack over plate; spoon on rum sauce. Let stand 2 hours, spooning with sauce occasionally. Before serving, spread with apricot glaze. May be frozen before glazing.

For rum sauce, simmer sugar, water and fruit for 5 minutes. Cool and strain and add rum as desired.

For apricot glaze, press jam through strainer and add lemon juice.

# Newbold Bread Pudding
A not-to-be-forgotton old favorite          Serves 8

4 c. milk
1 T. butter
1/4 t. salt
3/4 c. sugar
4 eggs, slightly beaten
1 t. vanilla
3 c. bread cubes

Scald milk and add butter, salt and sugar. Pour the milk mixture over the beaten eggs, vanilla and bread. Mix well. Pour into an 8-inch square baking pan and place pan into a larger pan, having about 2 inches of water in the larger pan. Bake at 325° for 50 minutes, or until firm. Serve warm with cream or lemon sauce; or sprinkle top with nutmeg and eat plain.

## Cherry-Berry Cobbler
May be doubled for a 9 x 13-inch dish                          Serves 6

1—21-oz. can cherry pie
   filling
1—10-oz. pkg. frozen red
   raspberries, thawed
   and drained
1 t. lemon juice
1/2 c. flour
1/4 c. sugar
1/4 c. butter
1/2 t. salt
whipped cream or ice cream

In a saucepan, combine pie filling, raspberries and lemon juice. Bring to a boil over medium heat. Pour into a greased 1-quart casserole dish. Mix flour, sugar, butter and salt until thoroughly blended and crumbly. Sprinkle over filling and bake at 375° for 30 minutes or until lightly browned. Serve warm with whipped cream or ice cream.

## Peachy Cobbler
Delicious with cinnamon ice cream                          Serves 8-10

2 c. drained, sliced
   peaches (or a 29-oz. can)
3 T. lemon juice
1 c. light brown sugar
1 t. cinnamon
3/4 c. flour
1/2 c. sugar
2 t. baking powder
1/4 t. salt
3/4 c. milk
1/3 c. melted butter

Arrange drained, sliced peaches in a 9-inch square baking pan. Sprinkle lemon juice and brown sugar over peaches. Sprinkle cinnamon over all. In a mixing bowl combine flour, sugar, baking powder and salt. Add milk and beat until smooth. Pour over peaches. Drizzle melted butter over batter. Bake at 350° for 35 minutes. Serve warm.

## Open Plum Kuchen
Apples or peaches work well, too                          Serves 12

1-1/2 c. flour
1/4 c. sugar
1/2 t. salt
1/2 c. butter or margarine
1 egg yolk
2 T. milk
1/4 c. cracker crumbs
4 c. halved, pitted plums
1 T. lemon juice
1/2 c. sugar
1 t. cinnamon
1 T. butter
1 c. whipping cream,
   whipped

Combine unsifted flour, sugar and salt in a bowl; cut in butter. Beat egg yolk and milk lightly; blend into flour mixture. Press into a 9-inch springform pan or pie plate, on the bottom and 1/2 inch up the sides. Sprinkle crumbs over the dough. Toss the plums with lemon juice; press into dough, open side up, in circles starting in the center. Sprinkle with sugar and cinnamon mixture; dot with butter.

Bake at 375° about 45 minutes; until crust browns and fruit is tender. Cool. Serve with whipped cream.

## Fresh Apple Pound Cake
May be made a day ahead                                      Serves 14

2 c. sugar
1-1/2 c. corn oil
3 eggs
2 t. vanilla
3 c. finely chopped
   apples
3 c. flour
1 t. baking soda
1 t. baking powder
1 t. salt
1 t. cinnamon
1/2 c. chopped nuts

Topping:
1/2 c. brown sugar
3/4 c. water
1/2 c. sugar
3 T. flour
1/4 c. butter

Cream together the sugar, oil, eggs and vanilla until fluffy. In a separate bowl, mix apples, flour, baking soda, baking powder, salt, cinnamon and nuts. Add creamed mixture to apple mixture and blend well. Pour into a greased and floured 10-inch bundt pan. Bake at 325° for 1 hour and 15-20 minutes. Cool on rack.

For topping, mix all ingredients in saucepan and cook until mixture is clear. Pour warm topping on cake and let it drizzle down the sides.

## Apple Cake
Serve as coffeecake or dessert                              Serves 16

Crust:
1 c. butter
2-1/2 c. flour
2 t. baking powder
4 t. milk
1/2 t. salt
2 T. sugar
1 t. vanilla
1 egg, lightly beaten
8 to 10 apples (or
   peaches or plums),
   peeled and sliced

Topping:
1 c. sugar
2-1/2 t. flour
3/4 T. cinnamon
4 T. melted butter

Cut butter into flour until mixture resembles cornmeal. Stir in baking powder, milk, salt, sugar and vanilla. Add egg and mix well. Flour hands and pat mixture onto 15 x 10-inch baking sheet. Arrange fruit attractively on crust. Mix together sugar, flour and cinnamon for topping; sprinkle over fruit. Drizzle melted butter over top. Bake at 375° for 40 to 45 minutes. Serve warm.

## Birthday Cake

Insert candles into maraschino cherries for decoration — Serves 10

3 pkg. ladyfingers
2—4-oz. bars sweet
  baking chocolate
4 T. sugar
4 eggs, separated
1 c. whipping cream,
  whipped

Line an 8-inch diameter mixing bowl with waxed paper. Separate the ladyfingers and line the bowl with them. Melt chocolate; add sugar and egg yolks. In a separate bowl, beat egg whites until stiff; fold into chocolate mixture. Layer ladyfingers and chocolate mixture until all are used. Refrigerate overnight.

Turn out on a serving plate and frost with whipped cream. Note: This cake can be made a day or two ahead, but must be served shortly after frosting with whipped cream.

## Whole Wheat Carrot Cake

This cake travels well — Serves 16

1 c. vegetable oil
1 c. sugar
1 c. brown sugar
4 eggs
1 t. vanilla
1 c. flour
1/3 c. non-fat dry milk
1 c. whole wheat flour
1 t. salt
1 t. baking soda
1 t. baking powder
2 t. cinnamon
1/8 t. allspice
1/8 t. ground cloves
3 c. finely grated carrots
1 c. chopped walnuts
1/2 c. raisins

Icing:
1—3-oz. pkg. cream
  cheese, softened
4 T. butter, softened
1 t. vanilla
2-1/4 c. powdered sugar
2 T. milk
1/4 c. chopped walnuts

In a large mixing bowl, beat together oil, sugars and eggs. Add vanilla; stir in dry ingredients and mix well. Stir in carrots and mix well. Stir in nuts and raisins. Pour into a well-greased 10-inch tube pan. Bake at 350° for 60 minutes. Cool in pan 10 minutes, then remove and cool completely.

For frosting, beat together cream cheese and butter. Beat in vanilla, powdered sugar, and enough milk to make a good spreading consistency. Frost cake and sprinkle with walnuts.

## Blueberry Cake
Can be made ahead and frozen                    Serves 12

1 c. sugar
1/2 c. butter, softened
2 eggs
2 t. baking powder
1/2 c. sweetened
  condensed milk
1-2/3 c. flour
1 t. vanilla
1 pt. fresh blueberries,
  lightly floured

Mix sugar, butter, eggs and baking powder in a bowl until creamy. Add milk and flour alternately, mixing well after each addition. Beat in vanilla. Fold in blueberries. Pour into a lightly greased 8 x 8-inch pan. Bake at 325° for 50-55 minutes.

## Butterscotch Nut Torte
Dazzling surrounded with fresh orange slices         Serves 10-12

6 eggs, separated
1-1/2 c. sugar
1 t. baking powder
2 t. vanilla
1 t. almond extract
2 c. graham cracker
  crumbs
1 c. finely chopped nuts
2 c. whipping cream
3 T. powdered sugar

Sauce:
1 c. brown sugar
1/4 c. butter
1/4 c. water
1/4 c. orange juice
1 T. flour
1 egg, well beaten
1 t. vanilla

Beat egg yolks well; add sugar, baking powder and flavorings. Beat egg whites until peaks form. Fold into yolk mixture; fold in graham cracker crumbs, then nuts. Line 2—9-inch layer cake pans with waxed paper; lightly flour paper. Pour in cake batter and bake at 325° for 30-35 minutes. Cool slightly; remove from pan and cool completely. Place 1 layer on serving plate. Whip cream with 3 T. powdered sugar; spread some of cream on bottom layer. Top with second layer and spread cream over the top and sides of cake. Refrigerate.

For sauce, mix all ingredients well and boil until thick enough to pour. Cool. Drizzle over whipped cream on top and down the sides of the cake. Refrigerate 1-2 hours, until ready to serve.

## Cheese Cupcakes
Easy and rich                                           Makes 24

3—8-oz. pkg. cream
  cheese, softened
1 c. sugar
5 eggs
1-1/2 t. vanilla
1 c. sour cream
1/4 c. sugar
1/2 t. vanilla
strawberry or blackberry
  preserves

Beat cream cheese with 1 cup sugar at low speed. Add eggs one at a time and beat well. Add 1-1/2 t. vanilla. Pour into 24 foil-lined cupcake cups, filling each half full. Bake at 300° for 40 minutes or until lightly browned. Cool 10 minutes.

Mix sour cream, 1/4 cup sugar and 1/2 t. vanilla. Spread over cupcakes. Place 1 t. preserves of your choice on the sour cream topping. Bake again for 5 minutes; cool.

## Fudge-Topped Chocolate-Cherry Cake
This moist cake takes only seconds in a food processor          Serves 16

1 c. sugar
1/2 c. butter, softened
1 egg
1-3/4 c. flour
1 t. baking soda
1/2 t. salt
1—1-oz. square
  unsweetened
  chocolate, melted
1 c. milk
1 T. lemon juice
25 maraschino cherries,
  quartered
1/4 c. maraschino cherry
  juice

Frosting:
1-1/2 c. sugar
6 T. milk
6 T. butter
1/2 c. chocolate chips

In mixing bowl or food processor, beat sugar, butter and egg. Beat in remaining ingredients until well blended. Pour into a greased and floured 9 x 13-inch baking pan. Bake at 350° for 30 minutes. Cool well in pan.

For frosting, mix sugar, milk and butter in saucepan; bring to boil, stirring constantly. Boil and stir for 3 minutes. Remove from heat and stir in chocolate chips (mixture will be thin). Continue to stir until mixture cools and thickens, about 5 minutes. When mixture appears shiny and reaches spreading consistency, quickly pour over cake and spread evenly. Let frosting harden for at least 30 minutes before serving. Frosted cake may be frozen.

## Chocolate Chip Cake
Rich, heavy and chocolatey                            Serves 16

1 c. sweetened
  condensed milk
2—1-oz. squares
  unsweetened chocolate
1/2 c. butter, softened
1-1/2 c. sugar
2 eggs
1 t. baking soda
1 c. milk
2-1/2 c. sifted flour
1 t. vanilla
12 oz. chocolate chips

In a saucepan, mix condensed milk and un-sweetened chocolate; bring to boil and stir until very thick. Remove from heat and cool. In mixing bowl, beat butter and sugar for 3 minutes. Add eggs; beat well. Add chocolate mixture. Dissolve baking soda in milk and add to batter alternately with flour. Mix well, stir in vanilla and chocolate chips. Pour into a greased and floured 10-inch tube pan. Bake at 350° for 55 minutes or until top springs back when touched. Cool 1 hour in pan; then remove and cool well. No icing is needed.

## Chocolate Torte
Recipe may be halved and molded in bread pan       Serves 16

3—4-oz. pkg. sweet
  baking chocolate
3 T. boiling water
2 eggs, separated
2 c. whipping cream,
  whipped
1/2 t. vanilla
1/2 t. almond extract
1 pkg. chocolate cookie
  wafers
1 c. whipping cream,
  whipped
1/4 lb. pistachio nuts,
  chopped

Melt chocolate in top of double boiler. Stir in boiling water; cool. Add slightly beaten egg yolks; beat until shiny. Beat egg whites until stiff; combine with whipped cream (2 cups); fold into chocolate mixture and add flavorings. Butter a 9-inch springform pan and alternate layers of wafers and cream mixture. Place in refrigerator for 24 hours. Remove to serving dish and frost with whipped cream (1 cup) and decorate with chopped nuts.

# White-Chocolate Mint Cake

Use liqueur of your choice in this glaze                    Serves 16

4 oz. white chocolate
1/2 c. boiling water
4 eggs
1-1/4 c. sugar
3/4 c. vegetable oil
1-1/2 t. vanilla
3/4 c. water
2-1/2 c. flour
1 t. baking soda
1—3-3/4-oz. pkg. instant
  vanilla pudding mix

Glaze:
2 c. powdered sugar
1/3 c. white creme de menthe

Melt white chocolate in boiling water in small saucepan. Cool slightly. Beat eggs in a large mixing bowl. Blend in sugar, oil, vanilla, water, flour, soda and pudding mix. Beat 2 minutes. Pour into a well-greased 10-inch tube pan. Bake at 350° for 55-60 minutes. While cake is baking, mix together glaze ingredients.

Remove cake from oven; let stand 5 minutes. Using a skewer, poke holes in cake and slowly pour the glaze mixture over the top. Let stand 3 to 4 hours; remove from pan. Slice and serve with or without ice cream.

# Cranberry Pudding Cake

Try this on a cold winter morning                          Serves 6

2 c. flour
3 t. baking powder
1/2 t. salt
1 c. sugar
1 c. milk
5 T. butter
2 c. raw cranberries

Sauce:
1 c. butter
2 c. sugar
1-1/2 c. half and half cream

In a large bowl, mix flour, baking powder, salt and sugar. Add milk, melted butter and cranberries. Mix gently. Pour into a greased and floured 9 x 13-inch pan. Bake at 350° for 40 minutes. Meanwhile, mix butter, sugar and cream in a saucepan. Bring to a boil and simmer 10 minutes. Remove from heat and cool slightly. Serve cake warm, passing sauce.

# Fruit-Filled Cake

Easy enough for the kids                                   Serves 10-12

1—10-inch chiffon cake,
  homemade or purchased
2 c. sour cream
1/4 c. brown sugar
1—20-oz. can crushed
  pineapple, well drained
1—3-1/2-oz. can flaked
  coconut
1—11-oz. can mandarin
  oranges, well drained.

Cut cake into 3 layers. Combine sour cream, sugar, pineapple and coconut. Place one cake layer on serving plate. Top with one-third of filling. Repeat twice more, ending with filling. Garnish with mandarin oranges. Refrigerate until serving time.

## Poor Man's Fruitcake

No eggs, butter or milk—reminiscent of depression times          Serves 8-10

1 c. water
1/4 c. lard
1-1/2 c. raisins
1-1/2 c. brown sugar
1/2 t. nutmeg
1/2 t. cloves
1 t. cinnamon
2 c. flour
1 t. baking soda
1/2 t. baking powder
1/4 t. salt
1-2/3 c. pecans or
    walnuts, chopped

Boil water, lard, raisins, sugar and spices together for 2 minutes. Let stand until cold (10-15 minutes in refrigerator).

Sift flour, baking soda, baking powder and salt together. Add to cold liquid. Beat well until well mixed. Add nuts.

Put into a greased and floured 6 x 10-inch pan. Bake at 325° for 45 to 60 minutes, or until cake springs back when touched in the center. Do not overbake. Cool well in pan. To serve, dust with powdered sugar, frost with a buttercream icing or top with whipped cream.

## Herrentorte

Gentlemen's Torte          Serves 12

6 eggs, separated
3/4 c. sugar, divided
1 T. rum
2/3 c. flour
1/3 c. unsweetened cocoa
1/4 t. baking powder
3/4 c. ground almonds
4 T. water
1 T. rum
1 c. whipping cream,
    whipped
2 T. powdered sugar
2/3 can whole cranberry
    sauce
1/3 c. strawberry jam
chocolate sprinkles

Beat egg yolks with 1/4 cup sugar until foamy; add rum. Beat egg whites with 1/2 cup sugar until foamy; add to egg yolks and mix together. Mix flour, cocoa and baking powder together; sift over egg mixture and fold in. Fold in nuts and water. Pour gently into a greased and floured 9-inch springform pan. Bake at 350° for 45 minutes. Cool; split cake into two layers.

Sweeten whipped cream with powdered sugar. Fill a pastry bag with whipped cream and make concentric circles of whipped cream, starting at the outside edge. In blender or processor, mix cranberry sauce and jam. Fill circles with the mixture. Put top layer of cake on; spread with cranberry mixture and use some of whipped cream to make a grid design on top. Frost sides with whipped cream. Press chocolate sprinkles onto the sides of the cake. Refrigerate until serving.

## Grandmother's Nut-Spice Cake

Seven-minute icing is perfect for this cake                Serves 12-16

1/2 c. butter
1 c. brown sugar
4 egg yolks, beaten
  lightly
1 t. baking soda
1/2 c. molasses
1 c. sour milk or
  buttermilk
2-1/4 c. cake flour
1 t. cinnamon
1/2 t. cloves
1/2 t. grated nutmeg
1 t. salt
1/2 t. baking powder
1/4 c. flour
1 c. chopped raisins
1/2 c. currants
1/2 c. finely chopped
  nuts

Cream butter; add sugar gradually, beating well. Add beaten egg yolks and beat thoroughly. Add soda and molasses to sour milk. Sift together the cake flour, cinnamon, cloves, nutmeg, salt and baking powder. Add liquid and dry ingredients alternately to butter mixture, beating after each addition. Mix 1/4 cup flour with fruits and nuts; mix floured nuts and fruits into batter, mixing thoroughly. Pour into two greased and floured 9-inch round cake pans. Bake at 350° for 45 minutes to 1 hour. Cool completely in pans. Frost as desired. May be frozen.

## Old Fashioned Jam Cake

Perfect for a picnic                Serves 12

1 c. butter
2 c. sugar
6 eggs, separated
1 c. blackberry jam
1 c. raisins
1 c. chopped nuts
3 c. flour
1 t. baking soda
1 t. ground cloves
1 t. ground allspice
1 t. nutmeg
1 t. cinnamon
1 t. ginger
1 c. buttermilk

Caramel Icing:
1 lb. light brown sugar
1/2 c. evaporated milk
1/2 c. butter

Cream butter and sugar until light and fluffy. Beat egg yolks; add to butter mixture. Add jam, raisins, and nuts. Mix well. Sift together flour, baking soda, and spices. Add alternately with buttermilk. Beat egg whites until stiff; fold into batter. Bake in four greased and floured 8-inch round cake pans at 325° for 30-35 minutes. Cool well.

For caramel icing, cook all ingredients over low heat, stirring constantly, until mixture reaches soft ball stage on candy thermometer. Remove from heat; allow to cool. When cool, beat with mixer until icing reaches spreading consistency. Use to fill and frost cake.

## Lemon Layer Cake

Plan brunch around this beautiful pale yellow cake        Serves 14

3 c. sifted cake flour
3 t. baking powder
3/4 c. butter
1-1/2 c. sugar
1 t. vanilla
3 eggs
1-1/4 c. milk
1-1/2 c. heavy cream
1/3 c. powdered sugar

Lemon Fill and Frost:
1 T. grated lemon rind
1/4 c. lemon juice
1-1/3 c. granulated sugar
1/2 c. butter
3 eggs, slightly beaten

Sift together the flour and baking powder. In a separate bowl, cream butter, sugar and vanilla. Thoroughly beat in the eggs, one at a time; stir in the flour mixture in 4 additions, alternately with the milk, just until smooth. Turn into 3 greased and floured 9-inch round cake pans. Bake at 350° until a cake tester inserted in cake comes out clean, 20-25 minutes. Cool cakes in pans on wire racks for 5 minutes. Turn out on racks and cool completely.

For lemon fill and frost, in a 1-quart saucepan over low heat, stir together lemon rind, lemon juice, sugar and butter until sugar is dissolved and butter melted. Off heat, gradually whisk in eggs. Over medium heat, stirring constantly, cook until slightly thickened; do not boil. Cover and chill.

Spread one layer with 1/2 cup of the lemon fill and frost. Add another cake layer and spread with another 1/2 cup of the lemon fill and frost. Top with last cake layer. Whip the cream with powdered sugar until stiff; fold in the remaining fill and frost and use to cover top and sides of cake. Store in refrigerator.

## Buttermilk Pound Cake

Equally good plain or with topping of your choice        Serves 16

1/2 c. butter
1/2 c. yellow vegetable
  shortening
3 c. sugar
5 eggs
2 t. vanilla
1/2 t. almond extract
3 c. flour
1/2 t. salt
1 c. buttermilk
1/2 t. baking soda
1 T. boiling water

In a large mixing bowl, beat butter, shortening and sugar for 4 minutes. Beat in eggs one at a time, beating well after each. Blend in vanilla and almond extract. Sift flour with salt; add to batter alternately with buttermilk. Dissolve baking soda in boiling water; stir into batter. Mix well and pour into a greased and floured 10-inch tube pan. Bake at 300° for 1-1/2 hours, testing after 1-1/4 hours (wooden pick inserted in cake should come out clean). Let rest 10 minutes before turning out of pan. Cool on rack. Freezes well.

## *Two-Tone Pound Cake*
May be tightly wrapped and frozen                    Serves 16

1-1/4 c. butter
2-1/2 c. sugar
5 eggs
2-1/2 c. sifted flour
1-1/4 t. baking powder
1/2 t. salt
1 c. less 2 T. milk
2 t. vanilla
1/4 c. unsweetened cocoa
powdered sugar

Cream butter; gradually add sugar, beating until light and fluffy. Beat in eggs, one at a time, creaming well after each addition. Sift together flour, baking powder, and salt; add alternately with milk and vanilla to the creamed mixture. Take out 2 cups batter and blend cocoa into it.

Alternately spoon light batter and chocolate batter into a greased and floured 10-inch tube pan.

Bake at 325° for 1 hour 10 minutes, or until toothpick inserted in cake comes out clean.

Cool in pan 10 minutes. Invert onto cake rack and cool completely. To serve, sprinkle with powdered sugar.

## *Pecan Praline Cake*
Topping cooks fast, so watch carefully              Serves 16

1 c. buttermilk
1/2 c. butter
2 c. light brown sugar
2 eggs
2 c. flour
1 t. baking soda
1/2 t. salt
3 T. unsweetened cocoa
1 T. vanilla

Topping:
1/2 c. butter
1 c. pecans, chopped
1 c. brown sugar
1/3 c. light cream or
  evaporated milk

In a small saucepan, warm buttermilk and butter just until barely warm. Pour into a large bowl; add brown sugar and eggs; beat well. Combine dry ingredients and sift into bowl. Mix until smooth. Stir in vanilla. Pour batter into a greased and floured 9 x 13-inch pan. Bake at 350° for 25 minutes.

For topping, combine all topping ingredients in a saucepan. Heat until butter melts. Spread mixture over hot cake in oven; put under broiler and cook until icing bubbles and turns golden, 1-2 minutes.

## Pumpkin Roll
Make several and freeze                                    Serves 10-12

3 eggs
1 c. sugar
2/3 c. pumpkin
1 t. lemon juice
3/4 c. flour
1 t. baking powder
2 t. cinnamon
1 t. ginger
1/2 t. nutmeg
1/2 t. salt
1 c. finely chopped
  walnuts

Filling:
1 c. powdered sugar
1—8-oz. pkg. cream
  cheese
4 T. butter
1/2 t. vanilla

Beat eggs on high for 3 minutes; gradually add sugar. Mix pumpkin and lemon juice together and add to egg mixture, beating until creamy. In a separate bowl, mix together dry ingredients. Gradually add flour mixture to the egg mixture. Spread in a greased and floured jelly roll pan and sprinkle with walnuts. Bake at 350° for 15 minutes.

Spread a large tea towel with powdered sugar. Turn cake, nut-side down, onto the towel. Roll towel up with cake, rolling from the shorter side. Cool for 3 hours.

For filling, beat powdered sugar and cream cheese; add butter and vanilla; mix until smooth. Unroll cake; spread with filling. Reroll cake and cover with plastic wrap. Chill at least 3 hours.


## Veiled Country Lass
From an old German recipe                                  Serves 8-10

4 lb. tart cooking
  apples, peeled
  and quartered
1/3 c. water
1/2 c. sugar
6 c. fresh white bread
  crumbs (12 slices)
1/3 c. brown sugar
1/8 t. cinnamon
1 c. chopped pecans
1 c. whipping cream,
  whipped
1—10-oz. jar raspberry
  jam
1/4 c. butter

Cook apples with water and sugar in a saucepan until apples form a pulp; cool. Melt butter in a frying pan; add bread crumbs and brown sugar. Saute until bread crumbs are golden and crisp. Add cinnamon and nuts. Place a layer of bread crumbs in a buttered 7-inch springform pan. Add a thin layer of applesauce and a layer of raspberry jam. Continue in thin layers, ending with a layer of bread crumbs. Bake for 20 minutes. Allow to cool thoroughly. Unmold and cover completely with whipped cream. Decorate with more whipped cream and raspberry jam, if desired. Must be served immediately after decorating.

# Schwarzwalder Kirsch Torte
Best possible combination of flavors · · · · · · · · · · · · · · Serves 16

1—16-oz. can pitted sour
  cherries, drained
1/3 c. Kirsch
3—1-oz. squares
  unsweetened chocolate
2-1/4 c. sifted cake flour
2 t. baking soda
1/2 t. salt
1/2 c. butter
2-1/4 c. brown sugar
3 eggs
1-1/2 t. vanilla
1 c. sour cream
1 c. boiling water
3—1-oz. squares
  semi-sweet chocolate
2 c. whipping cream
2 T. Kirsch
1/2 c. powdered sugar
maraschino cherries

At least 4 hours before baking cake, soak sour cherries and 1/3 cup Kirsch in a bowl, stirring occasionally. Drain and reserve juice. Melt unsweetened chocolate over hot water; cool.

Sift flour, baking soda and salt. Beat butter until soft; add brown sugar and eggs and beat until fluffy. Beat in vanilla; add cooled chocolate. Stir in dry ingredients alternately with sour cream, beating well with a wooden spoon. Stir in boiling water and drained cherries. Pour into two greased and floured 9-inch round cake pans. Bake at 375° for 25 minutes or until cakes test done. Cool in pans on wire rack 10 minutes. Remove from pans and cool well.

Soften semi-sweet chocolate in hands. With vegetable peeler, shave into curls for decoration. Set in cool place, but not refrigerator. Prick top of each cake layer and sprinkle 1 T. of reserved cherry marinade over each layer. Beat whipping cream with 2 T. Kirsch until stiff peaks form. Spread each layer with whipped cream, stack and top with maraschino cherries and chocolate curls. Frost sides with remaining whipped cream.

## Nut Torte
Will keep one week in refrigerator if well-wrapped          Serves 8-12

**Torte:**
4 eggs, separated
1 c. sugar
2 T. flour
1/2 t. baking powder
1 T. fresh orange juice
2 c. finely ground pecans
1/2 c. whipping cream, whipped
1-1/2 t. grated orange rind

**Frosting:**
1—6-oz. pkg. semi-sweet chocolate chips
1/2 c. sour cream
1/8 t. salt
whole pecans

For torte, beat egg yolks with sugar until thick and light-colored; add flour and baking powder; stir in orange juice and pecans. Beat egg whites until stiff; fold into nut mixture. Pour into two 8-inch round cake pans that have been greased and lined with wax paper. Bake at 350° for 25 minutes or until a finger leaves no dent. Cool; remove from pans. Two hours before serving, put layers together with whipped cream flavored with grated orange rind. Top with frosting.

For frosting, melt chocolate in top of double boiler over hot, not boiling, water. Stir in sour cream and salt. Spread over torte. Garnish with whole pecans. Refrigerate until serving time.

## Caramel Apple Cookies
Serve in miniature paper baking cups          Makes 3 dozen

1/2 c. butter
1/4 c. brown sugar
1/4 c. sifted powdered sugar
1/4 t. salt
1 egg
1/2 t. vanilla
2 c. sifted flour
1/2 c. miniature chocolate chips
3/4 c. evaporated milk
1—14-oz. pkg. caramels
3/4 c. ground pecans

Cream butter, sugars and salt. Add egg and vanilla. Blend in flour and mix well. Add chocolate chips. Form into 36 one-inch balls and place on greased cookie sheets. Bake at 350° for 15 to 18 minutes. Remove cookie sheets from oven. Immediately insert a round toothpick in the center of each cookie. Melt caramels and milk in the top of a double boiler or in microwave. Dip each cookie in melted caramel mixture. Let excess drip off. Dip in ground nuts to simulate caramel apple (nuts on bottom and half way up the sides). Place on waxed paper-covered cookie sheet. Refrigerate.

Note: To microwave caramels, place unwrapped caramels in a deep glass bowl. Add milk and cover with plastic wrap. Microwave on "roast" for 3 minutes. Stir and microwave 2 minutes longer or until melted.

## Apple Squares
Like a large apple pie                                        Serves 24

3 c. flour
1 c. lard
1 t. salt
1 egg, beaten
2/3 c. milk
2 c. cornflakes cereal
7 c. sliced apples, or
  more
1 c. sugar
1 t. cinnamon
2 T. butter

Frosting:
1-1/2 c. powdered sugar
1 t. vanilla
4 T. milk (approximate)

Cut together flour, lard and salt; add beaten egg and milk. If dough is sticky, add just enough flour so it can be rolled out. Divide dough into 2 balls. Roll out 1 ball to fit a 10 x 15-inch jelly roll pan; place in pan. Spread cornflakes over the crust. Spread apples over cornflakes. Sprinkle with sugar and cinnamon. Dot with 2 T. butter. Roll remaining ball of dough to fit the top of the pan and seal the edges. Bake at 350° for 45 minutes.

For frosting, mix powdered sugar and vanilla with enough milk to make a thin glaze. Drizzle on top of warm crust. Serve warm, cut into squares.

## Apple Cookies or Bars
Butterscotch chips are good in these, too          Makes 4 dozen

1/2 c. margarine
1-1/3 c. sugar
1 egg
1/4 c. milk
2 c. flour
1/2 t. salt
1 t. baking soda
1 t. cinnamon
1/2 t. nutmeg
1/2 t. ground cloves
1 c. chopped apples
1 c. chopped nuts
1 c. chopped raisins

Icing:
2 c. powdered sugar
1/4 c. butter
2 T. milk
1 t. vanilla

Cream margarine and sugar. Add egg and milk. Add sifted dry ingredients; stir in apples, nuts and raisins. For cookies, drop by teaspoons onto greased baking sheet; bake at 375° for 10 minutes. For bars, spread batter in greased 9 x 13-inch pan; bake at 375° for 20 to 25 minutes. Cool.

For icing, cream sugar and butter; add milk and vanilla. Use to frost cookies or bars.

# Chocoho-licks

Vary the liqueur to suit your fancy!                         Makes 24 pieces

1-1/2 c. sugar
3/4 c. butter
1/4 t. salt
3—1-oz. squares
  unsweetened
  chocolate, melted
3 eggs
1/2 t. vanilla
1 c. flour
1/2 t. baking powder
4 T. raspberry liqueur

Cream sugar, butter and salt. Add chocolate, eggs and vanilla and mix well. Mix in flour, baking powder and liqueur. Pour into greased 9 x 13-inch pan. Bake at 325° for 30 minutes. Cool and cut into 24 squares.

# Disappearing Marshmallow Brownies

These do disappear like magic                          Makes 18 pieces

1/2 c. butterscotch pieces
1/4 c. butter
3/4 c. flour
1/3 c. brown sugar
1 t. baking powder
1/4 t. salt
1/2 t. vanilla
1 egg
1 c. miniature
  marshmallows
1 c. semi-sweet chocolate
  chips
1/4 c. chopped nuts

Melt butterscotch pieces and butter in a heavy 3-quart saucepan over medium heat, stirring constantly. Remove and cool to lukewarm. Add flour, brown sugar, baking powder, salt, vanilla and egg to butterscotch mixture in pan. Fold marshmallows, chocolate pieces and nuts into the butterscotch batter; mixing about 5 strokes. Spread into a greased 9-inch square pan. Bake at 350° for 20 to 25 minutes; do not overbake. The center will be soft, but becomes firm upon cooling.

# Funny Fudge

The family can help with the kneading                  Makes 5 pounds

1 lb. American cheese
1 lb. margarine
4 lb. powdered sugar
1 c. unsweetened cocoa
1 t. vanilla
2 c. chopped nuts

Melt cheese and margarine; add to the sugar, cocoa, vanilla and nuts in a large bowl. Mix with hands, kneading until mixture feels smooth. Spread onto a lightly buttered 11 x 16-inch baking sheet with lightly greased hands. Chill; keep refrigerated until ready to serve.

## Heath Bar Candy

A nice finale when you don't want "dessert"        Makes 1 pound

1 c. sugar
1 c. butter
1 t. vanilla
1—6-oz. pkg. chocolate
   chips

Heat sugar and butter until light brown (about the color of peanut butter). Do not overcook. Add vanilla and pour onto buttered cookie sheet; melt chocolate chips and pour over the mixture. Put in freezer until hard. Remove and break into chunks. Store in refrigerator.

## Kolacky

Pretty on a tea table        Makes 3 dozen

1/2 c. sugar
1/2 c. margarine
1/2 c. shortening
1 egg plus 1 egg yolk,
   beaten
1 t. almond extract
2-1/2 c. flour
1—12-oz. can cake and
   pastry filling (prune or
   apricot)
powdered sugar

Cream sugar with margarine and shortening. Add beaten eggs and almond extract. Add flour gradually, stirring constantly. Make small balls the size of a walnut. Place on greased cookie sheets. Using a ketchup bottle cap, make a small dent in the ball (the sides will split a little). Fill each dent with 1 t. pastry filling. Bake at 350° for 20 minutes. Immediately remove cookies from pan and cool on racks. Sift powdered sugar over cooled cookies.

## Napoleon Creams

May be served as a candy in tiny pieces        Makes 24 pieces

1/2 c. butter
1/4 c. sugar
1/4 c. unsweetened cocoa
1 t. vanilla
1 egg, slightly beaten
2 c. graham cracker
   crumbs
1 c. flaked coconut
1/2 c. butter
3 T. milk
1—3-3/4-oz. pkg. instant
   vanilla pudding
2 c. powdered sugar
1—6-oz. pkg. chocolate
   chips
2 T. butter
1 T. milk

Mix 1/2 cup butter, sugar, cocoa and vanilla in a saucepan; heat until butter melts. Stir in egg. Cook and stir over low heat until it thickens; blend in graham cracker crumbs and coconut. Press firmly into a 9 x 9-inch pan. Chill slightly. Cream 1/2 cup butter; add 3 T. milk and instant pudding; add powdered sugar; beat well. Spread over chilled crust. Melt chocolate chips, 2 T. butter and 1 T. milk together. Cool slightly. Working quickly, spread over pudding mixture. Allow to stand 10-15 minutes. Cut into squares before top gets too hard. Chill until serving.

## Oatmeal Fudge Bars
For lunch boxes or picnic baskets                    Serves 10-20

1 c. butter
2 c. brown sugar
2 eggs
2 t. vanilla
2-1/2 c. flour
1 t. baking soda
1 t. salt
3 c. old-fashioned oatmeal

Filling:
1—12-oz. pkg. chocolate chips
1 can sweetened
   condensed milk
2 T. butter
2 t. vanilla
1/2 t. salt
1 c. chopped nuts

Cream butter and sugar; add eggs and vanilla. Sift in flour, soda and salt. Add oatmeal. Set aside and make filling. Mix all filling ingredients together in saucepan and cook over low heat until smooth. Add chopped nuts. Spread 2/3 of the oatmeal mixture in a 10 x 15-inch jelly roll pan. Cover evenly with filling. Put remainder of the oatmeal mixture on top. Bake at 350° for 20 to 25 minutes. Cool in pan; cut into squares.

## Oatmeal Sugar Cookies
Delicious with fresh fruit or sherbet               Makes 3 dozen

1/2 c. butter
1/2 c. margarine
1/2 c. sugar
1 c. flour
1-1/2 c. quick-cooking
   oatmeal
1/2 t. vanilla
powdered sugar

Cream butter, margarine and sugar together. Add flour, oatmeal and vanilla. Beat until well mixed. Shape into small balls, about 3/4 inch in diameter. Press onto a cookie sheet with a flat-bottomed glass which has been dipped into powdered sugar. Bake at 350° for 8 to 10 minutes. To prevent sticking, remove from pan after cookies cool a few minutes and place on waxed paper. Sift powdered sugar over cooled cookies.

## Old Fashioned Icebox Cookies
Nice to have on hand in the freezer                 Makes 4 dozen

1 lb. margarine
1 c. brown sugar
1 c. white sugar
2 eggs
5 c. flour
1 t. baking soda
1/8 t. salt
2 t. cinnamon
1/2 lb. chopped walnuts
   or pecans

Beat margarine with brown and white sugars; beat in eggs. In a separate bowl, mix flour, baking soda, salt and cinnamon. Add to margarine mixture gradually; add nuts and mix well. Form into 12-inch or smaller logs, in 2 x 3-inch ovals. Freeze logs. To bake, slice and place on greased cookie sheet. Bake at 350° for about 15 minutes or until slightly golden.

## Orange Cookies
A natural with lemonade

Makes 4 dozen

1 T. grated orange rind
1 c. shortening
1-1/2 c. brown sugar
2 eggs
1 t. vanilla
1 c. sour milk
3 c. flour

Icing:
4 T. butter
1/2 t. orange rind
3 T. orange juice
2 c. powdered sugar

Cream orange rind, shortening and brown sugar together. Add eggs and mix well. Add vanilla and sour milk; gradually add flour; mix well. Form cookies by placing a tablespoon of dough for each onto a greased cookie sheet. Bake at 375° for 10 minutes. Remove from pan and cool on racks.

For icing, mix all ingredients together and spread on cooled cookies.

## Peanut Butter Balls
These freeze well

Makes 6-8 dozen

4 T. butter
2 c. powdered sugar
2 c. peanut butter
2 c. pecans, chopped
4 c. crisp rice cereal
2—12-oz. pkg. semi-sweet
    chocolate chips

Mix butter and powdered sugar. Add peanut butter, pecans and rice cereal. Roll into tiny balls (approximately 1 t.) and put on a waxed paper-lined cookie sheet. Place in the freezer to harden. Melt chocolate bits in the top of a double boiler. Dip cold peanut butter balls into the chocolate and return to the waxed paper; refrigerate until set.

## Peanut Butter and Jelly Puffs
Great snacks

Makes 2 dozen

1-3/4 c. sifted flour
2 t. baking powder
1/4 t. salt
1 egg
1/2 c. sugar
1/2 c. peanut butter
1/2 c. milk
1 T. butter, melted
1/2 c. jelly, any flavor
peanut oil for deep
    frying
powdered sugar

Sift flour, baking powder and salt into a bowl. Beat egg; beat in sugar, peanut butter, milk and butter. Stir liquid ingredients into dry ingredients, blending well. Turn out onto lightly floured board or pastry cloth and roll out to 1/2-inch thickness. Cut into rounds with biscuit cutter. Place a spoonful of jelly in center of each round. Fold dough over to form half circles; seal edges well. Fry in 365° hot peanut oil until golden brown; turn to fry on other side. Drain on absorbent paper. Dust with powdered sugar.

## Pumpkin Bars
Everyone's fall favorite                                        Makes 40 pieces

4 eggs
1-1/2 c. sugar
1 c. vegetable oil
1—16-oz. can pumpkin
2 c. flour
2 t. baking powder
2 t. cinnamon
1 t. salt
1 t. baking soda

Frosting:
1—3-oz. pkg. cream
  cheese, softened
1/2 c. butter, softened
1 t. vanilla
2 c. powdered sugar

In large mixer bowl, beat together eggs, sugar, oil and pumpkin until light and fluffy. Stir together flour, baking powder, cinnamon, salt and baking soda. Add to pumpkin mixture and mix thoroughly. Spread in an ungreased 15 x 10-inch pan. Bake at 350° for 25 to 30 minutes. Cool and frost.

For frosting, cream together cream cheese and butter; stir in vanilla. Add powdered sugar a little at a time, beating well until mixture is smooth. Spread on bars.


## Butterscotch Sauce
Chopped pecans may be added                                        Makes 1 cup

1/2 c. sugar
1/2 c. brown sugar
1/4 c. butter
1/2 c. whipping cream

Mix all ingredients in saucepan. Heat, stirring constantly, until mixture boils; boil 2-3 minutes. Serve warm.


## Champagne Chocolate Sauce
Serve over strawberry ice cream in chocolate cups                  Serves 4

6 T. champagne
1—3-oz. extra bittersweet
  chocolate bar
1 T. fine-granulated
  sugar
2 T. butter, softened

Combine champagne, chocolate bar and sugar in saucepan. Heat over very low heat, stirring constantly, until melted and smooth. (Or, microwave on low power 1 minute.) Remove from heat; whisk in butter. Serve warm.

## Hot Fudge Sauce
The best you've ever indulged in                Makes 2 cups

1/2 c. butter
1 c. sugar
1/8 t. salt
1 t. instant coffee
1/3 c. unsweetened cocoa
1 c. whipping cream
2 t. vanilla
3 T. dark rum

In saucepan, melt butter; stir in sugar, salt, instant coffee and cocoa. Blend in cream. Bring to boil; simmer over low heat 5 minutes. Remove from heat; stir in vanilla and rum. Cool slightly or chill to serve. Sauce keeps 2 weeks in refrigerator, covered.

## Lemon Sauce
Best served warm over gingerbread or bread pudding       Makes 1-1/2 cups

1 c. sugar
1 T. cornstarch
1 c. hot water
2 T. fresh lemon juice
1 t. grated lemon peel
2 T. butter

Mix all ingredients in saucepan. Boil, stirring constantly, until thickened. Cool slightly before serving.

## Hot Buttered Rum Sauce
Delicious over apple pie                Makes 2 cups

1-1/4 c. brown sugar
1/2 c. honey
1/8 t. salt
1/2 c. butter
1/4 c. hot water
1/3 c. dark rum

In saucepan, mix brown sugar, honey, salt, butter and water. Heat, stirring constantly just until mixture comes to a boil. Remove from heat and stir in rum. Serve hot.

tom heflin

# Index

# Contributors

*Brunch Basket* gratefully acknowledges the following contributors and supporters of this recipe collection:

Mary Ann Ullrich Abate
Jean Simcox Adams
Jo Ann Norman Allen
Grace Radde Allison
Carolyn Mattison Allison
Jean Reynolds Anderson
Jean Wormley Anderson
Linda McDonald Anderson
Patricia Harris Anderson
Rae Kellner Anderson
Tressa Ginestra Anderson
Shirley Upchurch Ax
Donna Johnson Bader
Carolyn Kent Bailey
Donna Walker Bailey
Phyllis Marshall Bailey
Helen Smith Bailey
Sally Dickinson Baker
Harriet Bergren Barnard
Helen Scherwin Barrett
Patricia Price Bartlett
Georgeanne Call Bastian
Helen Wolfenspenger Beattie
Jane Groninger Bechaka
Lon Gersten Behr
Nadine Bright Bell
Norma Powers Bender
Jackie Busch Bernstein
Rosemary Kuhse Bieck
Lorraine Mittler Blackler
Debra Cain Blevins
Jean Thompson Bodorff
Isabelle Geithman Boehmen
Laura Smith Borghi
Suzanna Harrold Boswell
Joan Hopkinson Bowman
Ann Grady Bown
Barbara Knosp Boyce
Kay Anderson Boyer
Sally Bradley
Joan Doane Bradley
Julia Morley Brand
Debbie Beckstrand Brearley
Martha Howard Bremner
Marilyn Karrer Brown
Frances Smith Brown
April Smith Butitta

Nancy Lewis Butler
Elise Huckabee Cadigan
Elizabeth Sommer Canfield
Barbara Smith Capron
Elaine Sommer Carlson
Mary-Stuart Johnstone Carruthers
Mary Bartlett Caskey
Jo Sessions Castro
Barbara Sullivan Cavataio
Janice Swager Cheney
Ann Fetter Cherundolo
Ruth Scudder Clark
Mary Gardner Clarke
Paula Sommer Clise
Diana Gifford Cobb
Susan Kenkin Cody
Barbara Cole
Elizabeth Brown Coleman
Janet Brown Colman
Diane Snodgrass Conklin
Deborah William Connolly
Mary Loughry Cook
Becky Byrd Cook
Marcia Kaney Cook
Nancy Kozminske Coole
Margaret Cooney
Donna Peterson Cornwell
Theodora Mollenhuer Countryman
Susan Flink Cowman
Barbara Stone Craig
Easton McNabb Crawford
Patty Roderick Crow
Janet Geiger Currier
Carol Chandler Dasenbrook
Linda Johnson Dawson
Jan Buckingham DeBruyne
Gloria Lester Dermer
Bobbe Cohen Deutchman
Joyce Blum DeWallace
Elizabeth Quest Dickinson
Nancy Ghent Donohue
Virginia Kenney Dorighi
Darcy Isaacs Dougherty
Mary Condon Downey
Kirby Johnson Doyle
Marilyn Waling Doyle
Barbara Platt Dudgeon

Jan Bauer Dunbar
Deidre Early Eberhart
Georganne Hinchliff Eggers
Shirley Fivek Eighmy
Susan Caldwell Eissens
Lucy Goetz Eklund
Marjorie Anderson Elliot
Sandra Howe Elliott
Barbara Whitty Erickson
Joan Matthews Erkert
Ellen Battinger Erkert
Charlotte Sweeney Ernster
Jean VanHara Fadden
Katherine Eastman Faith
Artina Phillips Finkenstaedt
Amy Younglove Fish
Penny Hummel Fisher
Margaret More Fourie
Susan Frame
Penny Knecht France
Ann Perry Krugler Frankenthal
Andi Simmons Freed
Sondra Hartley Frus
Darlene Koning Furst
Barbara Feldman Gagliano
Barbara Ferrell Gaines
Barbara Bennett Galloway
Kay Lievens Galloway
Barbara Brockmeier Gambino
Maureen Connell Gaudreau
Marylou Linsinger Gault
Nan McDonald Geddeis
Judy Lundeen Geissler
Jan Rebman George
Georgalee George
Karen Henschel Gilbert
Anne Gilberti
Sue Munson Gilmore
Marilyn Guzzardo Ginestra
Kathleen Leonard Giovingo
Kathleen Keller Giovingo
Nancy Monday Glass
Patricia Meyers Gleichman
Allison Furst Goddard
Sally Kumkle Goddard
Mary Kay Meixner Grans
Judy Woker Greier
Sue Brannen Groff
Maureen Lundquist Gustafson
Gloria Mortellaro Gustafson

Geraldine Nosalik Gustafson
Kathy Ginestra Guzzardo
Miriam Negin Halle
Missy DiSalvo Hand
Darlene Myers Hanna
Joan Berquist Harding
Joan Terrell Hardy
Marjorie Chandler Harnois
Marcella Eason Harris
Mary Schindel Harris
Jane Wilhelmus Hawkins
Diane Anderson Hedberg
Barbara Stumkle Heinzeroth
Patricia Hembrough
Jean Carlson Hembrough
Marsha Lewis Hess
Vivian Veach Hickey
Roz Castrogiovanni Hill
Helen Chung Hill
Nancy Logan Hill
Joan Otis Hinken
Judy Vosburg Hirsch
Judy Healey Holder
Barbara Ernstein Holmstrom
Jessica Dickinson Holt
Shirley Sommer Holzwarth
Betsy Nash Homewood
Sue Dundore Hudson
Suzanne Ralston Humphris
Jane Wortham Hunter
Susan Brostedt Huntting
Martha Ashley Hutt
Nancy Guyer Hyzer
Jeanne Grahn Ilseman
Terry O'Donnell Ingrassia
Leslie Carter Jackson
Jill Fritzler Jackson
Laura Swenson Jacobsen
Margaret Halversen Jeffrey
Phoebe Johnson Jeffreys
Marge Stranik Joehnk
Patricia Michaels Johnson
Ana Jinkins Johnson
Barbara Johnson
Julie Holmberg Johnson
Georgann Allen Johnson
Diane Lovett Jones
Ruth Lilja Joslyn
Nancy Morris Kase
Lynda Peterson Kennedy

Carla Shaff Kieckhefer
Lesley Bork Killoren
Patricia King
Sharon Klint
Jeanne Delong Knowland
Fran Castrogiovanni Knutson
Sylvia Bruscato Koberg
Vicki Nichols Kolhbacher
Pauline Koplos Kostantacos
Jean Wheeler Kramer
Lauren Kapper Kronenberg
Barbara Duda Kullberg
Gloria Nelson Kullberg
Nancy Novinski Lacey
Judith Ann Langewisch
Jean Jackson Larsen
Wendy Coretz Larson
Barbara Tarabori Lasalle
Jean Wilkinson Lathrop
Deb VanAtta Laughlin
Betsy McCoy Laven
Elizabeth Rhodes Lawton
Ellen Teevan Letourneau
Sanchia Bruer Leach
Grace Hartman Leighton
Jane Shew Lenz
Helen Leonard
Betty Thorpe Lillie
Jeanne Anderson Lindman
Terri Green Lindmark
Kathleen Clausen Lindsay
Kathryn Wiley Link
Joan Ralston Lippincott
Pamela Johnson Livingston
Galey Shappert Lucas
Nancy Hovet Lundstrom
Rosalind Lyons
Jane Lyons
Kathleen Ellis Maher
Jane Smith Marlowe
Penny Unger Martenson
Mary Glen Foster Marth
Lynn Morley Martin
Gale Reid Marzorati
Terry Abruzzo Mathiesen
Katrina Mattison
Kathryn Rundquist Mattison
Marie Buchmann Mattison
Nancy Shappert Mattison
Jean Leland Mattison

Elaine Brown Mayfield
Beverlie Briggs Maynard
Joyce Myers Mazzola
Carroll Adams McCarthy
Diane Faber McConville
Elizabeth Brearley McDonald
Wilma Schrag McNess
Marilyn Stone McPherson
Frances Frisbie Miller
Diane Dal Pra Mitchell
Sharon Michel Montalbano
Janet Larsen Moore
Judith Sprague Moore
Ann Bluth More
Caryl Obrecht Morgan
Kathleen Lerche Morman
Nadia Bilys Morrison
Anne Keegan Morrow
Doris Clausius Mosser
Catherine Oliver Mott
Martha Taxon Mott
Phyllis Mark Mott
Janet Conley Murray
Julie Barber Murray
Margit Neumeister Naden
Jo Needham Nash
Marjorie Salisbury Needham
Linda Groff Nelson
Lois Sandy Nelson
Pat Banner Nelson
Constance Stanley Nethercut
Susan Lundeen Nethery
Carole Sanders Newcomer
Ruth Whitehead Nicholas
Rachel Brauchle Nichols
Sally Hobson Nihan
Sandra Jacobson Nilsson
Jody Stafford Nordlof
Patricia Fedro Norten
Beverly Barber North
Peggy Clark Northrop
Gwendolyn Jacobs Novak
Kristine O'Rourke
Mary Alice Egan Odling
Lois Starr Ogilby
Elizabeth McBride Olin
Denise Countryman Oliver
Cheryl Gaer Olson
Nancy Nichols Olson
Courtney Read Olson

Ellen Bradford Olson
Lucretta Smith Paddock
Marilyn Le Febve Paladino
Dee Baluh Pallasch
Cynthia Koerber Patterson
Jo Moerschel Paul
Debbi Reitsch Pauletto
Lisbeth Lindquist Pearson
Dale Hart Peel
Judy Mette Pember
Renate Fischer Pendleton
Claire Bandelin Perkins
Carlyn Bruce Peterson
Kathryn Dalvey Peterson
Sharon Bressler Pierce
Sally Winkleman Pike
Sue Feldman Pisano
Norma Futherman Polcek
Susan Stolar Polivka
Carol Pollock
Martha Brown Porter
Mary Bodaken Powell
Joan Behr Powell
Edna Harrison Powell
Barbara Lace Pozzi
Beverly Hughes Preiss
Lucy Pritz
Becky Boyden Pschirrer
Linda Lee Ream
Jean Whitehead Reese
Mary Reeves
Jacqueline Grear Reitsch
Enrica Gianoli Reitsch
Gertrude Grassman Reynolds
Carol Kendall Roseberg
Beverly Bennett Rosecrance
Winifred Smith Rosecrance
Barbara Bell Ross-Shannon
Shirley Johnson Rundquist
Nancy Kraffert Russo
Marjorie Tullock Ryan
Beato Battrud Rystrom
Connie Steward Sabatino
Joan Wilson Salamone
Bonnie Goldberg Saliman
Pat Davis Sanderson
Joan Slausen Schmidt
Pamela Antrim Schmidt
Gretchen Cruver Schmidt
Nancy Little Schroeder

Nancy Hobson Schroeder
Patricia Gilmour Schueller
Marilyn Bygrave Schweisberger
Dianne Wiley Seim
Susan Kohlhorst Shaffer
Lorraine Shipley Shaffer
JoAnn Cox Shaheen
Norma Bailey Shelden
Judi Hoover Sheley
Karen Reinhold Shifo
Peg Cavitt Showers
Jennifer Shriner
Nancy Schmeling Shugart
Dorothy Rudat Shumway
Genny Bradley Sjostrom
Mary Elizabeth Schmitz Skerkoske
Julie Lundeen Slack
Bev Phillips Slayton
Nancy Smith
Barbara Bygrave Smith
Jane Liljedahl Smith
Betty Burrows Smith
Lou Craft Smith
Jayne Barden Smith
Patricia Murphy Sneed
Julie Smith Snively
Eleanor Anderson Snyder
Evelyn Merrifield Sommer
Mary O'Connor Sparks
Lynn Jacobson Spaulding
Debbie Wallk Speer
Pam King Spengler
Lynn Kania Splinter
Annette Bert Stegall
Marion Dooley Sterling
Sally Black Stevens
Sue Berns Stieber
Sally Champman Stone
Helen Dasenbrook Street
Marjorie Goembel Summerfield
Linda Wantz Summerfield
Coline Hampton Sutherland
Susan Christopher Swift
Sue Fivaz Symes
Carol Giovingo Taphorn
Susan Nelson Taylor
Melissa Mehall Teske
Marilyn Norris Thayer
Cathie Wahlstrom Thiede
Margaret Powell Thienemann

# Contributors ⸻⸻⸻⸻⸻ 339

Dorothy Barber Thomas
Elizabeth Shriner Thompson
Nancy Johnson Thorell
Becky Aplington Thorsen
Karyl Yost Thorsen
Ruth Bonnell Torrence
Sandra Dolezal Tower
Ruth Colman Tower
Ann Cummings Towne
Betsie Kramp Trejo
Cathy Whitney Trost
Gayle Noble Truitt
Shirley Estwing Tuckett
Francine Williams Tuite
Susan Milligan Turner
Prudence Ross Twitchell
Marcia Millspaugh Tyrrell
Carol Sargant Valaitis
Sally Countryman Varland
Lynne Denham Vass
Barbara Giorgi Vella
Maureen O'Brien Volkmann
Ann Miller Waddell

Ann Schabrau Wadlington
Eleanor Harms Wales
Mary Lee Wantz
Patricia Collier Waters
Susan Heege Weiss
Dimmis Lathrop Weller
Joan Selimos Welsh
Sue Shellenberger Welsh
Laurie Fuller Wharton
Mary Elizabeth Nobles Wheeler
Beverly Williams Whitehead
Harriet Burpee Whitehead
Lois Blue Williams
Audrey Roberts Williams
Georgia Wolf
Sarah Beekman Wolf
Mary Margaret Mulnix Wolfley
Claudia Katz Woodward
Jeanine Carlson Wortmann
Sue Frandsen Wulf
Judy Pieper Wyatt
Nancy Hasen Yde
Karen Wiesand Zander

## Restaurants:

Bellamy's
Chez Gerlinde
China Palace
Figg's
Giovanni's
Grampa's
Jungle Jim's
Maria's
Mauh-Nah-Tee-See Country Club
Mayflower
Old Rock River Deli
Pie Shell
Royal Dragon
YMCA River Room

### The Junior League of Rockford, Inc.
### 4118 Pinecrest Road
### Rockford, Illinois 61107

Please send _____ copies of *Brunch Basket* at $16.95 each, plus $2.50 postage and handling per book. For Illinois delivery, add $1.06 (6.25% sales tax) per book. Make checks payable to Brunch Basket, The Junior League of Rockford, Inc.

Name _____

Street _____

City _____

State _____ Zip _____

### The Junior League of Rockford, Inc.
### 4118 Pinecrest Road
### Rockford, Illinois 61107

Please send _____ copies of *Brunch Basket* at $16.95 each, plus $2.50 postage and handling per book. For Illinois delivery, add $1.06 (6.25% sales tax) per book. Make checks payable to Brunch Basket, The Junior League of Rockford, Inc.

Name _____

Street _____

City _____

State _____ Zip _____

### The Junior League of Rockford, Inc.
### 4118 Pinecrest Road
### Rockford, Illinois 61107

Please send _____ copies of *Brunch Basket* at $16.95 each, plus $2.50 postage and handling per book. For Illinois delivery, add $1.06 (6.25% sales tax) per book. Make checks payable to Brunch Basket, The Junior League of Rockford, Inc.

Name _____

Street _____

City _____

State _____ Zip _____